About the Editor

Bertil Dunér is a political scientist educated at the University of Uppsala. He is the author of several books and articles in English on conflict in the South, including *Military Intervention in Civil Wars: The 1970s* (Gower, 1985) and *The Bear, the Cubs and the Eagle: Soviet Bloc Interventionism in the Third World and the US Response* (Gower, 1987).

Since 1991 he has headed the Human Rights Programme of the Swedish Institute of International Affairs in Stockholm, and has published a number of books in Swedish on the subject of human rights, including *Free and Equal in Dignity and Rights* (1992) and *The UN and Human Rights* (1995). His current research concentrates on non-governmental organizations and the problems posed by human rights for foreign policymaking.

Zed Titles on Human Rights

Zed Books, as part of its programme of publishing on international and Third World issues, has long published in the field of human rights. Our list is now a significant contribution not only to our understanding of this subject, but to the diverse struggles and strategies that exist to ensure greater respect for the rights of people.

I. Agger, *The Blue Room: Trauma and Testimony among Refugee Women*

Agger and Jensen, *Trauma and Healing under State Terrorism*

British Medical Association, *Medicine Betrayed: The Participation of Doctors in Human Rights Abuses*

Susan Forbes Martin, *Refugee Women*

Gordon and Marton (eds), *Torture: Human Rights, Medical Ethics and the Case of Israel*

Hardon and Hayes (eds), *Reproductive Rights in Practice: A Feminist Report on the Quality of Care*

David Keen, *Refugees: Rationing the Right to Life: The Crisis in Emergency Relief*

Joanna Kerr (ed.), *Ours by Right: Women's Rights as Human Rights*

W. Myers (ed.), *Protecting Working Children*

Petchesky and Judd (eds), *Negotiating Reproductive Rights: Women's Perspectives across Countries and Cultures*

S. Pritchard (ed.), *Indigenous Peoples, the United Nations and Human Rights*

Eric Prokosch, *The Technology of Killing: A Military and Political History of Anti-Personnel Weapons*

W. Courtland Robinson, *Terms of Refuge: The Indochinese Exodus and the International Response*

Jamil Salmi, *Violence and Democratic Society: New Approaches to Human Rights*

Bernard Schlemmer (ed.), *The Exploited Child* (in preparation)

Katerina Tomasevski, *Women and Human Rights*

World University Service, *Academic Freedom*, Volumes 1, 2, 3, 4

For full details of this list and Zed's other lists (including Development Studies, Economics, Politics, Environment Studies, Health, Women's Studies, and Cultural Studies and Anthropology) titles, please write to:

Marketing Department, Zed Books, 7 Cynthia Street, London N1 9JF, UK or email Sales@zedbooks.demon.co.uk.

Visit our website at: http://www.zedbooks.demon.co.uk

An End to Torture

Strategies for its Eradication

Edited by Bertil Dunér

ZED BOOKS
London & New York

An End to Torture was first published by
Zed Books Ltd, 7 Cynthia Street, London N1 9JF, UK,
and Room 400, 175 Fifth Avenue, New York, NY 10010, USA in 1998

Distributed exclusively in the USA by St Martin's Press, Inc.,
175 Fifth Avenue, New York, NY 10010, USA

Typeset by Lucy Morton & Robin Gable, Grosmont
Cover designed by Lee Robinson
Printed and bound in the United Kingdom
by Biddles Ltd, Guildford and King's Lynn

A catalogue record for this book is available from the British Library

Library of Congress Cataloging-in-Publication Data
An end to torture : strategies for its eradication / edited by Bertil Dunér.
    p.   cm.
Includes bibliographical references and index.
ISBN 1–85649–621–X. — ISBN 1–85649–622–8 (pb)
1. Torture.   2. Torture—Prevention.   3. Torture victims.   4. Torture
(International law).   I. Dunér, Bertil, 1942–   .
HV8593.E53   1998   98–8239
323.4'9—dc21   CIP

ISBN 1 85649 621 X (Hb)
ISBN 1 85649 622 8 (Pb)

Contents

Editor's Preface

This book aims to provide a comprehensive account of torture in today's world, demonstrating the multifaceted nature of the practice and assessing the prospects for change. The enterprise is especially opportune, being published in the year in which we celebrate the fiftieth anniversary of the Universal Declaration of Human Rights. Eighteen authors from ten countries have cooperated in this effort, not only in preparing their respective contributions but also by helping to finance the free distribution of copies to institutions, organizations and individuals in countries where torture is a more or less common occurrence.

Thanks are due to the Swedish Government for its generous contribution of author fees. Thanks also go to the authors for their equally generous attitude in using their honorariums to finance the free distribution of bulk copies of the book. I am greatly indebted to Diana Madunic for invaluable editorial assistance throughout, and for research assistance on Chapter 5.

Bertil Dunér

Foreword

Nigel S. Rodley

Professor of Law, University of Essex;
United Nations Special Rapporteur on Torture

> No-one shall be subjected to torture or to cruel, inhuman or degrading
> treatment or punishment.
>
> Universal Declaration of Human Rights, Article 5

Despite the prohibition of torture contained in the Universal Declaration
of Human Rights, the world is far from seeing the end of the practice as
the Declaration's fiftieth anniversary approaches. Indeed, the year 2000 –
which will mark the twenty-fifth anniversary of the adoption by the
General Assembly of the Declaration on the Protection of All Persons
from Being Subjected to Torture or Other Cruel, Inhuman or Degrading
Treatment or Punishment – cannot be expected to herald better tidings.

The fact remains that states are unwilling to take the necessary measures to ensure that their law-enforcement officials and other security or
military personnel involved in maintaining public order do not succumb
to the temptation to commit crime to combat it. For many years torture
was thought of as being something used to respond to an organized
political challenge to the existing authorities. Indeed, it is very much the
case that torture is frequently used as a part of counter-insurgency operations, where the political challenge takes the form of armed activity,
which may or may not be of terrorist nature. The purpose of the torture
will usually be aimed at securing intelligence about the 'enemy' or to
intimidate perceived actual or potential supporters of the opposition, as
well as to obtain confessions. Sometimes even non-violent dissent will
attract the same treatment, usually for securing confessions or information about confederates, but also as a means of *de facto* punishment.

With the decline of authoritarian regimes, political dissent becomes
something integral to the political process rather than a challenge to it.
When armed insurgencies subside, there will be no continuing need to

combat them by whatever means the security forces believe necessary. As the political manifestation of the problem therefore disappears or substantially abates, so we are beginning to identify a problem of torture or ill-treatment in the context of repression of common criminality. We can only speculate on the extent to which such torture or ill-treatment are the inheritance of practices followed by way of response to political challenges or are a phenomenon that has persisted over the decades but has been overlooked because of the focus on the more visible political dimension.

In the final analysis what is incontestable is that torture can be stopped or at least reduced to the occasional aberration, if states are willing to do so. It is mainly a question of breaching impunity. Impunity can be tackled preventively and repressively. Preventive measures are aimed at removing the opportunity for torture. Anyone who has studied the problem knows that torture typically takes place when the victim is at the unsupervised mercy of his or her captors and interrogators, without access to the outside world – notably, family and lawyers. This condition is often called incommunicado detention. Any state that permits such detention for more than a matter of hours is intentionally choosing to open the doors to potentially undetectable abuse by its law-enforcement officials. The longer the period of incommunicado detention, the likelier it is that abuse will occur.

Repressive measures are those brought to bear by the criminal justice system (and, to some extent, by disciplinary procedures of the law-enforcement agency in question). Again, the more police, prosecutors and judges contrive to turn a blind eye to crimes committed by law-enforcement officials (usually abetted by the screen of incommunicado detention), the more those officials will have reason to believe that their criminal practices are tolerated or even expected.

In the end, it boils down to a matter of political will. Unfortunately, politicians frequently think in terms of a cost–benefit calculation, often in the context of short-term political advantage. The challenge to the international community is to find means of increasing the political costs to governments when they give a 'green light' to their law-enforcement officials to combat crime by resorting to crime. This means that all who wish to see an end to the affront to our civilization and common humanity that is torture must redouble their efforts to expose it wherever it occurs. Vigorous exposure can involve real costs. That is why governments often go to great lengths to conceal or deny it.

The chapters in this volume will provide the reader with many ideas as to what else is being done or can be done to make the political costs of torture unacceptably high.

Glossary of Acronyms

ABF	Arbetarnas Bildningsförbund (Workers' Educational Association)
ACAT	Action of Christians for the Abolition of Torture
AI	Amnesty International
APT	Association pour la Prévention de la Torture (Association for the Prevention of Torture)
AVRE	Association pour les Victimes de la Répression en Exil
BIM	Ludwig Boltzmann Institute of Human Rights
CAT	Committee Against Torture
CCPR	Covenant on Civil and Political Rights (= ICCPR)
CDDH	Comité Directeur pour les Droits de l'Homme (Council of Europe's Steering Committee for Human Rights)
CICR	Comité International de la Croix-Rouge (International Committee of the Red Cross)
CPT	European Committee for Prevention of Torture
CPTRT	Centre for the Prevention, Treatment and Rehabilitation of Victims of Torture and their Families
CRC	Committee on the Rights of the Child
CSCE	Conference on Security and Cooperation in Europe
CSCT/APT	Comité Suisse Contre la Torture/Association pour la Prévention de la Torture
DANIDA	Danish International Development Assistance
ECHR	European Convention for the Protection of Human Rights and Fundamental Freedoms
ECOSOC	Economic and Social Council
ESG	Emergency Services Group
EU	European Union
FEBEM	Fundação Educacional do Bem Estar do Menor (Foundation for the Welfare of Minors)

FIDH	Fédération Internationale des Droits de l'Homme (International Federation of Human Rights Leagues)
FMLN	Frente Farabundo Martí de Liberación Nacional (Farabundo Martí National Liberation Front)
GSS	General Security Service
HAS	Hamilton Anxiety Scale
HDS	Hamilton Depression Scale
HRFT	Human Rights Foundation of Turkey
HRW	Human Rights Watch
ICCPR	International Covenant on Civil and Political Rights
ICJ	International Court of Justice
ICJ	International Commission of Jurists
ICRC	International Committee of the Red Cross
IFACAT	International Federation of Action of Christians for the Abolition of Torture
IGO	Inter-Governmental Organization
IHD	Insan Haklari Dernegi (Human Rights Association)
IMF	International Monetary Fund
IRA	Irish Republican Army
KGB	Komitet Gosudarstvennoi Bezopasnosti (Committee for State Security)
NAMDA	National Medical and Dental Associations
NATO	North Atlantic Treaty Organization
NGO	Non-Governmental Organization
NIEO	New International Economic Order
NSAID	Non-Stereoid Anti-Inflammatory Drug
OAS	Organization of American States
OECD	Organization for Economic Cooperation and Development
OASSA	Organization for Appropriate Social Service in South Africa
OMCT	Organisation Mondiale Contre la Torture (World Organization Against Torture)
OSCE	Organization for Security and Cooperation in Europe
PKK	Kurdistan Workers' Party
PTSD	Post-traumatic stress disorder
RCT	Rehabilitation and Research Centre for Torture Victims
RCT/IRCT	Rehabilitation and Research Centre for Torture Victims/ International Rehabilitation Council for Torture Victims
SCT	Swiss Committee against Torture
SI	Survivors International
SIM	Netherlands Institute of Human Rights at the University of Utrecht
PHR–Israel	Physicians for Human Rights – Israel
TTB	Turkish Medical Chamber

UDHR	Universal Declaration of Human Rights
UN	United Nations
UNDP	UN Development Programme
UNESCO	UN Educational, Scientific and Cultural Organization
UNHCR	UN High Commissioner for Refugees
WHO	World Health Organization

Part I
International Law

1
Torture:
International Rules and Procedures
Love Kellberg

Historical Background

It is a striking fact that prior to the beginning of the nineteenth century, within the international community and in the field of international relations, individuals – if they were taken into account at all – were treated not as subjects but as objects dominated by sovereign states, who were the real and only actors in the world arena. As such, individuals were subjected to the whims of rulers, and ownership of them could pass from one to the other, as for example after a war, when the spoils were distributed between the victorious powers. However, slowly and as a result of the many declarations of rights, written into a number of constitutions – especially the American and French ones at the end of the eighteenth century – recognition of the equal right of every individual to life, liberty and property (and, later on, the protection thereof) began to be established within international relations. An early example is the Declaration on the Abolition of the Slave Trade, announced at the Vienna Congress in 1815. This was followed by the Treaty of London in 1841 on the same subject.

The second half of the century witnessed great strides in the mitigation of the plight of soldiers through the conclusion of a number of treaties, starting with the Geneva Convention of 1864. That was followed four years later by the Declaration of St Petersburg, which prohibited the use of explosive or inflammable projectiles. This latter Declaration is of particular interest inasmuch as it states that the use of such arms would henceforth be contrary to the laws of humanity: one of the first occasions this notion was incorporated in a treaty text. A reference to this fundamental principle was also made in the Hague Declaration of 1899 on the prohibition of the use of so-called dum-dum bullets.

The principle was further elaborated in the preamble to the Fourth Hague Convention respecting the Laws and Customs of War on Land of 1907, where it is stated that 'in cases not regulated in the convention, the populations and belligerents remain under the protection and control of the principles of international law/law of nations as they result from the usage established among civilised nations, from the *laws of humanity* and the dictates of the public conscience' (emphasis added).

Its lasting importance is evidenced by the fact that it is quoted word for word in the denunciation clauses of the 1949 Geneva Conventions – the so-called 'Red Cross' Conventions – as well as in Article 1:2 of the 1st Additional Protocol and in the Preamble of the 2nd Additional Protocol of 1977, reminding those governments who renounce the Conventions that they are nevertheless bound by the enshrined principles in the conduct of warfare.

These principles are even more valid in peace time. This was stressed by the International Court of Justice (ICJ) in the Hague in the Corfu Channel case between the UK and Albania in 1949: 'certain general and well-recognized principles, like elementary considerations of humanity, are even more absolute in peace time than in war time'. Furthermore, the principle of humanity has also been inscribed in the UN Charter (Articles 55:c and 56) as an overarching maxim restricting the domain otherwise reserved for states' exclusive jurisdiction.

Finally, states' duties to observe the fundamental principle of humanity do not rest on reciprocity or on the maintenance of a perfect contractual balance between rights and duties, but have now acquired the weight of *jus cogens* – peremptory law – endowed with special legal force, which is valid for all (*erga omnes*) with no exception and from which no opting out or derogation is possible. The result of this development is that states can no longer hide behind the principle of sovereignty and refuse scrutiny of the way they deal with human rights issues – for example, how they treat their own nationals or non-nationals – measured by the standards and yardsticks accepted by the community of nations.

The breakthrough in this focus on the human being rather than on the state came after World War II and was given expression in the UN Charter (for example, Articles 1:3, 13 and 55) and particularly in the Universal Declaration of Human Rights of 1948, which broadened the body of international rules on human rights.

This emergence of the human being as a subject of international law and not merely an object – at least in some areas of the law – does not mean that the individual can be said to be on a par with states on all counts. There will be a long process of gestation before the individual achieves that status – if, indeed, it ever comes about. Nevertheless, it is important to note that to a certain extent and for certain groups of states, in particular for those countries within the sphere of the Council of Europe, in the human rights field the individual has been granted formal *locus standi* in proceedings before the appropriate international bodies.

In what follows, a survey is presented of the international mechanisms available (i) to an individual who alleges that one of his or her most basic human rights has been violated, viz. respect for his or her physical integrity has been denied – in other words, the individual has been subjected to torture or other forms of serious ill treatment or punishment; (ii) to a state which wants to complain about another state's failure to honour its treaty obligations or, more generally, to comply with its duties under international law. Subsequent consideration is given to definitional issues and to case law jurisprudence. Included is an analysis of monitoring systems that have been accepted by states as a general undertaking or could be agreed to by them on an *ad hoc* basis.

General Remarks on Supervisory and Enforcement Bodies in the Field of Human Rights

Since the adoption by the UN General Assembly in 1948 of the Universal Declaration of Human Rights – which did not at the time, and was not intended to, impose legal obligations on states, and consequently did not establish any supervisory facility for monitoring and enforcement – there has been a vast expansion of the human rights field, generating a network of bodies, organs, institutions and complaints procedures of almost impenetrable diversity and complexity. Most are of a non-judicial character, and use techniques of verification that tend to be more inquisitorial than adversarial: that is, they eschew the system whereby contending parties vie for a result favourable to themselves. Another significant feature is that they only issue legally non-binding recommendations, reports and opinions. Some of these bodies are the product of the very instrument, the compliance of whose provisions they have been mandated to control.

A few of the bodies have a judicial or quasi-judicial function, conducting their examinations and investigations in the form of proceedings between two opposing parties who make submissions to them in oral hearings. The proceedings are concluded with a legally binding appraisal of proffered and alleged facts – often called a judgement (examples are the European Commission of Human Rights/European Court of Human Rights and the Inter-American Commission and Court of Human Rights).

Most of the bodies are offshoots of United Nations activities; some belong to regional organizations. Within the United Nations distinction can be made between those functions which emanate from and are based directly on the UN Charter itself, and those mechanisms which derive from a treaty proper. Thus two distinct spheres of UN human rights activity are discernible: 'charter-based' and 'treaty-based'; both will be considered later. Within a regional organization such as the Council of Europe, one can also discern two spheres of activity: one emanating from the Statute of the Council and the other treaty-based.

UN International Instruments Containing Torture-Prohibiting Clauses

The notion of 'laws of humanity' was not specific enough to indicate what kinds of acts were prohibited. A first attempt at clarification was made in the 1929 Geneva Convention concerning the treatment of prisoners of war, where it is stated that 'all kinds of corporal punishment, incarceration in localities without natural light and, generally, all forms of cruelty' are prohibited (Article 46:3) In 1943 the three Allied powers (UK, USA and the Soviet Union) issued the so-called Moscow Declaration on account of evidence from many quarters of German atrocities, massacres and cold-blooded mass executions, declaring that the perpetrators would be sent back to the scene of their crime and judged on the spot. As regards major war criminals 'whose offences have no particular geographical localiza-tion', it was decreed that they should be punished by the joint judgement of the Allied governments: this foreshadows the constitution of the Nuremberg Tribunal, which in its charter was given jurisdiction over 'war crimes', including 'ill-treatment' of civilian populations, as well as 'crimes against humanity' – 'murder, extermination ... and other inhumane acts' committed on political, racial or religious grounds.

This, then, is the context that influenced the decision to grant a particularly prominent place to the promotion of human rights in the new organization of the world, and that was the driving force behind the subsequent drawing up of the *Universal Declaration of Human Rights* (UDHR), adopted on 10 December 1948 by the UN General Assembly. It was obvious that an essential element of the UDHR would be a provision prohibiting torture and other forms of severe ill-treatment. The formulation that was finally decided upon, as Article 5, is this: 'No one shall be subjected to torture or to cruel, inhuman or degrading treatment or punishment.' This wording, with a degree of variation, has since become the model for the plethora of international instruments that have articles on torture. The article does not define any of the concepts used, or give a clear indication what the drafters had in mind. However, proposals were tabled to prohibit medical or scientific experimentation against the subject's will, in response to the heinous experiments that had been forcibly conducted on concentration camp inmates. The Universal Declaration did not set up any enforcement mechanism, since it did not impose legal obligations on states.

Eighteen years later, in 1966, the General Assembly adopted two covenants: one on civil and political rights and another on economic, social and cultural rights; both introduced as implementation machinery a duty on states to report to different UN organs how they had fulfilled their obligations under the covenants. With regard to the Covenant on Civil and Political Rights (CCPR), the duty to report was complemented by the establishment of a Human Rights Committee (as distinguished from the UN Commission of Human Rights, the UN's main body, which was set up in 1946 by the Economic and Social Council to deal with all matters relating to human rights – the Commission is 'charter-based'; the Committee is 'treaty-based'). The Committee was granted the power to deal with so-called inter-state complaints, on condition that the states concerned recognized its competence. It was also empowered – in an Optional Protocol to the CCPR – to receive and consider complaints from individuals alleging violations of the Covenant by states which had accepted this right of petition by their ratification of the Protocol.

However, ten years passed before the covenants came into force, in 1976. And it is a regrettable fact that fewer than half the states which ratified them have accepted the inter-state complaints procedure or the right of individual petition, in spite of fervent and repeated appeals by the UN General Assembly and by the World Conference on Human Rights in Vienna in 1993 (Vienna Declaration and Programme of Action). Unfortunately, some states have also appended extensive reservations to their ratifications, thereby appreciably eroding the scale of their commitments. Nevertheless, the delay of almost thirty years, between the adoption of the UDHR and the two covenants, compounded by the reluctance of many states to comply with the implementation mechanisms, have led to the UDHR acquiring a juridical status more important than was originally intended. It is thus gratifying that the UDHR, although it does not lay down enforceable legal obligations, is widely used as a means of judging compliance with human rights obligations under the UN Charter. Its impact has been considerable: references to the UDHR are, for example, to be found in the American Convention on Human Rights of 1969, as well as in the African Charter on Human and Peoples' Rights of 1981. What is more, the Declaration serves as a point of reference for domestic courts, inasmuch as the international prohibition on torture is unequivocally established in the law of nations.

The important question as to whether the UDHR has become

customary law with regard to the rights enshrined therein has not yet received a final answer. At the Tehran Conference on Human Rights in 1968 it was proclaimed that 'UDHR constitutes an obligation for the members of the international community'. However, the World Conference on Human Rights in Vienna in 1993 took a more cautious approach, stating instead that it 'constitutes a common standard of achievement for all peoples and all nations' and 'has been the basis for the United Nations in making advances in standard setting as contained in the existing international human rights instruments', in particular the two covenants. A judgement based on the stringent standards of the classical doctrine on the determination of the elements which form international customary law – that is, the convergence of extensive, continuous and reiterated practice and of *opinio juris* – a measured standpoint would be that the UDHR does not in its entirety constitute customary international law.

For the purpose of this survey, however, it suffices to assert that very few states would deny that a state is in violation of international law if it practises, encourages or condones torture or other cruel, inhuman or degrading treatment or punishment (the possible exception being certain Muslim states, such as Iran, which has indicated to the UN Human Rights Committee that it does not consider itself bound by human rights provisions that conflict with Iran's interpretation of Islamic law). An important piece of evidence on the present attitude of states is Chapter II B 5, entitled Freedom from Torture, of the 1993 Vienna Declaration and Programme of Action, in which it is emphasized that 'one of the most atrocious violations against human dignity is the act of torture' and that freedom from torture is a right which 'must be protected under all circumstances, including in times of internal or international disturbance or armed conflict'. States are being urged 'to put an immediate end' to this practice and to 'eradicate this evil for ever' through the full implementation of the Universal Declaration as well as the relevant conventions.

The Genocide Convention of 1948, which was approved by the General Assembly the day before the UDHR was adopted, that is 9 December 1948, came into force in 1951. It is, unlike the UDHR, a legal compact, which pledges every Contracting Party to punish or to extradite for punishment any person committing genocide, as well as conspiracy, incitement or attempt thereto or complicity therein, 'whether they are constitutionally responsible rulers, public officials or private individuals'. It is applicable in peacetime as well as in times of war and encompasses those acts that aim to obliterate, in whole or in part, ethnic, racial or religious groups by 'causing serious bodily or mental harm' to their members, as well as outright killing. Other punishable acts covered by the Convention include the sterilization of members of a given group;

the separation of men and women and their transfer to different camps or places of banishment; removal of children from one group to another and to other countries (as was the case with thousands of Greek children during the Second World War); incitement of a population to abuse narcotics in poisonous doses (practised by the Japanese in China); removal of groups to regions with forbidding climatic conditions or denial of elementary means of sustenance.

The General Assembly's basic resolution on genocide, unanimously adopted on 11 December 1946, declares that genocide 'is a crime under international law, contrary to the spirit and aims of the United Nations and condemned by the civilized world'. This is reinforced by Article 1 of the Convention, which adds 'in time of peace or in time of war' – an important extension of the Nuremburg Tribunal Charter, which was only applicable to crimes committed during a war. The General Assembly resolution and the Convention are therefore clear expressions of the view that genocide is a crime even for those states which have not ratified the Convention; the consequence of this is that a national of such a state cannot escape criminal responsibility. Furthermore, it means that an accusation of genocide – quite independently of the Convention – cannot be rebutted by a state with reference to Article 2:7 of the UN Charter (the domestic jurisdiction clause), whether that state is a Contracting Party to the Convention or not. Disputes on the interpretation, application or fulfilment of the Convention shall be submitted to the ICJ under Article IX, which implies an acceptance of the compulsory jurisdiction of the ICJ on the basis of Article 36:1 of the Court's Charter (the so-called optional clause). If a party to a case before the Court fails to carry out the obligations incumbent upon it under a judgement by the Court, the other party may seek recourse to the Security Council in accordance with Article 94 of the UN Charter. In this way the Security Council may be forced to deal with genocide cases which do not endanger international peace and security (Articles 34 and 39 of the UN Charter).

The time-limit for the prosecution and punishment of war crimes and crimes against humanity has been an issue of considerable contention. It began to receive attention during the mid-1960s in those countries, such as Sweden, which in their national laws provided for different periods of limitation for various crimes, with no exception made for war crimes or crimes against humanity. This caused deep concern within the UN Commission of Human Rights, which on 9 April 1965 adopted a resolution that no one guilty of such crimes 'shall escape the bar of justice wherever he may be and whenever he may be detected'. This resulted in a convention dated 26 November 1968 on the *Non-Applicability of Statutory Limitations to War Crimes and Crimes against Humanity*, which affirms 'in international law, through this Convention, the principle that there is no period of limitation for war crimes and crimes against humanity, and [pledges] to secure its universal application'. Some countries, however, have been reluctant to waive the time limitation in their national laws, on the grounds that not only was this founded on a deep-rooted principle of criminal law but also because obvious evidentiary difficulties would arise, with the growing risk of miscarriage of justice as time goes by. It is also a fact that to date only some forty states have ratified this Convention: of the five permanent members of the Security Council, only Russia/the states of the former USSR have signed; as have the states of the former Warsaw Pact bordering the West; Germany has signed but not Japan; all the new states of the former Yugoslavia are signatories. (Some 115 states have ratified the Genocide Convention; those failing to sign include Japan).

The chronological nature of this survey demands that mention be made of the *Standard Minimum Rules for the Treatment of Prisoners* of 1955. These Rules prohibit, *inter alia*, corporal punishment (Rule 31).

The Covenant on Civil and Political Rights of 1966 (CCPR) has been mentioned cursorily above. The CCPR came into force in 1976. Together with its Optional Protocol, the CCPR establishes different accountability procedures; these will be dealt with later. The article prohibiting torture and other forms of severe ill-treatment (Article 7) carries the same general wording as Article 5 of UDHR, with the addition of a sentence covering medical and scientific experimentation. Article 7 reads:

> No one shall be subjected to torture or to cruel, inhuman or degrading treatment or punishment. In particular, no one shall be subjected without his free consent to medical or scientific experimentation.

Linked to this article prohibiting torture and inhuman treatment is Article 10:1, which lays down the positive requirement for the humane treatment of detained persons:

> All persons deprived of their liberty shall be treated with humanity and with respect for the inherent dignity of the human person.

The two articles have notable differences. First, whereas Article 7 is of general application (*lex generalis*), Article 10 targets only persons in detention (*lex specialis*). Second, and perhaps surprisingly, whereas Article 7 is non-derogable – that is, states must comply with it even in time of public emergency – Article 10:1 is not protected from infringement in times of crises; measures of derogation may, however, only be taken 'to the extent strictly required by the exigencies of the situation' and may not involve discrimination (Article 4). The observance of this principle of proportionality is also subject to control and review by the Human Rights Committee under Article 40, as is the principle of non-discrimination. Many situations will involve both principles at the same time and therefore require their simultaneous application.

The articles do not contain any definition of the different terms and notions used, but the Committee has set out its views on certain aspects (General Comment 20/44 of 3 April 1992 on Article 7 and General Comment 21/44 of 6 April 1992 on Article 10). The Committee emphasizes that Article 7 allows of no limitation, that no derogation is allowed at any time, and that no justification or extenuating circumstances may be invoked to excuse a violation of Article 7 for any reason, including receipt of an order from a superior officer or public authority.

The non-justification principle has been affirmed also by other international judicial and official bodies as well as in international instruments – with one notable exception: the UN Convention Against Torture of 1984, which permits the infliction of pain and suffering as part of the imposition of lawful sanctions (see below). Some of the paragraphs may be quoted here: they set out in summary and competent form the standard of conduct that most international bodies monitoring a state's behaviour consider to be common ground as regards the standards states should uphold and abide by in order to comply with their obligations under Article 7:

4. The Covenant does not contain any definition of the concepts covered by article 7, nor does the Committee consider it necessary to draw up a list of prohibited acts or to establish sharp distinctions between the different kinds of punishment or treatment; the distinction depends on the nature, purpose and severity of the treatment applied.

5. The prohibition in article 7 relates not only to acts that cause physical pain but also to acts that cause mental suffering to the victim. In the Committee's view, moreover, the prohibition must extend to corporal punishment, including excessive chastisement ordered as punishment of a crime or as an educative or disciplinary measure. It is appropriate to emphasise in this regard that article 7 protects, in particular, children, pupils and patients in teaching and medical institutions.

6. The Committee notes that prolonged solitary confinement of the detained or imprisoned person may amount to acts prohibited by article 7. As the Committee has stated in its general comment No. 6 (16), article 6 of the Covenant refers generally to abolition of the death penalty in terms that strongly suggest that abolition is desirable. Moreover, when the death penalty is applied

by a State party for the most serious crimes, it must not only be strictly limited in accordance with article 6 but it must be carried out in such a way as to cause the least possible physical and mental suffering.

7. Article 7 expressly prohibits medical or scientific experimentation without the free consent of the person concerned.... The Committee also observes that special protection in regard to such experiments is necessary in the case of persons not capable of giving valid consent, and in particular those under any form of detention or imprisonment. Such persons should not be subjected to any medical or scientific experimentation that may be detrimental to their health....

9. ... States parties must not expose individuals to the danger of torture or cruel, inhuman or degrading treatment or punishment upon return to another country by way of their extradition, expulsion or *refoulement*....

11. In addition to describing steps to provide the general protection against acts prohibited under article 7 to which anyone is entitled, the State party should provide detailed information on safeguards of the special protection of particularly vulnerable persons. It should be noted that keeping under systematic review interrogation rules, instructions, methods and practices as well as arrangements for the custody and treatment of persons subjected to any form of arrest, detention or imprisonment is an effective means of preventing cases of torture and ill-treatment. To guarantee the effective protection of detained persons, provisions should be made for detainees to be held in places officially recognized as places of detention and for their names and places of detention, as well as for the names of persons responsible for their detention, to be kept in registers readily available and accessible to those concerned, including relatives and friends. To the same effect, the time and place of all interrogations should be recorded, together with the names of all those present and this information should also be available for purposes of judicial or administrative proceedings. Provisions should also be made against incommunicado detention. In that connection States parties should ensure that any places of detention be free from any equipment liable to be used for inflicting torture or ill-treatment. The protection of the detainee also requires that prompt and regular access be given to doctors and lawyers and, under appropriate supervision when the investigation so requires, to family members.

In General Comment 21/44 of 6 April 1992 the Committee takes up the rights of detainees under Article 10 combined with Article 7.

4. Treating all persons deprived of their liberty with humanity and with respect for their dignity is a fundamental and universally applicable rule. Consequently, the application of this rule, as a minimum, cannot be dependent on the material resources available in the State party. This rule must be applied without distinction of any kind, such as race, colour, sex, language, religion, political or other opinion, national or social origin, property, birth or other status....

7. Furthermore, the Committee recalls that reports should indicate whether the various applicable provisions form an integral part of the instruction and training of the personnel who have authority over persons deprived of their liberty and whether they are strictly adhered to by such personnel in the discharge of their duties. It would also be appropriate to specify whether arrested or detained persons have access to such information and have effective legal means enabling them to ensure that those rules are respected, to complain if the rules are ignored and to obtain adequate compensation in the event of a violation.

So far as I know, the CCPR is the only international instrument drafted within the UN that contains a specific reference to 'medical and scientific experimentation' as being prohibited if performed without a person's free consent. The clause bristles with difficulties; this is amply illustrated by the discussions and the many proposals that were submitted during the drafting procedure, such as the distinction between treatment and experimentation, the need to outlaw criminal experimentations without hindering legitimate scientific and medical research and practices (psycho-surgery, foetal experimentation, etc.). The problem of free consent is equally thorny: what about sick, mentally retarded, or unconscious persons, for example; how do we safeguard against dubious or extorted consent?

One tried to compile an exhaustive list of generally recognized exceptions but the difficulties were so numerous – a fact also recognized by the WHO, which had been consulted – that the idea had to be abandoned. The Human Rights Committee comments only sparingly on this problem, noting the paucity of information available. It may be added here that in the first Additional Protocol of 1977 to the Geneva Conventions of 1949 there is laid down in Article 11:2 a prohibition on medical or scientific experiments, *even with the consent* of the person concerned. As regards medical or scientific experimentation it should also be added that a European Convention on Human Rights and Biomedicine was opened for signature on 19 November 1996, dealing *inter alia* with consent to medical interventions (chapter II), scientific research on human beings (chapter V), organs and tissue transplantation (chapter VI); no complaints mechanism has been established.

On 9 December 1975 the *Declaration on the Protection of all Persons from being subjected to Torture and other Cruel, Inhuman or Degrading Treatment or Punishment* was adopted by the General Assembly. It is a recommendation that lacks legally binding force, but its moral and political impact may, however, be considerable. On 10 December 1984 the *Convention Against Torture and other Cruel, Inhuman or Degrading Treatment or Punishment* (CAT) was opened for signature; it came into force on 26 June 1987. To date some ninety-five states have ratified the Convention. Whereas the

Convention confers obligations only on the Contracting Parties, the Declaration addresses itself to all states members of the United Nations that have taken part in its adoption – in this case the whole community of nations of the world. These two instruments are the only ones within the UN system that contain definitions of 'torture'. These definitions, which some prefer to call descriptions, are similar but not identical. Both refer also to 'cruel, inhuman or degrading treatment or punishment', without offering any definition.

The two instruments contain a wide range of obligations incumbent on states in the fight against torture. These obligations apply in principle also to *cruel, inhuman or degrading treatment or punishment*, although the applicability of some was left unresolved during the drafting of the Convention. Almost all the provisions of the Declaration have their equivalent – albeit differently formulated – in the CAT. But the CAT has also taken up the issues of 'non-*refoulement*', 'non-extradition' and 'non-expulsion', where there is a risk of torture if the person is returned to a particular country (Article 3, based on the jurisprudence of the European Commission and Court of Human Rights); it also deals in some detail (basing itself on the principle of *aut dedere aut punire*) with the question of establishing universal jurisdiction over acts of torture, so that a suspected offender will either be proceeded against where he is found or in his own country or where the offence has been committed. This principle had already been embodied in a number of conventions against terrorism. And it is rightly considered as a keystone in the fight against torture as well.

Both instruments stress the necessity for properly trained staff, the requirement to keep under systematic review interrogation methods and practices, arrest and custodial procedures to avert cases of ill-treatment, and effective complaint procedures, as well as adequate means of redress and compensation to victims of torture.

The *Code of Conduct for Law-Enforcement Officials* was adopted by the General Assembly on 17 December 1979. The term 'code' may suggest that this set of rules is legally binding on its target group, namely police officers, but it is not. However, the rules set standards of professional practice and behaviour which have a strong morally binding force without being a legal code, unless they are incorporated into national legislation. Each of the eight articles of the Code is accompanied by commentaries to facilitate its use. One, Article 5, contains a prohibition on the use of 'torture or other cruel, inhuman or degrading treatment or punishment', which is derived from the Declaration against Torture of 1975. It is interesting to note that the article also prohibits the use, in defence, of the 'superior order' plea, which is missing in the 1975 Declaration but was included later in the CAT.

In Article 8 the duty is laid down for law-enforcement officials not only to prevent but also rigorously to oppose any violations of the Code as well as to report those they believe have occurred or are about to occur, both to their superiors and to other higher authorities, external to the police force, invested with the power to review grievances and complaints. The bringing of violations to public attention through the mass media may also be justified as a last resort, according to the commentaries to the article.

The commentaries to Article 5 indicate that 'cruel, inhuman and degrading treatment or punishment has not been defined by the General Assembly but should be interpreted so as to extend the widest possible protection against abuses, whether physical or mental'. This formulation is further developed in a later UN instrument, which will be dealt with below. It has also become the guiding maxim for the European Committee for Prevention of Torture and inhuman or degrading treatment or punishment.

On 18 December 1982 the General Assembly adopted the *Principles of Medical Ethics* bearing on the role of health personnel, particularly physicians charged with the medical care of prisoners and detainees. Principle 2 declares that 'it is a gross contravention of medical ethics, as well as an offence under applicable instruments ... to engage, actively or passively, in acts which constitute participation in, complicity in, incitement to or attempts to commit torture or other cruel, inhuman or degrading treatment or punishment'.

In the resolution by which the General Assembly adopted these Principles reference was made to the 1975 Declaration against Torture as well as to the so-called *Tokyo Declaration by the World Medical Association* in 1975, which begins with a definition of torture:

> the deliberate, systematic or wanton infliction of physical or mental suffering ... to force another person to yield information, to make a confession, or for any other reason

and thereafter describes in some detail how the definition shall be understood ('not countenance, condone or participate in the practice of torture' – 'not provide any premises, instruments, substances or knowledge to facilitate the practice of torture' – 'not be present during any procedure during which torture or other forms of cruel, inhuman and degrading treatment or punishment is used or threatened').

On 8 December 1988 the General Assembly adopted the *Body of Principles for the Protection of All Persons under any Form of Detention or Imprisonment*, which may be considered as the beginning of a founding charter on prisoners' rights. Principle 6 contains an unequivocal prohibition on torture:

No person under any form of detention or imprisonment shall be subject to torture or to cruel, inhuman or degrading treatment or punishment. No circumstance whatever may be invoked as a justification for torture or other cruel, inhuman or degrading treatment or punishment.

In the same way, but in a more elaborated form than in the Code of Conduct for Law-Enforcement Officials, 'cruel, inhuman and degrading treatment and punishment' has been explained thus:

The terms 'cruel, inhuman or degrading treatment or punishment' should be interpreted so as to extend the widest possible protection against abuses, whether physical or mental, including the holding of a detained or imprisoned person in conditions which deprive him, temporarily or permanently, of the use of any of his natural senses, such as sight or hearing, or of his awareness of place and the passing of time.

As in the Code of Conduct for Law-Enforcement Officials, arresting and prison officers are enjoined in Principle 7 to report violations to higher authorities – both internal and external – with reviewing or remedial powers.

The Convention on the Rights of the Child of 1989, which came into force on 2 September 1990, has been ratified by some 190 states. Article 37 lays down a prohibition against 'torture, and other cruel, inhuman or degrading treatment or punishment' in the same way as the CCPR; but states are also under a positive obligation to take 'all appropriate legislative, administrative, social and educational measures to protect the child from all forms of physical or mental violence, injury or abuse' (Article 19).

UN Procedures: Supervisory and Enforcement Mechanisms

Certain of the treaties discussed above have set up monitoring organs: these will be dealt with first. Thereafter an account will be given of charter-based organs.

1. Treaty-based bodies

The Human Rights Committee was established in 1977 under the CCPR. Its eighteen members are elected by secret ballot by the States Parties to the CCPR for a four year term. They serve in their personal capacity – that is, they shall not be under instruction from other bodies or agencies – and may be re-elected.

The task of the Committee is threefold. First, there is the mandatory *reporting procedure* under Article 40, according to which states undertake to submit reports on the measures they have adopted to give effect to the

rights recognized by the CCPR and on the progress made in the enjoyment of those rights. Following an initial report, to be submitted during
the first year in which a state has become a party to the CCPR, a five-
year rule applies. Adherence to this rule is not impressive. Many states
delay reporting – sometimes inordinately – in spite of reminders. What
is more, reports are often inadequate and incomplete and supplementary
information is often not forthcoming, although the Committee strives to
elicit more during meetings with states' representatives, as well as through
follow-up requests. Since tardiness and inadequacy in reporting entails no
sanctions, the risk arises that immunity from review and accountability
will result. It must be said that, on the whole, the reporting system falls
considerably short as a means of raising human rights standards and
preventing violations.

Second, an optional *inter-state complaints procedure* is laid down in Articles
41–43. Only some 45 states out of 145 have accepted this procedure,
which as a result seems to have become a dead letter.

Third, there is also, in an Optional Protocol to the CCPR, a procedure for *individual complaints*, to which some 90 states have adhered. Under
this protocol the Committee may be seised by individuals claiming that
their rights under the CCPR have been violated. The main features of the
procedure are as follows:

(i) The Committee is competent to deal with a complaint if all
domestic channels have been exhausted and if the matter is not being
examined under another procedure of international investigation or
settlement; a complainant may be excused from having to exhaust
such channels if this would entail unreasonably prolonged procedures.

(ii) A complaint which has been declared admissible shall be communicated to the state concerned, which shall within sixth months submit
to the Committee written explanations or statements clarifying the
matter; it shall also indicate what measures it may have taken to remedy
the situation (Article 4). On completion of the case-file, the Committee
examines in camera the documentation submitted by both parties,
after which it forwards its views to the state concerned (Article 5:4).

(iii) Although not provided for in the Protocol, a state may be asked
to stay the proceedings against a complainant by so-called 'interim
measures', which are not, however, binding. Nor do the final views
expressed by the Committee constitute legally binding decisions; nevertheless, because of the moral weight they carry, based as they are on
impartial and objective assessment of the facts as presented, many
states act on and in accordance with the findings of the Committee.

If the mainly written procedures were to be complemented by oral hearings, the Committee's views would probably assume even greater authority with states.

Since its foundation in 1977 the Committee has been petitioned with increasing numbers of complaints, indicating that the procedure is considered a valid and worthwhile one by complainants.

The Committee Against Torture was established pursuant to Article 17 of the CAT and began to function in 1988. It has ten members who are elected – in the same way as the members of the Human Rights Committee – by the States Parties to the CAT for a four-year term. They likewise serve in their personal capacity and may be re-elected.

The Committee has a fourfold task. Three of these functions are formulated in the same way – with only minor variations – as the three responsibilities of the Human Rights Committee: examination of reports from states (Article 19); examination of inter-state complaints (Article 21); examination of individual complaints (Article 22). In addition, the committee has a mandate to conduct confidential inquiries, if it has received well-founded indications of systematically practised torture (Article 20).

It is mandatory for states to submit reports from the moment they have adhered to the CAT, but acceptance of inter-state and individual complaints is optional and dependant upon special declarations. As regards the inquiry procedure, states must cooperate with the Committee if they did not at the time of adherence make a declaration in accordance with Article 28 ('opting-out clause'); the duty to cooperate does not, however, include *per se* 'visits to the territory' of the state, for which special agreements are necessary.

The number of states adhering to the CAT reached one hundred in December 1996. Of those, some forty states have accepted the inter-state complaints procedure; the same states with two exceptions (the USA and UK) have also accepted the individual complaints procedure. The USA has also registered an elaborate general reservation. This contains not only formal reservations, referring *inter alia* to the 4th, 5th and 14th Amendments of the US Constitution, but also interpretive 'understandings' as well as 'declarations'; this has moved some countries, including the Netherlands, Finland and Sweden, to submit objections to the Secretary-General regarding the reservations.

The procedure for *examining reports* from states is very similar to that provided for in the CCPR and submission is subject to the same periodicity. And, likewise, within the CAT system states are failing in their responsibilities: 'a high number of reports have not been submitted', noted the UN General Assembly in December 1996. As a means to prevent torture the system is as anodyne as reporting within the CCPR.

The *inter-state complaints* procedure is modelled on, *inter alia*, the CCPR by way of an *ad hoc* Conciliation Commission, and is based on the expectation that a friendly solution will be achieved. If it is not, the Committee can only submit a report containing the facts with the submissions of the states concerned and communicate it to them through the Secretary-General. It is doubtful that this procedure will prove any more attractive than that used by the CCPR.

However, in the area of *individual complaints* the CAT procedure has attracted a number of cases. Article 22 contains provisions which regulate the procedure along the same lines as laid down in the Optional Protocol to CCPR Articles 2–5. In the clause on the exhaustion of internal remedies (Article 22:5 (b)), there is however an interesting addition: observation of the rule ceases to be mandatory not only where application of such remedies is unreasonably prolonged but also if they are 'unlikely to bring effective relief to the person who is victim' of a violation. One seldom finds this general rule of international law spelt out so explicitly in a treaty text. Grounds for admissibility are (Article 22:5 (a)) not only that the same matter *is not being*, but also that it *has not been* examined by another international investigatory body.

Many individual complaints relate to expulsion cases, where it is maintained that the complainant will be subjected to torture if sent back to a particular country in violation of Article 3 of the Convention. The procedure is less cumbersome than that involving the European Commission on Human Rights, and since knowledge has spread of a number of successful complaints, the CAT procedure is gaining in favour with those at risk. Governments are more restrained since they prefer full contradictory proceedings in the presence of both parties at oral hearings. There must be a threat of torture: cruel, inhuman or degrading treatment or punishment is not sufficient ground for applying Article 3 (in contrast to the European Commission's and Court's jurisprudence, where threats of inhuman and degrading treatment may constitute obstacles to expulsion).

The confidential *inquiry procedure* (Article 20) caused much controversy during drafting, up to the very last moment. This was settled by insertion of an 'opting-out clause' in Article 28. Article 20 authorizes the Committee to institute, on its own initiative, an inquiry if it receives reliable information containing well-founded indications of a systematic practice of torture. Again, the article is applicable only to 'torture', not to 'cruel, inhuman or degrading treatment or punishment'. It shall in such a case seek the cooperation of the state concerned and, in agreement with that state, the inquiry may include a visit to its territory. After the completion of the investigation the committee may decide as a 'reward' to keep the entire matter confidential. Nevertheless it has the option of 'going public' by including a summary of the results of the inquiry in its annual report to the General Assembly, as a means of pressure to induce the state to cooperate.

The difficulties the Committee encounters in cases of this kind are amply shown in its Annual Report for 1996, where a summary account of the results of the proceedings concerning the inquiry on Egypt is given: long-drawn-out negotiations on an *in situ* investigation ended in failure and Egypt made known its opposition to publication; the Committee, however, concluded that publication was 'necessary in order to encourage full respect for the provisions of the convention in Egypt'.

The Committee on the Rights of the Child was established pursuant to Article 43 of the Convention on the Rights of the Child. It has ten members elected by the States Parties and they serve in their personal capacity for four-year terms. They may be re-elected. The Committee monitors the progress made by states in fulfilling their obligations. States have to submit a first report within two years of ratifying the convention and then subsequently at five-year intervals. States shall make their reports 'widely available to the public in their own countries'.

The Convention is a cover-all treaty, encompassing the whole range of human rights – civil, political, economic, social and cultural – as well as humanitarian law relevant to children in armed conflicts, thus bringing together the rights of the child expressed in many treaties and declarations, from the UDHR of 1948 onwards. However, it does not establish any right of petition either in the form of an inter-state or an individual complaints mechanism. Aggrieved parties must resort instead to, for example, the grievance procedures available within the monitoring systems of the Human Rights Committee or the Committee Against Torture.

2. Charter-based bodies

The Commission on Human Rights, which was set up in 1946, is the United Nations' central policy organ in the field of human rights. It makes, *inter alia*, recommendations and drafts international instruments relating to human rights; it also investigates allegations concerning violations of human rights and handles communications relating to such violations. It is composed of fifty-three member states' representatives, elected for three-year terms.

The Commission has established a number of subsidiary bodies: in 1947 it set up the Sub-Commission on the Prevention of Discrimination and Protection of Minorities, which has twenty-six (sitting) experts nominated for a four-year term by governments, though they act in their personal capacity and not as representatives of states. In recent years the

Commission has set up organs to investigate human rights problems in specific countries or on thematic situations: special rapporteurs, representatives or other designates.

As for the Commission itself, elaborate provisions have been laid down in several resolutions by the Economic and Social Council on its competence to study situations 'which reveal a consistent pattern of violation of human rights' (Resolution 1253/XLII of 6 June 1967), as well as to consider communications 'which appear to reveal a consistent pattern of gross and reliably attested violations of human rights' (Resolution 1503/XLVIII of 27 May 1970). If it finds an investigation warranted, it may appoint an *ad hoc* committee to conduct it 'with the express consent of the state concerned' and 'in constant cooperation with that state and under conditions determined by agreement with it' and only after 'all available means at the national level have been resorted to and exhausted'; all proceedings in accordance with Resolution 1503 shall remain confidential until such time as the Commission decides to make recommendations to the ECOSOC; in contrast, the debates on situations under Resolution 1253 are in public.

A Special Rapporteur on Torture (and Country Rapporteurs) was appointed by the Commission on Human Rights in 1985 to examine questions relevant to torture; he was empowered to seek and receive credible and reliable information on such questions and to respond to such information without delay ('the urgent action procedure'). The Special Rapporteur corresponds with governments on measures they have taken or plan to take to prevent or combat torture. Requests for urgent action received by him are brought to the attention of the government concerned to ensure protection of the individual's right to physical and mental integrity. He also holds consultations with governments who express the wish to meet with him, and visits countries where torture occurs or is alleged to occur.

The Special Rapporteur submits an annual report to the Commission of Human Rights. In those reports he has taken the view that, although the mandate is limited to torture as opposed to cruel, inhuman or degrading treatment or punishment, that distinction is a matter of degree and a matter of intent – both highly subjective notions. There is thus a 'grey area regarding the degree of pain and suffering, which distinguishes torture from other treatments'. If a difference of opinion were to arise over whether a particular situation actually constitutes torture, the Special Rapporteur would be acting within his mandate if information relating to events in this hazy area were brought to the attention of the government with a request for comments. He has also made recommendations on the broader problem of detainees; these are in line with what other bodies dealing with the same questions are suggesting.

The difference between the country-oriented and the thematic approach is that a country rapporteur deals with the violation of all human rights in one specific country, whereas a thematic rapporteur deals with the violation of one specific human right all over the world. All countries in the world are therefore affected by the appointment of an issue-oriented rapporteur. Furthermore, although the thematic mechanisms are created on the basis of Resolution 1253, which explicitly refers to 'situations which reveal a consistent pattern of violations of human rights', their mandate is not restricted to such situations. Indeed, special rapporteurs often take up violations which are not part of a systematic practice but may constitute the sole incident of its kind.

The High Commissioner for Human Rights is a post which was created with General Assembly Resolution 48/141 of 20 December 1993 in the wake of the Vienna World Conference on Human Rights of 14–25 June 1993. It may be recalled that the idea of a High Commissioner had been mooted several times since the mid-1950s by, in particular, Latin American countries, but had always been sunk in the Cold War morass.

The High Commissioner's tasks are formidable: promoting effective universal enjoyment of all civil, cultural, economic, political and social rights; carrying out the tasks assigned to him or her by the competent bodies of the United Nations system in the field of human rights and making recommendations to them; promoting the realization of the right to development and encouraging enhanced support from relevant bodies of the United Nations system; providing, through appropriate institutions, advisory services and technical and financial assistance, at the request of the state concerned and, where appropriate, the regional human rights organizations; coordinating relevant United Nations education and public information programmes in the field of human rights; playing an active role in removing current obstacles and meeting challenges to the full re-alization of all human rights and in preventing the continuation of human rights violations throughout the world; engaging in a dialogue with all governments regarding the implementation of his/her mandate with a view to securing respect for all human rights; enhancing international cooperation for the promotion and protection of all human rights; co-ordination of human rights promotion and defence activities throughout the United Nations system; rationalization, adaptation, strengthening and streamlining of the United Nations machinery in the field of human rights; overall supervision of the Centre for Human Rights.

It is too early to evaluate the likely impact of the High Commissioner in the field of torture. Much depends on the resources states are willing to allocate. For the present it seems obvious that the office is under-resourced.

The Council of Europe

Rules: international instruments

The Statute of the Council of Europe of 5 May 1949 proclaims as one of its aims the maintenance and further realization of human rights and fundamental freedoms; every member of the Council 'must accept the principles of the rule of law and of the enjoyment by all persons within its jurisdiction' of the said rights and freedoms. Any member which seriously violates those principles may be suspended from its right of representation and requested to withdraw; if such a member does not comply with a request to withdraw, a decision may be taken that he has ceased to be a member (Article 8). That article was applied when Greece in 1969, after lengthy proceedings before the European Commission of Human Rights, was found guilty of torturing and ill-treating detainees – opponents of the military junta which had seized power in April 1967 – in police stations and prisons. Greece was readmitted in 1974 after the junta's downfall.

The European Convention for the Protection of Human Rights and Fundamental Freedoms (ECHR) was adopted in 1950, and came into force in 1953. Article 3 of the ECHR provides that 'No one shall be subjected to torture or to inhuman or degrading treatment or punishment.' The text is, save for the omission of the word 'cruel' before 'inhuman', identical with Article 5 of UDHR. As is the case with the corresponding Article 7 of the CCPR, the rule is absolute in the sense that no derogation may be made from it (Article 15). The dropping of the word 'cruel' is nowhere explained: experts have subsequently agreed that the difference in wording does not signify any difference in substance.

Proposals were also made for the inclusion of a prohibition on physical mutilation as well as medical or scientific experimentation against one's will. Other proposals were also put forward in exemplification of the 'basic' prohibition – such as sterilization, beating, forcible drug administration, imprisonment with an excess of light, darkness, noise or silence to cause mental suffering – but they were not adopted.

The void created by the lack of definition in the article itself has in some measure been filled by a rich jurisprudence created by the two supervisory bodies: the European Commission and the European Court of Human Rights. The ECHR also entrusts the Committee of Ministers as well as the Secretary-General with powers of supervising states' observance of their engagements under the Convention.

In 1979 a *Declaration on the Police* was adopted by the Parliamentary Assembly. It covers 'all individuals and organizations, including such bodies as secret services, military police forces, armed forces or militias performing police duties, that are responsible for enforcing the law, investigating offences, and maintaining public order and state security'. It declares that 'torture and other forms of inhuman or degrading treatment or punishment remain prohibited in all circumstances. A police officer is under an obligation to disobey or disregard any order or instruction involving such measures'. The Committee of Ministers has not been able to give the Declaration its unqualified support due to hesitations on certain points, but it has raised no objection to the rule on 'torture'.

In 1987 the *European Prison Rules* were adopted by the Committee of Ministers. Rule 37 'completely' prohibits 'corporal punishment, punishment by placing in a dark cell, and all cruel, inhuman or degrading punishment ... as punishments for disciplinary offences'.

The *European Convention for the Prevention of Torture and Inhuman or Degrading Treatment or Punishment* was adopted on 26 November 1987 and came into force in February 1989. It is a procedural convention with no substantive provisions, setting up a Committee with wide supervisory powers and performing its mandate through inspection visits to states which have ratified it. Such states are under an obligation to open up for inspection and control all places of detention, under whatever name or style, where they house persons deprived of their liberty by a public act (houses of arrest, jails, police prisons, remand prisons, ordinary prisons, mental hospitals, military barracks, refugee centres etc.). The Committee's right of inspection remains in force also in wartime and during other emergencies or crises.

Procedures: supervisory and enforcement mechanisms

The *European Commission of Human Rights* is composed of the members that constitute the Contracting States. They are elected in their individual capacity for a period of six years and may be re-elected. Any violation of the Convention alleged to have been committed by a Contracting State may be referred to the Commission. The Convention grants this right of petition to a Contracting State against another Contracting State (inter-state procedures under Article 24 are mandatory) as well as to individuals, non-governmental organizations or groups of individuals (Article 25), if the state concerned has recognized the Commission's competence to receive such individual complaints. Most states have satisfied this condition.

The Commission, which meets in camera, examines first the admissibility of an application. Necessary conditions for inter-state as well as individual applications are (i) exhaustion of all domestic remedies, and (ii) submission of the complaint within six months of the date of the final domestic decision. For individual petitions further requirements are that they are not (i) anonymous, (ii) abusive, (iii) incompatible with the provisions of the Convention, (iv) manifestly ill-founded or (v) substantially the same as a matter which has already been examined by the Commission or has formerly been submitted to another procedure of international investigation or settlement.

On admission of an application, the Commission ascertains the facts of the case together with the parties through the written exchange of information and by way of oral hearings; on-site investigations may also take place. The Commission may also 'indicate' interim measures to be taken by the parties (e.g. stay of proceedings in expulsion cases), which, however, carry only advisory status.

Before the Commission formulates its legal opinion on the case it places itself at the parties' disposal with a view towards securing a friendly settlement of the matter on the basis of respect for human rights. If no friendly settlement is reached, the Commission draws up a report on the facts, stating its legal opinion as to whether they disclose a violation. At this point the task the Convention has assigned to the Commission ends. The decision on the merits of the case (i.e. breach or no breach) is taken either by the Court of Human Rights or by the Committee of Ministers, if the case has not been referred to the Court within a period of three months by the parties to the case or the Commission itself. Since 1994 the right to refer cases to the Court has also been granted to individuals.

The *Committee of Ministers*, which is composed of the Ministers of Foreign Affairs or their deputies, is the executive organ of the Council of Europe. In the ECHR it has also been given a judicial role, since it shall rule on the merits of a case where the Commission has handed down its opinion and where the case has not been referred to the Court. If the Committee by a two-thirds majority finds for a violation, it shall prescribe a period within which the state must take the measures required by the Committee's decision. The Committee's decisions are binding on states. The Committee also supervises the execution of the Court's judgements.

The *Court of Human Rights* consists of a number of judges, one from each member country of the Council of Europe. They are elected for a period of nine years and may be re-elected. The Court works in Chambers composed of seven judges. The judge who is a national of a state that is a party to a case shall always take part in the examination of that case. The procedure falls into two stages: the written stage, when those appearing before the Court file memoranda; and the oral hearings, where the parties plead in public before the Court, unless the Court in exceptional circumstances decides otherwise.

The Court's decision, taken by a majority vote, is reasoned and final. If a violation has been found, the Court may also afford just satisfaction to the injured party (e.g. pecuniary compensation). The states concerned must abide by the Court's decision/judgement. The judgement is transmitted to the Committee of Ministers, which supervises its execution.

It should be noted that an important restructuring of the complaints machinery under the Convention will take place when a new protocol, No. 11, to the Convention enters into force. This Protocol establishes a single Court, which will operate on a full-time basis and replace the present Commission and Court.[1] The new Court will be competent to receive individual as well as inter-state complaints; admissibility criteria will be the same as before and friendly settlement proceedings will take place as before and be conducted confidentially. Otherwise, hearings shall be public. Just satisfaction may be afforded. Judgements will be final and – as before – transmitted to the Committee of Ministers, which shall supervise their execution. This is the only function that remains with the Committee.

Appeals ('referrals') within the Court from one of its Chambers (seven judges) to its Grand Chamber (seventeen judges) are possible, if a case raises a serious question affecting the interpretation or application of the convention, or a serious issue of general importance. The Protocol comes into force when all States Parties to the ECHR have ratified it.

The *Secretary General* of the Council of Europe has, in Article 57[2] of the ECHR, been granted a modicum of monitoring powers, in that he may request states to 'furnish an explanation of the manner in which their internal laws ensure the effective implementation of any of the provisions of the Convention'. Such requests have been few and far between and the impact negligible.

Unlike the Commission and the Court, the *Committee for the Prevention of Torture* (CPT) is not a judicial body empowered to settle legal disputes or redress legal wrongs – that is, determine claims *ex post facto*. The CPT is a mechanism intended first and foremost to prevent ill-treatment from occurring (although it may in special cases intervene after the event). Its activities aim at 'conflict avoidance' on the practical level, whereas the Commission and the Court aim at 'conflict solution' on the legal level. In other words, the Commission and the Court can only intervene after having been petitioned by individuals or states, which also have to conform to certain procedural criteria; the CPT intervenes *ex officio* through periodic, follow-up and *ad hoc* visits, and states are under an obligation to permit visits as well as allow access to any and all places of detention whether public or private, as long as the deprivation of rights results from an action taken by a public authority. And the CPT has the right to visit such institutions at any time (e.g. police stations in the middle of the night); there is no obligation to give advance notice. During visits it has the right to interview any detainee in private. But it also has the right to interview police and prison officers and other guardians, as well as doctors, social workers, lawyers, and so forth. The right of access includes all kinds of written information which may be relevant to achieve the purpose of the visit: for example, custody records, medical files, complaints records, disciplinary registers.

Following a visit the CPT draws up a report, which is confidential and contains its findings and its recommendations. This is transmitted to the government concerned, which is asked for a detailed response within a specified time limit. If a government refuses to cooperate the CPT may make a public statement on the situation in the country concerned. This has to date only happened twice – albeit with regard to the same state. Almost all states have realized the importance of openness in these matters and have agreed to publish the CPT's visiting reports.

Given the nature of its functions, the CPT consists of members from various walks of life: medical doctors, psychiatrists, psychologists, experts in penitentiary matters, prison chaplains, lawyers, and so on; it may also engage additional expertise on an *ad hoc* basis.

As can be inferred from this very short description, the CPT is unprecedented not only in terms of its mandate but also in terms of its composition and its powers. And it should be stressed that for the CPT to carry out its preventive functions effectively, it must aim at a degree of protection which is greater than that upheld by the Commission and the Court when adjudging cases of ill-treatment of detainees: to fulfil its tasks it must identify situations which are not violations and may not even be critical but which nevertheless show signs of potentially degenerating into ill-treatment if allowed to develop. That is also why the CPT was very wisely granted a great deal of latitude as regards the standards it could apply: it is not bound by the case law of judicial or quasi-judicial bodies working in the same field, but can use this as a starting point when making its assessments.

This new approach to the fight against the scourge of torture is worthy of being tried out in other parts of the world; in this connection one may recall that the 1993 World Conference on Human Rights reaffirmed 'that efforts to eradicate torture should, first and foremost, be concentrated on prevention', and to this end called for 'the early adoption of an optional protocol to the convention against torture', to establish 'a preventive system of regular visits to places of detention'.

Finally, it is obvious that the CPT will be confronted with formidable challenges, once the Russian Federation and Ukraine sign up to the

Convention, since this will mean a doubling of the prison population falling within its mandate, while only adding two more members to the CPT. It is a moot question whether this enormous increase of the CPT's workload can be handled within its present structure.

Other Regional Instruments and Bodies

The American Convention on Human Rights, which was signed in November 1969 by the Latin American states as well as the United States, came into force in July 1978. Article 5, Paragraph 2 reads: 'No one shall be subjected to torture or to cruel, inhuman, or degrading punishment or treatment. All persons deprived of their liberty shall be treated with respect for the inherent dignity of the human person'.

The Convention also incorporated the Inter-American Commission on Human Rights – which had existed since 1948 – as an organ for the Convention's implementation, and established the Inter-American Court of Human Rights. The Convention gives the right of petition to individuals, groups of individuals and non-governmental organizations; inter-state complaints operate only among states that have expressly agreed to such a procedure. These bodies have developed an extensive jurisprudence.

Mention should also be made of the *Inter-American Convention to Prevent and Punish Torture*, which was adopted in 1985 and came into force on 28 February 1987. Article 2 contains this definition of torture:

> For the purposes of this Convention, torture shall be understood to be an act intentionally performed whereby physical or mental pain or suffering is inflicted on a person for purposes of criminal investigation as a means of intimidation, as personal punishment, as a preventive measure, as a penalty, or for any other purpose. Torture shall also be understood to be the use of methods upon a person intended to obliterate the personality of the victim or to diminish his physical or mental capacities, even if they do not cause physical pain or mental anguish.
>
> The concept of torture shall not include physical or mental pain or suffering that is inherent in or solely the consequence of lawful measures, provided that they do not include the performance of the acts or use of the methods referred to in this article.

However, a former president of the Inter-American Court has characterized this convention as a 'disappointing instrument', since it has eliminated the reaffirmation of torture as an international crime and also allows for continued application of the right of asylum, thereby suggesting that torture may be considered as a political crime, excluding it from the application of extradition treaties as well as eroding the principle of universal jurisdiction.[3]

The African Charter on Human and People's Rights, which was adopted in 1981, came into force on 21 October 1986. Most of the fifty countries in the African region have ratified it. Article 5 of the Charter is worded as follows:

> Every individual shall have the right to the respect of the dignity inherent in a human being and to the recognition of his legal status. All forms of exploitation and degradation of man particularly slavery, slave trade, torture, cruel, inhuman or degrading punishment and treatment shall be prohibited.

An *African Commission on Human and People's Rights* is established by the Charter to ensure the promotion and the protection of the rights. The task of promotion involves functions relating to studies, research, information, 'training and further training' – that is, a pedagogical function. It also has quasi-legislative functions, such as proposing and preparing draft laws on human rights or defining the principles that should apply.

The task of protection consists of examining complaints of human rights violations, submitted either by states or by individuals (so-called 'other communications'). The proceedings are in writing and confidential. The Commission's factual reports, accompanied by its findings and recommendations, shall be submitted to the *Assembly of Heads of State and Government*, which may decide that it should be published. No Court is established, since – as it is said – African customs and traditions emphasize mediation, conciliation and consensus rather than the adversarial and adjudicative procedures common to Western legal systems. A draft protocol on the creation of an African Court of human rights is, however, being discussed.

In 1981 the *Universal Islamic Declaration of Human Rights* was issued. It states, in Article 7, that 'No person shall be subjected to torture in mind or body, or degraded, or threatened with injury either to himself or to anyone related to or held dear by him.'

The *Final Act of the Conference on Security and Cooperation in Europe* (CSCE) was signed in Helsinki on 1 August 1975 by thirty-five states: all the countries of Europe (except Albania) plus the USA and Canada. Since 1 January 1995 the CSCE has been called the Organization for Security and Cooperation in Europe (OSCE). At the end of the third follow-up meeting of the Helsinki Conference held in Vienna in 1986–89, a Concluding Document was adopted, on 19 January 1989, which established a procedure for the continuous monitoring of the human rights dimension of the CSCE/OSCE (the *Vienna Human Dimension Mechanism*); this has only undergone minor alterations since coming into being. The procedures are cast in a traditional form based on reciprocity between two or more states for the settling of differences or disputes regarding the fulfilment of commitments. Individuals have no direct access to the Vienna mechanism, but may – like NGOs – provide information in general or on individual cases.

International Humanitarian Instruments and Bodies

International humanitarian law developed during the nineteenth century in conjunction with the laws of warfare (*jus in bello*), of which, according to some scholars, it even formed a part. With the sweeping development of the wider concept of human rights, certain notions – in particular with regard to acts prohibited under international law – are used interchangeably in human rights instruments as well as in humanitarian law instruments. Furthermore, prohibition of the said acts is absolute – that is, non-derogable and therefore applicable also in wartime – in the human rights instruments and without any designation of particular categories, as is often the case in humanitarian law instruments. This means that the said categories are doubly protected, and that others are safeguarded by relevant human rights instruments.

The concepts alluded to are *inter alia* the following: cruel treatment, torture, humiliating and degrading treatment, medical or scientific experiments, corporal punishment. Some concepts, like rape and enforced prostitution, in some of the humanitarian law instruments may be subsumed under one or several of the aforementioned. The same may be the case with regard to (physical) mutilation.

The *Geneva Conventions of 1949 on the Protection of War Victims*, and the Additional Protocols of 1977, consider 'torture or inhuman treatment, including biological experiments, wilfully causing great suffering or serious injury to body or health' to be 'grave breaches', the perpetrators of which states are under an obligation to search for, regardless of their nationality, and to bring them before their courts or hand them over to another High Contracting Party for trial (i.e. the principle of *aut punire aut dedere* that is also laid down in the UN Convention Against Torture).

In 1991 an optional *'International Fact-Finding Commission'* was established under Article 90 of the First Additional Protocol, and granted the competence to enquire into alleged grave breaches or other serious violations of the conventions and protocols.

Inspection of places of detention where persons affected by the events of war are being held (prisoners of war, detainees or civil internees) can be carried out *inter alia* by the *International Committee of the Red Cross* in accordance with the 1949 Geneva Conventions and the Additional Protocols of 1977. The Red Cross has a right to visit all places of detention in cases of international armed conflicts and may, in cases of non-international armed conflicts, based on its right of initiative, propose to the conflicting parties that it visits such places.

As regards situations characterized by internal disturbances or tension the Red Cross has – outside the convention framework – acquired a right of humanitarian initiative that allows it to offer its services to governments. This right originates in the very Statutes of the International Red Cross and Red Crescent Movement, which have been approved by the States Parties to the Geneva Conventions; consent on a case-by-case basis is needed.

Since the International Red Cross carries out functions and uses methods similar to those of the CPT Committee, it became necessary to make a distinction between the Geneva Conventions and the CPT Convention. This was achieved by a special provision in the latter to the effect that the CPT shall not visit places which the Red Cross representatives 'effectively visit on a regular basis' by virtue of the Geneva Conventions and the Additional Protocol. Hence the CPT shall not inspect places of detention where there is an armed conflict (international or internal) and the Red Cross effectively and regularly performs visits. Nevertheless the Red Cross protection does not cover common-law detainees and prisoners, but only those who are victims of armed conflicts; nor does it formally cover situations of internal disturbance and tension.

Definitional Issues and Case Law Jurisprudence

International instruments

Both in the *UN Declaration* and the *UN Convention Against Torture*, 'torture' is defined or described as having the following elements:

1. The *nature* of the act: an act by which severe physical or mental pain or suffering is inflicted upon a person.
2. The *perpetrator* of the act: he is a public official or any other person acting in an official capacity.
3. The perpetrator's *aim*: his acts are intentional and executed for the purpose, in particular, of obtaining from the victim or a third person information or confessions, or for the purpose of punishing him for an act, which he or a third person has committed or is suspected of having committed, or generally, for the purpose of discrimination of any kind.

The text of Article 1 in the Declaration and the Convention is reproduced below:

1. For the purpose of this *Declaration*, torture means any act by which severe pain or suffering, whether physical or mental, is intentionally inflicted by or at the instigation of a public official on a person for such purposes as obtaining from him or a third person information or confession, punishing him for an act he has committed or is suspected of having committed, or intimidating him or other persons. It does not include pain or suffering arising only from, inherent in or incidental to, lawful sanctions to the extent consistent with the Standard Minimum Rules for the Treatment of Prisoners.

2. Torture constitutes an aggravated and deliberate form of cruel, inhuman or degrading treatment or punishment....

1. For the purposes of this *Convention*, the term 'torture' means any act by which severe pain or suffering, whether physical or mental, is intentionally inflicted on a person for such purposes as obtaining from him or a third person information or a confession, punishing him for an act he or a third person has committed or is suspected of having committed, or intimidating or coercing him or a third person, or for any reason based on discrimination of any kind, when such pain or suffering is inflicted by or at the instigation of or with the consent or acquiescence of a public official or other person acting in an official capacity. It does not include pain or suffering arising only from, inherent in or incidental to lawful sanctions.

One important difference between the two instruments is the formulation of the 'escape clause' at the end of the first sub-paragraph of Article 1, which exempts 'lawful sanctions' from what are otherwise coverall definitions: in the Declaration, pain and suffering arising from such sanctions is not considered to be torture 'to the extent [they are] consistent with the Standard Minimum Rules for the Treatment of prisoners' adopted by the UN in 1955; these rules contain *inter alia* a clause number 31, which 'completely prohibits as punishments for disciplinary offences': 'corporal punishment, punishment by placing in a dark cell and all cruel, inhuman or degrading punishment'. Attempts were made to reproduce the formulation of the Declaration in the Convention; this was not accepted because it was argued that the Convention did not purport to recommend reform of the system of penal sanctions in different countries and that therefore the formulation would not be acceptable to a range of states. In the Convention this limitative description of lawful sanctions had to be left out! There therefore exists a regrettable void: how to qualify as punishment in some countries, for example, strict solitary confinement, in particular for longer periods, or mutilations and indeed stoning as a form of execution or, for that matter, public whipping and flogging. Some hold that such punishments are *per se* prohibited by international law and therefore not covered by the exception – a view which is certainly not accepted in some parts of the world.

The Declaration – but not the Convention – contains in its second sub-paragraph a summary definition of torture, which is often quoted by judicial as well as other bodies, and is formulated as follows: 'Torture constitutes an aggravated and deliberate form of cruel, inhuman or degrading treatment or punishment.' Some call this a 'definition proper' because the first paragraph of Article 1 in both instruments is more of a description than a real definition, to be used as an aid to interpretation when implementing the Convention.

In neither instrument is there a reference to 'medical and scientific experimentation', as we have found in the CCPR, Article 7. Nevertheless it can be argued that such treatment, in particular if it reaches a certain level of severity, is also covered by Article 1 of the Declaration and the Convention.

In connection with Article 1 of the Convention it is important to draw attention to Article 2, which contains a *respondant superior* clause, laying down that 'an order from a superior officer or a public authority may not be invoked as a justification of torture' – a principle which had already been enshrined in Article 8 of the Nuremberg Tribunal Charter of 1945, with the added rider that such an order could be 'considered in mitigation of punishment if the Tribunal determines that justice so requires'. It is important to note that this does not shatter the 'non-justification' principle, which must be applied. It is only when meting out a punishment that the 'superior order' plea may be taken into account. No similar provision is to be found in the Declaration.

As was remarked earlier, neither of the instruments defines or describes the phrase 'cruel, inhuman and degrading treatment or punishment'.

The torture clause in the *Inter-American Convention of 1985* is reproduced above. Although the Convention has been criticized for having impaired the international fight against torture, the said clause contains a valuable description of inadmissible methods, to which there is no equivalent in the UN Declaration or in the UN Convention. This reads as follows:

> Torture shall also be understood to be the use of methods upon a person intended to obliterate the personality of the victim or to diminish his physical or mental capacities, even if they do not cause physical pain or mental anguish.

This focuses attention on the fact that the aim of torture is not merely to extract a confession or obtain information from a victim, but to destroy a human being, his personality and identity, for example by chemical mind-control techniques.

The escape clause of lawful sanctions also has an important qualifying proviso – unfortunately lacking in the two UN instruments – which takes much of the sting out of this obnoxious clause:

The concept of torture shall not include physical or mental pain or suffering that is inherent in or solely the consequence of lawful measures, provided that they do not include the performance of the acts or use of the methods referred to in this article.

The official General Assembly commentary to the *Code of Conduct for Law-Enforcement Officials and Body of Principles for the Protection of Detained or Imprisoned Persons* has provided an interpretation of the phrase 'cruel, inhuman or degrading treatment or punishment', according to which it 'should be interpreted so as to extend the widest possible protection against abuses, whether physical or mental'; with regard to the Body of Principles, the commentary has been supplemented with an exemplifying addition. The European Committee for the prevention of torture has adopted this interpretive statement as its guiding maxim.

International Monitoring Bodies

Judicial and other monitoring bodies established under international instruments other than the ones mentioned, and in which there are only straightforward clauses prohibiting torture, inhuman or degrading treatment or punishment without any definitional or descriptive additions, have developed their own jurisprudence or case law germane to their understanding of how to interpret the torture prohibition laid down in the instruments the compliance of which they are monitoring. Some examples of this, from what may be called 'leading cases', should be compared with the 'treaty definitions/descriptions' given above.

Judicial bodies

The *European Commission for Human Rights* was the first to make a reasoned formal finding in the case of Greece (1969) that torture and ill-treatment had taken place, when applying Article 3 of the ECHR; it indicated as its view that 'torture' comprises inhuman and degrading treatment and that 'inhuman treatment' comprises degrading treatment; it thereafter went on to describe its notion of 'inhuman treatment', as well as 'degrading treatment', in the following way:

> The notion of inhuman treatment covers at least such treatment as deliberately causes severe suffering, mental or physical which, in the particular situation, is unjustifiable.
> The word 'torture' is often used to describe inhuman treatment, which has a purpose, such as the obtaining of information or confessions or the infliction of punishment, and it is generally an aggravated form of inhuman treatment.

Treatment or punishment of an individual may be said to be degrading if it grossly humiliates him before others or drives him to act against his will or conscience.

The Commission was criticized for contemplating the possibility of 'justification' of inhuman treatment. Therefore it elaborated on this issue in a later case, that of Northern Ireland (1976), concluding 'that the prohibition under Article 3 of the Convention is an absolute one and that there can never be, under the convention or under international law, a justification for acts in breach of that provision'. It must be said, however, that what was in mind was the mitigation possibility referred to above, as well as the fact that the kind of ill-treatment that constitutes inhuman treatment of torture will depend upon its character (degree of severity) and the circumstances in which it is inflicted: then the notion is not absolute. It is a question of relativity of assessment, often perceived subjectively.

The aforementioned case of Northern Ireland offers an illustration of this point, in that the European Commission unanimously had found the methods (the so-called 'five techniques') used at interrogation centres for IRA detainees to be torture, whereas the European Court to which the case was referred 'reduced' this finding to 'ill-treatment'. It is no secret that this 'downgrading' caused some surprise within the Commission, since it had heard all the witnesses (some 150), which the Court had not; to add to that, the UK Government had accepted this unanimous finding by the Commission. The five techniques have been described as follows:

(a) wall-standing: forcing the detainees to remain for periods of some hours in a 'stress position', described by those who underwent it as being 'spreadeagled against the wall, with their fingers put high above the head against the wall, the legs spread apart and the feet back, causing them to stand on their toes with the weight of the body mainly on the fingers';

(b) hooding: putting a black or navy coloured bag over the detainees' heads and, at least initially, keeping it there all the time except during interrogation;

(c) subjection to noise: pending their interrogations, holding the detainees in a room where there was a continuous loud and hissing noise;

(d) deprivation of sleep: pending their interrogations, depriving the detainees of sleep;

(e) deprivation of food and drink: subjecting the detainees to a reduced diet during their stay at the centre and pending interrogations.

For the Commission, those methods, euphemistically called 'interrogation in depth', involved sensory deprivation (prevention of the use of one's senses) which directly affected the personality physically and mentally and was sufficient to break the will of the detainee for the purpose of obtaining information and confessions. The commission considered that 'the systematic application of [these] techniques ... shows a clear resemblance to those methods of systematic torture which have been known over the ages'. The Court did not quarrel with the Commission on this point but took another line: for the Court the crucial issue was the distinction to be drawn between torture and inhuman or degrading testament, which 'derives principally from a difference in the intensity of the suffering inflicted'. It continued: 'it appears ... that it was the intention that the Convention, with its distinction between "torture" and "inhuman degrading treatment", should by the first of these terms attach a special stigma to deliberate inhuman treatment causing very serious and cruel suffering.' And, 'although the five techniques, as applied in combination, undoubtedly amounted to inhuman and degrading treatment ... they did not occasion suffering of the particular intensity and cruelty implied by the word torture as so understood'. The Court's view has been criticized *inter alia* because the 'special stigma' notion has no legal significance or implications, and also because of the unexplained assertion that the techniques did not cause suffering sufficiently intense to be labelled torture.

Other bodies

The interpretive philosophy of the *UN Human Rights Committee* is reflected in its General Comments 20/44 1992, where it is stated that it does not 'consider it necessary ... to established sharp distinctions between different kinds of punishment or treatment'. Although its practice is not entirely consistent, it seems to tend to the use of general terminology, finding 'violations of Article 7', without indicating under which of the notions used in the article the treatment or punishment should be put.

As was pointed out earlier, the *European Committee for the Prevention of Torture* (CPT) performs no judicial functions. Its tasks are fact-finding and preventive: on the basis of information collected during visits it shall make recommendations with a view to strengthening the *cordon sanitaire* which separates permissible and inadmissible behaviours, attitudes and actions.

As a yardstick for its own work and as a guide for states that have accepted the CPT's visitorial mandate, it has laid down in successive Annual Reports a number of standard recommendations dealing with such matters as rights possessed by persons deprived of their liberty, custody and interrogation procedures, disciplinary procedures, avenues of complaints, physical conditions of detention, regime activities, health care and standards of hygiene, and so on.

The CPT has always stressed that these issues must be viewed not only individually but also cumulatively. The 'totality of conditions' approach is therefore a lodestar for its work: conditions taken one by one may not be inhuman or degrading, but they may well be or become so if combined or interacting. The CPT does not hesitate to say this in its Reports, without however referring to any particular treaty provision prohibiting such treatment or punishment.

The 1949 Geneva Conventions, on the basis of which the International Committee of the Red Cross (ICRC) performs its inspection visits, do not contain any definition or description of the concept of torture other than saying that 'torture' or inhuman 'treatment' shall be considered as 'grave breaches' for prosecution purposes. And the ICRC has not formulated its own definition but uses, when necessary, those already established. The one generally accepted today is that of the UN, which defines torture as an aggravated form of cruel, inhuman and degrading treatment.

The Problem of Overlapping Competences of Different Supervisory Bodies

Since a number of states have signed several treaties providing for individual as well as inter-state complaints procedures before different supervisory bodies, with regard to the same or similar rights or sets of rights, some have made attempts to guard against a duplication of procedures before different bodies by the same complainant in the same case. Thus, when ratifying the Optional Protocol of the CCPR, some states – such as Denmark, Norway and Sweden – entered reservations, saying that the Human Rights Committee should not have competence to consider a communication from an individual, unless it has ascertained that the same matter is not being and has not been examined under another procedure of international investigation or settlement. In the CAT convention a provision containing those two provisos for admissibility of individual complaints was inserted in its Article 22:5(a).

Concluding Remarks

This survey provides evidence of the amplitude and complexity of the subject, which some say has grown to 'nightmarish' proportions and others consider to have produced an 'implementation crisis'. Indeed, there is no denying the fact that states experience increasing difficulties in coping with all the tasks imposed on them by various categories of human rights instruments and by different types of monitoring bodies handing out 'fiats' which enjoy different degrees of authority. The UN has repeatedly warned against duplication of work and overlapping of mandates, and it has also issued guidelines on the need for consistency in standard-setting (e.g. resolution 41/120 of 4 December 1986, reaffirmed by the Vienna Declaration of 1993).

The winner, though, is the individual, who has been granted a new standing in international law and also been given a variety of routes by which he or she can fight for the upholding of his or her dignity as a human person.

One of the most important challenges in the years to come will be to achieve a fair balance between the all-important concern for effective protection of the individual against human rights violations and the legitimate concern of states regarding the possible overloading of the system – which would lead to increasing indifference and lassitude (already discernible) towards sustained promotive actions in the human rights field.

A plurality of proceedings in the same case before different organs adds to this problem. Some states have tried to avoid this along the lines indicated above; nevertheless it remains the case that they must each time engage in time-consuming procedural representations with the supervisory body concerned, which is the ultimate judge of the admissibility of such cases.

Notes

1. The new Court will be formally inaugurated on 1 November 1998.

2. According to Protocol 11 (see above) this Article has been given a new number – 52.

3. Pedro Nikken, 'L'action contre le système interaméricain des droits de l'homme', in Antonio Cassese, ed., *The International Fight Against Torture*, Nomos Verlagsgesellschaft, Baden-Baden, 1991.

2

An Optional Protocol,
Based on Prevention and Cooperation

Ann-Marie Bolin Pennegård

Background to the New Protocol

This chapter is intended to present the history and the outline of a proposed new Protocol to the Convention Against Torture, whereby a new international committee would be established with a mandate to inspect places where persons deprived of their liberty by a public authority are held. The aim of the inspections would be report to and advise States Parties to the Protocol how they can further protect from torture and ill-treatment those persons deprived of their liberty.

International law is clear and unequivocal on outlawing torture. A number of the most important international and regional conventions and declarations in the field of human rights and international humanitarian law contain an absolute prohibition against torture and other cruel, inhuman or degrading treatment or punishment. Despite these legal obligations and the many political commitments made, violations of the most gruesome nature, including torture and other forms of ill-treatment, continue to plague the world. Innovative approaches are therefore called for to complement the human rights mechanisms already in place, which consist first and foremost of supervision by treaty bodies or UN organs, such as those of the Commission on Human Rights. In order that the implementation of human rights might be more effective, existing work practices should be supplemented with more developed approaches focusing on prevention and early action, including through observation and presence in the field, as well as technical assistance, where needed.

Preventive action is often called for, but this has proved more difficult to realize on the ground, especially when a situation has already deteriorated to a certain degree or even turned into open conflict. For example, once torture is practised with impunity in a country, the situation is likely to produce contempt and distrust among the general public for the authorities. Vicious circles are set in motion, including cover-ups at various levels of decision-making. In the case where a new government is confronted with such problems, it is of the utmost importance that it does not get caught up in the old pattern. Here the international community must be more effective in reaching out and offering assistance that will be of value to a government that wishes to change unpopular structures and attitudes inherited by its authorities from the past. There are many examples where a government, despite initially committing itself in words and deeds to improving the human rights situation in the country, gradually becomes caught up in situations where over time inaction on its part turns into complacency and acceptance of abuses by that same government. Strategies and concrete methods of work focusing on fact-finding and prevention are ways whereby the international community could be of assistance to such governments.

Torture and ill-treatment by state agents of persons deprived of their liberty is a subject that ought to be at the forefront of preventive action undertaken by the United Nations. Work has been ongoing both within and outside the United Nations since the 1970s to establish a system of preventive visits to places of detention. It is the hope of many that a new legal instrument on the prevention of torture and ill-treatment can be open for signature and ratification around the turn of the new millennium.

Jean-Jacques Gautier: the originator

The ideas embodied in the proposed Optional Protocol to the Convention Against Torture is attributable to the pioneering work of Jean-Jacques Gautier (1912–1986). Gautier was a successful private banker in Geneva with a deep Christian commitment. He was committed to using his wealth to assist his fellow human beings. In 1973, having followed Amnesty International's worldwide Campaign for the Abolition of Torture (1972), he decided to devote himself to the struggle against torture. He became firmly convinced that the prohibition of torture in international law needed more effective control.

Gautier thought that by establishing, through a convention, an impartial body of persons authorized to visit places of detention, states were likely to take their legal undertakings with regard to the prohibition of torture more seriously. He was struck by the fact that Germany – notwithstanding the Holocaust, the extermination of Jews at civil concentration camps – treated its prisoners of war of Jewish descent comparatively well.

He attributed this fact not least to the ability of the International Committee of the Red Cross (ICRC) to visit prisoner-of-war camps; whereas the ICRC was excluded in principle from inspection visits to civilian camps such as the concentration camps of Auschwitz and Buchenwald.[1]

Gautier had also followed events closely when the Council of Europe put Greece under strong pressure following the military junta's seizure of power in 1967, finding the government guilty of torturing and ill-treating detainees. Greece subsequently, in 1969, allowed the ICRC to visit prisoners; Gautier noted the reported immediate reduction in cases of torture following that decision. When Greece later withdrew from the Council of Europe and also closed its prisons to the ICRC, torture once again became a practice until the fall of the junta regime.[2]

Gautier became convinced of the need for a convention of a preventive nature whereby states agreed in advance to inspection visits. States should allow an international delegation to visit all places within their jurisdiction where persons deprived of their liberty were being held. States should be able to count on the confidentiality of the mission and its findings, and only in cases of refusal and non-cooperation on the part of a state should the international delegation go public. These ideas won considerable support in Switzerland. In 1977 Gautier founded the Swiss Committee Against Torture (SCT) (which in 1992 became the Association for the Prevention of Torture (APT)). A draft Convention based on these ideas was subsequently produced.[3]

However, before the international community began to focus on how to realize Gautier's vision, another path in the struggle against torture opened up. In 1973 a resolution was introduced in the General Assembly of the UN by Sweden, Austria, Costa Rica, the Netherlands and Trinidad and Tobago, requesting the Assembly to examine the question of torture. Subsequently the Fifth UN Congress on the Prevention of Crime and the Treatment of Offenders, held in Geneva in 1975, elaborated a draft Declaration on the Protection of All Persons from Being Subjected to Torture and Other Cruel, Inhuman or Degrading Treatment or Punishment, on the basis of a Swedish draft. The Declaration was adopted by the General Assembly of the UN in 1975. In 1977 the General Assembly of the UN requested its Commission on Human Rights to prepare a draft Convention Against Torture and Other Forms of Cruel, Inhuman or Degrading Treatment or Punishment in the light of the principles embodied in the Declaration.

At that time several draft texts for such a Convention were circulating. Apart from the text by Gautier and the Swiss Committee Against Torture there were two others: one was presented by the Swedish government and the other by the International Association of Penal Law. These last two were subsequently merged into a revised version of the Swedish text. Naturally, both texts also aimed at strengthening the existing prohibition against torture through a number of concrete measures. Both foresaw a public reporting procedure, which through its various phases of preparation, examination and public exposition was regarded as one effective way of bringing about conformity in national law and practice to international standards. With regard to on-site inspections, neither went as far as the text provided by Gautier and the Swiss Committee Against Torture, though the Swedish draft provided for an inquiry procedure in cases where there was evidence of 'systematic torture'.[4]

At that crucial juncture it was proposed by Niall MacDermot, secretary-general of the International Commission of Jurists, that the draft convention proposed by Gautier and the Swiss Committee could be transformed into an Optional Protocol. Thus, the main Convention Against Torture would be elaborated based on the revised Swedish draft and the text proposed by Gautier and the Swiss Committee would be seen not as a competing but rather as a complementing project. In 1979 such a text for an Optional Protocol was drafted; this was published and widely distributed as a pamphlet.[5]

The idea of an Optional Protocol gradually gained support in many quarters. But there was also concern regarding the possible negative effect that the submission of a draft Optional Protocol to the Commission on Human Rights might have on the difficult negotiations taking place at that time in the open-ended working group established to elaborate, based on the Swedish draft, a draft Convention Against Torture, especially with regard to implementation provisions.[6] On 6 March 1980 the government of Costa Rica formally submitted the draft Optional Protocol to the Commission on Human Rights. In order that it should not disturb the ongoing negotiations, Costa Rica requested explicitly that consideration of the draft be deferred until the Convention Against Torture had itself been adopted.[7]

The United Nations adopted the United Nations Convention Against Torture and Other Cruel, Inhuman or Degrading Treatment and Punishment (referred to in this chapter as the Convention Against Torture) on 10 December 1984. The Convention came into force on 26 June 1987. By November 1997, ten years later, 104 states had ratified the Convention. Although this is indeed an achievement, it should nevertheless be noted that this is the lowest ratification total amongst the six major human rights instruments. It is to be hoped that greater efforts will be made by the United Nations, its member states, non-governmental organizations and media, to increase the level of ratification until the Convention Against Torture achieves universal adherence.

Regional and national efforts and visits by the International Committee of the Red Cross

Realization of Gautier's idea at a regional level was one way of establishing its viability and value to the world. Noël Berrier, a French senator and medical doctor, who at the time was chairman of the Legal Affairs Committee of the Council of Europe, proposed in a memorandum in 1981 that the 'countries of Europe might set an example and institute such a system among themselves in the framework of the Council of Europe, without waiting for the proposal to be implemented at world level'.[8]

In 1983 the Parliamentary Assembly recommended that the Council of Ministers adopt a regional instrument. Attached to the recommendation was a proposal for a regional instrument put forward by the Swiss Committee Against Torture and the International Commission of Jurists (ICJ); it essentially followed the elements of the proposed UN Optional Protocol, but was adapted to fit regional circumstances. The Committee requested that the Steering Committee for Human Rights (CDDH) submit proposals for a possible follow-up to the recommendation of the parliament.

A subsidiary Committee of Experts (Committee DH-EX) under the Steering Committee began to work on the proposal for a regional instrument in 1984. In 1986 the Steering Committee presented to the Committee of Ministers a Draft European Convention for the Prevention of Torture and Inhuman or Degrading Treatment or Punishment. After the Assembly had approved the text on 27 March 1987, the Convention as prepared by the Steering Committee was adopted by the Committee of Ministers on 26 June 1987 and opened for signature on 26 November the same year. The Convention was accompanied by an Explanatory Report, regarded as an important and integral part of the system. The Convention has subsequently been amended through its Protocol 1 with regard to election and re-election of members to the Committee and through its Protocol 2 with regard to the opening up of the Convention for non-member states of the Council of Europe.

To compare the original draft and the final Convention with its Explanatory Report gives an interesting insight into the transformation of the provisions in the original draft Convention submitted by the Swiss Committee Against Torture and the International Commission of Jurists. That draft was designed primarily to provide a mechanism intended to combat possible practices of torture and physical mistreatment of detainees. During the negotiations the focus gradually shifted towards the drafting of an instrument concerned with conditions of detention and practices surrounding the use of custody. This development and the innovative procedures adopted by the European Committe for the Prevention of Torture (CPT), established under the Convention, have resulted in an instrument that today, after ten years of practice, has proved to have more far-reaching significance in the area of protection than was originally conceived. In fact, the Committee, in order to fulfil its preventive function and to emphasize the non-judicial character of its work, has set a higher level of protection for detained persons than that upheld by the judicial organs of the Council of Europe (the Commission and the Court), and its work has proved to be of great value and help to the member states of the Council of Europe.

The UN Commission on Human Rights returned briefly to the issue of an Optional Protocol in 1986. Noting that a draft European Convention based on similar ideas to those found in the draft Optional Protocol had been submitted, it encouraged other regions to consider the possibility of preparing a draft convention containing similar ideas.[9]

The American Convention on Human Rights of 1969 contains a prohibition against torture and ill-treatment, but no mechanism similar to the European Committee for the Prevention of Torture. Neither did the Inter-American Convention to Prevent and Punish Torture, which had been signed at Cartagena de Indias, Colombia, on 9 December 1985, include a system of inspection visits of that kind. A regional colloquium was organized in April 1987 in Montevideo by the Swiss Committee Against Torture and the International Commission of Jurists, where some thirty experts discussed a draft for an Inter-American convention along the same lines as the European Convention, but achieved no outcome.

Today the Inter-American Commission on Human Rights carries out *ad hoc* country visits, including through a special working group focusing on conditions in prison and places of detention. The visits differ from those envisaged in the Protocol in that they are not made on a regular basis and are less systematic. Also, since the regional efforts in the Inter-American system did not materialize into any final results with regard to a specific convention, many governments in that part of the world are today among the greatest supporters of a global instrument along the lines of the proposed Optional Protocol. Tribute should be paid in particular to the government of Costa Rica for its tireless efforts for the Protocol.

In Africa, the adoption in 1981 of the Charter on Human and Peoples' Rights, included a provision prohibiting torture and cruel, inhuman or degrading punishment and treatment. The Charter, which came into force on 21 October 1986, establishes the African Commission on Human and Peoples' Rights. The Commission was not, however, given any role that can be compared to the European Committee for the Prevention of

Torture. One interesting new development is that the Commission in 1996 decided to appoint a Rapporteur, charged with undertaking efforts aimed at improving conditions in places of detention in African countries.

In addition to these regional efforts, in many countries independent visits to places of detention are undertaken through national efforts by the judiciary, national institutions of human rights, non-governmental organizations and others. Such visits are called for by the United Nations Standard Minimum Rules for the Treatment of Prisoners and the United Nations Body of Principles for the Protection of All Persons under Any Form of Detention or Imprisonment, adopted by the General Assembly in 1988.[10] Both the former and current Special Rapporteur on Torture, appointed by the Commission on Human Rights, have in their yearly reports emphasized the value of such preventive visits. The system of visits under the proposed Optional Protocol, by an international team, is to be seen as an important complement to visits already undertaken at regional and national levels.

The visits to places of detention by the International Committee of the Red Cross (ICRC) is another independent mechanism of vital importance. To allow for visits by ICRC to places of detention follows either from the obligations of States Parties to the four Geneva Conventions of 1949 and their Additional Protocols of 1977 or from the possibility for any state to authorize the ICRC to visit places of detention in situations not covered by international humanitarian law. In the proposed new Protocol recognition is explicitly made of this ICRC regime for visits to places of detention. The ICRC, furthermore, has for many years been an active participant in and supporter of the proposed Protocol, provided that it results in obligations for all States Parties to grant a visiting inspection team freedoms and conditions that do not go below the standards set for the ICRC's own visits.

Back to work on a global mechanism

In 1987 a workshop, organized by the Austrian Committee Against Torture, was convened in Graz, Austria. Among the participants were the Swiss Committee Against Torture and the first UN Special Rapporteur on Torture, Professor Peter Kooijmans, who in his report to the Commission on Human Rights in 1987 had advocated the Optional Protocol and stated that the establishment of regional systems would not necessarily stand in the way of a global instrument on the subject.[11] It was decided in Graz that the time was ripe to discuss further the establishment of a global mechanism in UN fora and to draw up a revised draft Optional Protocol, taking recent developments into account. In its 1989 session, the Commission on Human Rights decided to postpone discussion of the Costa Rican draft Protocol until its session in 1991 to give more time for the preparation of a new version.[12] The updated version was the result of work by several academicians and non-governmental organizations. In particular, it was elaborated by a group of experts, convened in Geneva in 1990 at the iniative of the Swiss Committee Against Torture and the International Commission of Jurists. That updated draft Optional Protocol was submitted by Costa Rica to the 1991 Commission on Human Rights together with a letter and introductory memorandum.[13] The Commission decided to consider the question at its next session in 1992 in order to give states an opportunity to study the new proposal.[14]

Due not least to strong lobbying and effective work by a number of non-governmental organizations, the Commission on Human Rights took a favourable decision in 1992. Unanimously, it decided to entrust an open-ended intersessional working group with the mandate to elaborate a draft Optional Protocol to the United Nations Convention Against Torture, on the basis of the draft proposed by Costa Rica, and to consider the implications of the Optional Protocol, regional instruments and the Committee Against Torture.

An intersessional working group has subsequently met for two weeks in October since 1992. In 1995 it concluded the first reading of the text of the draft Optional Protocol, and in 1996 embarked on the second and final reading. The work has so far been organized in a plenary session, where general discussions take place, while most of the actual drafting takes place in a drafting committee of a more informal character. The working group has since its inception in 1992 reported to the Commission on Human Rights, which, on the basis of these annual reports, has renewed the mandate of the working group.

It is envisaged that the effort to bring the negotiations to a successful conclusion will require one or two more sessions of the open-ended working group, provided that agreement can be reached on the remaining outstanding issues, or alternatively that those countries which continue to have doubts about some of the fundamental objectives inherent in the Protocol will decide not to stand in the way of its adoption, given its optional character. Important headway was made at the 1997 session of the open-ended working group.

Agreement still remains to be reached on a number of crucial issues. These relate in particular to how far-reaching the obligations of a State Party are with regard to the new committee; whether or not prior consent is necessary for each visit or whether ratification itself entails such consent; what services and freedoms a State Party has to grant a visiting delegation; whether or not the new committee in cases of non-cooperation of a State Party, as a last resort, can go public about its findings; and whether or not a State Party should be allowed to lodge reservations to the new Protocol.

Some Basic Elements of the New Protocol

The aim of a new Optional Protocol is to enhance protection for detained persons against torture and ill-treatment. A procedure and a new committee will be proposed to this end. That new committee is referred to in the proposed Protocol as the Sub-Committee to distinguish it from the Committee Against Torture. In what follows, therefore, the proposed new committee is referred to as the Sub-Committee.

The Protocol is of a procedural character, and does not contain any new substantive provisions. The Convention Against Torture and Other Cruel, Inhuman or Degrading Treatment or Punishment, as well as other relevant legal instruments serve as its points of reference; these latter include the UN Standard Minimum Rules for the Treatment of Prisoners, the UN Code of Conduct for Law Enforcement Officials, the UN Principles of Medical Ethics relevant to the Role of Health Personnel, and the UN Standard Minimum Rules for the Administration of Juvenile Justice. These and other documents will provide the substantive basis for the new Sub-Committee and the government concerned in a given case.

The innovative aspects of the Protocol, in comparison with other human rights instruments of a global nature, lie in its emphasis on a series of important principles. These will now be considered.

Prevention

One can argue that all human rights instruments, from the Universal Declaration of Human Rights onwards, aim at preventing violations through curtailment of possible abuse of power by setting forth what kind of standards and rights governments are to accord the people residing within their respective jurisdictions.

The basic means deployed by the six major human rights treaties with treaty bodies to ensure compliance are through supervision tied to a reporting system. Whereas this system has proved valuable, it nevertheless exhibits drawbacks with regard to securing follow-up. Additional mechanisms for ensuring compliance are provided for in those treaties or protocols that set out individual or state complaint procedures. Compliance or not by a State Party is decided in such cases by procedures of a judicial or quasi-judicial nature. In a global perspective, relatively few governments are as yet party to this kind of complaint procedure. The lack of more effective means for the international community to promote implementation and ensure compliance has been at the heart of the human rights debate during the last decade. The Protocol offers a new way forward.

The basic approach is to encourage states to abide by their treaty obligations with regard to the prohibition on torture and ill-treatment with the help of the new Sub-Committee. Through visits of a preventive nature, submission of confidential reports and dialogue, a State Party will become more aware of practical measures it can take in order to improve conditions in places of detention and prevent torture and ill-treatment.

Any closed institution where persons deprived of their liberty are held is an environment that can lend itself to torture and ill-treatment. That fact has unfortunately been proved over and over again in every country and in all parts of the world. Advice from an international body on minimizing the risk of abuse in a particular place can serve as an important complement to other measures. It is intended for those governments that possess a genuine will to combat torture and ill-treatment. Through the new procedure they can obtain independent and confidential advice from recognized international experts on the practices in their closed institutions and on ways to improve the treatment of detainees.

On-site visits

The basic requirement by a State Party in the Protocol is to 'permit visits to any place within their jurisdiction where persons deprived of their liberty by a public authority or with its consent or acquiescence are held or may be held.'[15] Only a true picture of the situation in places of detention and inprisonment will be of use to a government. The full cooperation of all competent authorities is essential. That includes information on and access to all places where persons deprived of their liberty are held. It also includes unlimited access to all persons that have any information of interest to the delegation, including to any person deprived of their liberty as well as to lawyers, doctors and relatives of detained persons.[16]

Cooperation

An essential prerequisite for effective results under the new procedure is the establishment of trust and cooperation between the Sub-Committee and the State Party. The State Party has, for its part, to extend to the Sub-Committee before, during and after visits to its territory all the facilities required for a proper fulfilment of its function; these are expected to be spelled out in some detail in the Protocol. The Sub-Committee has, for its part, to be guided in its work by the principles of 'confidentiality, impartiality, universality and objectivity'.[17] The Sub-Committee, and indeed its visiting delegation, must be composed in such a way that they contain the necessary expertise and therefore gain the confidence of the State Party. Provisions with regard to the qualifications to be taken into account in the nomination of members of the Sub-Committee and to the scope for consultation with the Sub-Committee about the participation of delegation members who do not sit on the Sub-Committee are intended to ensure that such confidence exists.

Confidentiality

During negotiations on the Protocol, the element of confidentiality has been emphasized as being of great importance to many states. Many states consider it almost revolutionary to open up to international observers their police stations, prisons, military barracks, mental hospitals or any other place where persons deprived of their liberty are held as a result of decisions by a public authority. At the same time, it has also been widely recognized by many states that they might greatly benefit from allowing such outside and independent inspections of their closed facilities, conducted according to agreed principles. This is evidenced by the high regard the European states have for the work of the committee set up by the Council of Europe, a system which has worked very well for nearly ten years. In that system, confidentiality has unexpectedly ceased to be a crucial issue: many countries have requested instead that the report of the European Committee be made public. Nevertheless, also in the European Convention confidentiality remains a core functional principle at the disposal of the States Parties as an option, should they so wish.

Confidentiality, in order to serve the purpose of the Protocol, can also be seen to have its limits. In the draft text of the Protocol it is proposed that in cases of obstruction and non-cooperation by a State Party, the Sub-Committee may as a last resort issue a public statement.[18] In addition to the pressure this places on a State Party, the Sub-Committee should be permitted to inform the outside world that its inability to act is due not to its own shortcomings but to obstruction by a State Party. Also, taking into consideration the optional character of the Protocol, it seems reasonable that a State Party which is no longer willing to extend its cooperation to the Sub-Committee, in violation of its obligations under the Protocol, should not benefit from the rule of confidentiality in order to retain a good reputation. In such a case it is to be preferred that the State Party instead avails itself of the procedure according to which it may register an objection and withdraw from membership of the Protocol.[19]

There still exists a divergence of opinion among the governments participating in negotiations in the open-ended working group as to provision under the Protocol for issuing a public statement in cases of non-cooperation.

Recommendations

The means at the disposal of the Sub-Committee are the making of observations of fact during visits and the submission of recommendations to the State Party. The aim is not to produce charges and accusations, but rather to observe, conclude and cooperate with the State Party. The Sub-Committee is not a judicial or quasi-judicial body; its role will be to perform non-judicial tasks intended to be of assistance to states. Its observations and recommendations will be based on and evaluated against the standards contained in treaty law and other relevant international instruments that the international community has developed and agreed upon, relating to the prohibition of torture and ill-treatment and to the conditions in places of detention, prisons and other institutions that fall within the scope of the Protocol. These standards will serve as points of reference for both the Sub-Committee and the States Parties.

It is important to realize that if a report is to have maximum impact, its submission will mark not the end but the beginning of a dialogue between the Sub-Committee and a State Party. Various measures to ensure follow-up are likely to be elaborated and agreed upon; each actor will be expected to prove its willingness to cooperate and achieve results.

Financial and other assistance

For some years now the UN regular budget has covered the cost of all six treaty bodies under human rights conventions. This was only achieved after amendments were approved with regard to the Convention Against Torture and the Convention on the Elimination of Racial Discrimination, which formerly were financed jointly by the States Parties. Agreement was reached at the 1997 session of the open-ended working group to include a provision in the Protocol whereby costs directly linked to the Sub-Committee's performance of its functions under the Protocol were to be borne by the regular UN budget.[20]

Another interesting aspect of financing has come to the fore: namely, assistance to States in the implementation of recommendations. It is well known that the poor conditions that prevail in many closed institutions around the world are in part due, not simply to lack of training, regulations and safeguards, but to the limited public resources at the disposal of governments. It has been argued that if the aim of the Protocol, to enhance protection for detainees, is to be put into practice and made relevant, it must be accompanied by a willingness on the part of the international community to assist those states which, though they adhere to the Protocol and demonstrate the political will to improve conditions of detentions in accordance with the recommendations of the Sub-Committee, nevertheless may lack the financial means to implement some of them.

To this end, on the basis of a proposal made by several nongovernmental organizations and governments and submitted to the openended working group by the government of South Africa, a provision has been agreed upon regarding the establishment of a special fund. The aim of the fund should be to help finance implementation of the recommendations made by the Sub-Committee to 'a State Party expressing the need for additional assistance for its ongoing efforts to improve the protection of persons deprived of their liberty'.[21] The wording is intended to reflect that a State Party has to give clear signs of its positive attitude through its own contribution and participation in the implementation of the recommendations made by the Sub-Committee. Also, it is intended to acknowledge that many recommendations may not require a great amount of financial or special technical assistance; they may relate to changes in training, or to procedures and regulations regarding detention and arrest whose fulfilment may actually entail no or very little cost.

Assistance to governments in the course of improving conditions in closed institutions may, however, in other cases entail large investments. In view of the scale of need in many countries, where conditions at closed institutions are sometimes deplorable, the great degree of assistance required to improve conditions will probably continue to be provided in national, bilateral or multilateral programmes outside the scope of the proposed new Protocol.

There are many good reasons for linking certain funds for assistance to the Protocol, to secure the implemention of the Sub-Committee's recommendations. The confidential nature of these recommendations, which a State Party may wish to conceal from the outside world or from development agencies, might be one such reason. Another is the incentive of such a fund for those states considering becoming Parties to the Protocol.

Other Essential Components for an Effective Protocol

Effective missions and cooperation

A *sine qua non* of an effective Protocol is that the Sub-Committee is able to base its recommendations on an accurate picture. To that end the Sub-Committee must be able to organize missions to a State Party with no strings attached. The simple requirement is that each State Party shall permit visits to any place within its jurisdiction where persons are deprived of their liberty by a public authority. To require prior consent for a mission or negotiations as to what the mission will be allowed to do or not to do would raise serious doubts about the effectiveness of the new body. A few governments participating in the negotiations still want to resolve the question of consent in different ways from that proposed by the vast majority. The majority advocates provisions in the Protocol that ratification of the Protocol entails prior consent by a State Party to missions by the Sub-Committee, with the possibility, in exceptional circumstances as defined in the Protocol, to make representations to the Sub-Committee against a particular visit.

In order to be useful to a State Party, the Sub-Committee must also be able and willing to organize missions other than regular or periodic ones. It has therefore been proposed that it should be free to enact such extra missions to a State Party as it desires, either of a follow-up character or on an *ad hoc* basis.

The nature of the task requires that the Sub-Committee and the State Party need to be in regular contact before and during a mission with regard to practical issues entailed. These will include information about the Sub-Committee's arrival, consultation where necessary when the delegation includes personnel other than members of the Sub-Committee, and an outline of its proposed schedule. On the basis of such notification, the government needs to take measures in order to supply the necessary logistical support to the visiting delegation and ensure the full cooperation of its police, prisons and other affected authorities. It is also essential that a visiting delegation is able, if it so wishes, to make a surprise visit outside its proposed schedule as an additional means of securing as accurate a picture as possible.

It is important that the obligations of the State Party towards the visiting delegation during a mission be clearly spelled out in the Protocol. This is essential since the work of the Sub-Committee is performed under confidentiality. All states contemplating adherence to the Protocol must have a clear picture as to the obligations they undertake to fulfil. If a state decides to adhere to the Protocol, it also has to provide the authorities concerned with exact information as to what is expected of them. The system would be not only less effective but also more cumbersome for both the Sub-Committee and States Parties if the Protocol – as is suggested by some – left open the possibility of States Parties renegotiating the conditions before each mission.

It has been emphasized by many, including members of the European Committee, that it is essential that the Sub-Committee avail itself of the opportunity to attach necessary expertise to its mission. These experts will remain under the authority and supervision of the Sub-Committee. At the 1997 session of the open-ended working group, agreement was reached on provisions allowing the Sub-Committee to be assisted by experts, if needed, as well as on the establishment of a list from which the Sub-Committee would normally select its experts.

The basic obligations of a State Party towards a visiting delegation have to include the right to travel without retriction, unlimited access to places of detention, the ability to interview in private detainees as well as all other persons the delegation might want to meet with. Only if such circumstances exist will the visiting delegation be able to assess in the most accurate way the conditions of detention in a country. The example of the Theresienstadt concentration camp, the only such camp offered by the Nazis for inspection by the Red Cross as a model of the conditions prevailing at concentration camps, must never be repeated. It must be the Sub-Committee, rather than the visiting country, that decides where to go and who to meet in order to obtain an accurate picture. Unfortunately, the open-ended working group has not yet resolved this fundamental issue.

It is very likely that the Protocol will contain a provision whereby a State Party, in 'exceptional circumstances', may 'make representations to the Sub-Committee or its delegation against a particular visit'.[22] An important proposal by Chile, which won acceptance in the first reading text, is that 'the existence or (formal) declaration of a State of Emergency as such shall not be invoked by a State Party as a reason to object to a visit.'[23] Still open for final discussion is the list of grounds that may be invoked against a particular visit. In this context, it may be noted that the European Convention for the Prevention of Torture contains very broad grounds in this regard.[24] On the other hand, these grounds have in practice not been readily invoked.

The size, composition and election of the Sub-Committee

According to the text that has been agreed upon in the open-ended working group, the Sub-Committee shall initially consist of ten members. After the fiftieth accession to the Protocol, the numbers of the Sub-Committee shall increase to twenty-five. The members shall serve in their individual capacity, shall be independent and impartial, and shall be able to serve the Sub-Committee effectively.[25] It will probably be a very time-consuming task for the individuals who serve on the Sub-Committee.

It has also been agreed that the members of the Sub-Committee shall be chosen from among 'persons of high moral character, having proven professional experience in the field of the administration of justice, in particular in criminal law, prison or police administration or in the various medical fields relevant to the treatment of persons deprived of their liberty or in the field of human rights'.[26] The persons nominated should possess the nationality of a State Party to the Protocol.[27]

One interesting feature of the text is that one of the two candidates that can be nominated by a State Party can possess the nationality of another State Party. This is done in order to recognize that today, when migration between countries is greater than ever, many persons suitable to serve on the Sub-Committee may live and practise their expertise in countries other than the one of which they are the national. This provision helps to enlarge the group from which selection can be made in order that suitable and competent persons willing and able to serve in the Sub-Committee might be found.

Elections are to be held at meetings of the States Parties every second year. In the election of members, States Parties shall give primary consideration to the criteria of competence as set out in the Protocol. States Parties shall also give due consideration to a proper balance among the various fields mentioned and of women and men, as well as to an equitable geographical distribution of membership.[28] Agreement has been reached on all questions relating to the nomination of candidates and the election process, including the procedure when a member dies or where two nationals receive the same number of votes, given that no two members of the Sub-Committee may be nationals of the same state.[29]

The Sub-Committee's relationship to other bodies

Although the Optional Protocol will be connected to the Convention Against Torture, it seems likely that the Sub-Committee will have very limited links to the Committee Against Torture. It is seen as important to safeguard the distinct and different mandates of the two bodies. Nor is it desirable to increase through the workings of the new Protocol the already heavy workload of the Committee Against Torture.

The main role of the Committee Against Torture in the new Protocol, it is envisaged, is connected with receiving reports from the Sub-Committee, and in particular its annual reports. Discussions have yet to reach a conclusion on whether the Committee Against Torture or the Sub-Committee itself should issue a public statement, if it is to be issued, when a State Party fails to cooperate.[30]

According to Article 20 of the Convention Against Torture, the Committee may, if it receives reliable information that appears to contain well-founded indications that torture is being systematically practised in the territory of a State Party, decide to undertake a confidential inquiry, which may include a visit to the territory of the concerned State Party. If such a visit has been agreed and is scheduled, it seems inappropriate that the Sub-Committee should undertake a mission to that country at the same time. In has therefore been agreed that in such a case the Sub-Committe may wish to postpone its own mission.

It is important that any new body takes fully into account all ongoing efforts to prevent torture and improve conditions in detention centres. Many international and regional organs already undertake important work in the area. Among them are the Special Rapporteur on Torture, the International Committee of the Red Cross (ICRC), the European Committee for the Prevention of Torture (ECPT), the Crime Prevention Branch in Vienna, UNDP, as well as other regional organizations. It is crucial that the new body enters into cooperation with these organs in order to avoid duplication of work and ensure that there exists, wherever possible, coordination of effort.

When a visit is made to a detention centre of a State Party under a regional convention to which the state is also a party, the principle of universality and the global character of the Protocol require that the State Party also receive missions of the Sub-Committee. Only such an approach can assure the universal application of the Protocol. In order to avoid unnecessary overlap and duplication of tasks, cooperation and consultation are encouraged between the Sub-Committee and such regional bodies.[31]

With regard to the work of the International Committee of the Red Cross (ICRC), it is explicitly recognized that the provisions of the Protocol do not affect the obligations of States Parties to the four Geneva Conventions of 1949 or the two Additional Protocols of 1977, or the possibility of any State Party authorizing the ICRC to visit places of detention in situations not covered by international humanitarian law.[32] The ICRC has been a participant in the sessions of the working group, and is actively promoting the establishment of the new Sub-Committe. The ICRC has also repeatedly reminded the participants that the Sub-Committee, in order to be effective and helpful to States Parties, must be granted the freedom found in Article 12 of the original Costa Rican text governing the conduct of visits. These stipulations are similar to the procedure the ICRC follows for its visits to places of detention, a procedure which stems from specific provisions in international humanitarian law and which is non-negotiable and regarded as a prerequisite for effective action.

Report and procedures

Following each mission the Sub-Committee has to draw up a report containing its observations and findings, which shall be submitted to the

State Party for comments. The Sub-Committee shall thereafter finalize its report after fair consideration is given to the comments submitted, within a reasonable time, by a State Party. The report shall contain any recommendations the Sub-Committee considers necessary to improve the protection of persons deprived of their liberty.[33] The Sub-Committee and the State Party then enter into a confidential dialogue on the implementation of the recommendations, including the ways and means in which the State Party can be assisted. The effectiveness of the Protocol will depend on the calibre of the Sub-Committee's recommendations and the quality of this dialogue. The dialogue may include several phases, including missions. It may take the form of a follow-up programme, enabling both the Sub-Committee and the State Party to assess progress in implementation in accordance with a realistic time frame.

Although the rule of confidentiality protects proceedings under the Protocol, three exceptions are under discussion. The first is that the Sub-Committee should publish the report at the request of the State Party concerned. The second is that, if the State Party decides to publish part of the report but in doing so gives a distorted picture of the report's content, the Sub-Committee may go public so as to ensure a balanced presentation of the contents of the report.[34] The third exception covers the eventuality where a State Party fails to cooperate or refuses to improve the situation in the light of the recommendations of the Sub-Committee; most governments participating in the negotiations want the Sub-Committee itself or, by request, the Committee Against Torture to be free to make a public statement or publish the report of the Sub-Committee.[35] No final agreement has yet been reached on these provisions.

The Protocol is unlikely to be very specific about the procedures that the Sub-Committee shall apply in its internal work, apart from a few provisions about election of officers, decision-making and quorum.[36] It is widely felt that working methods should instead be decided upon by the Sub-Committee itself in its rules of procedure. Flexibility in this regard should thus be given to the Sub-Committee. After all, the meetings of the States Parties will provide a forum for discussion and provision of the necessary guidance to the Sub-Committee.

Concluding Remarks

Whether or not a Protocol will be adopted along the lines set forth in this chapter is still an open question. Negotiations on several fundamental issues remain to be concluded in the open-ended working group. When this has been achieved, a draft Protocol must be approved by the Commission on Human Rights, ECOSOC and the General Assembly, before it can be opened up for signature and ratification by states. If agreement can be found on all issues in the open-ended working group, it is expected that approval by the higher bodies will follow.

Every country and a number of relevant organizations are invited, in accordance with established practice, to participate in the open-ended working group. The negotiations take place over two weeks during annual sessions of the open-ended working group. The very limited time alloca-tion, which are in accordance with standard practice for working groups of this kind under the UN Commission on Human Rights, shall be kept in mind when assessing the pace of the negotiations and the progress made. Notwithstanding the political difficulties, many issues relating to the Protocol also require time and careful consideration from both legal and practical points of view. It should be acknowledged that, as the negotiations have evolved, guidance on the framing of a number of provisions has not always been found in the draft text, since alternative solutions may have been agreed upon by the working group.

At the time of writing, early 1998, there still remain certain fundamen-tal issues on which there is a divergence of views among countries. As indicated above, the most important of these issues relate to the need or not for prior consent before each mission; what degree of prescribed obligations a State Party and its authorities should have towards the Sub-Committee, including a visiting delegation; whether or not a public state-ment should follow in cases of non-cooperation of a State Party; and whether reservations to the Protocol shall be allowed or not.

It is clear that one or two more sessions of the working group will be needed to try to resolve the remaining provisions of the Protocol. If a resolution has not been found by that time, the proponents of a new effective Protocol would need to reflect on different strategies. One would be to conclude that not every country is yet prepared to allow the inter-national community to realize the idea of Jean-Jacques Gautier. If only a small minority of countries are known to oppose the adoption of the Protocol, a vote might be considered. Another strategy would be to put the almost finished Protocol on hold and pursue other avenues in the struggle against torture and ill-treatment, and wait until changes in those countries bring about support for adoption. It is not advisable to push for finalization of the Protocol at any cost, as this could have negative repercussion in the human rights field, including on the work of other human rights and humanitarian bodies.

Another strategy would be to try to convince those few states committed to a different development of key concepts in the Protocol to accept the wording supported by the great majority of states and – bearing in mind the optional character of the Protocol – agree not to block its adoption. The many incentives for governments and the international community alike that lie in the adoption of a Protocol will hopefully convince them. For governments it is an opportunity to adhere to a basically confidential procedure that will provide advice on how to improve conditions in places of detention in the light of observation and assessment by an international body of experienced men and women. In addition, governments might receive help, where necessary, in remedying their situation in line with the recommendations of the international body.

Adoption of an effective Protocol would demonstrate the international community's willingness to develop new means to address urgent needs in the field of human rights. Conditions in places of detention and efforts aimed to prevent torture and ill-treatment of detained persons continue to be of great relevance. It would also signal that, fifty years after the adoption of the Universal Declaration of Human Rights and its prohibition of torture and ill-treatment, new means are still being developed to grant everyone the right to a life free from torture and abuse.

The new Protocol would also demonstrate that, even though the level of material conditions in places of detention may vary, it is the duty of each state to promote and create conditions that ensure that each person, including those deprived of their liberty, is treated with respect for his or her inherent human dignity.

Notes

1. The ICRC was permitted to visit only the civilian concentration camp Theresienstadt. For a more detailed account, see Malcolm Evans and Rod Morgan, 'The Origins and Drafting of the ECPT: A Salutary Lesson?', in *20 ans consacré à la réalisation d'une idée*, ATP, Geneva, 1997; J.-C. Faveze, *Une Mission Impossible? Le CICR, les déportations et le camps de concentration nazis*, Editions Payot, Lausanne, 1988.

2. F. de Vargas, 'Bref Historique Du CSCT/APT', *20 ans consacré à la réalisation d'une idée*, p. 28. Greece was readmitted to the Council of Europe in 1974 following the downfall of the junta.

3. F. de Vargas, 'History of a Campaign', *Torture: How to Make the International Convention Effective*, International Commission of Jurists and Swiss Committee Against Torture (1980), revised and enlarged edition, Geneva, 1979, p. 43.

4. J.H. Burgers and H. Danelius, *The UN Convention Against Torture*, Martinus Nijhoff, Dordrecht, 1988, p. 26.

5. *Torture – How to Make the International Convention Effective: A Draft Optional Protocol*, International Commission of Jurists and Swiss Committee Against Torture (1980), revised and enlarged edition, Geneva, 1979.

6. Burgers and Danelius, p. 28.

7. Ibid.

8. Council of Europe doc. AS/Jur (33) 18, 9 September 1981, para. 13.

9. Resolution 56/1986 of the Commission on Human Rights.

10. Rule 55 of the UN Standard Minimum Rules for the Treatment of Prisoners,

and Principle 29 of the UN Body of Principles for the Protection of All Persons under Any Form of Detention or Imprisonment.

11. For a more detailed account of the drafting history of the Optional Protocol at this stage, see R. Kicker: 'A Universal System for the Prevention of Torture: Discussion and Proposals Within the Austrian Committee Against Torture', *20 ans consacré à la réalisation d'une idée*, pp. 61–2, and F. Vargas, 'Bref Historique Du CSCT/APT', ibid., pp. 27–46.

12. Resolution 104/1989 adopted by the Commission on Human Rights.

13. The draft texts of the Protocol, the letter and memorandum are contained in U.N. Doc. E/CN.4/1991/66.

14. For a more detailed account, see Kicker, 'A Universal System', pp. 61–4, and Vargas, 'Bref Historique Du CSCT/APT', pp. 35–7.

15. Article 1 of the Draft Optional Protocol, as submitted by Costa Rica, contained in U.N. Doc. E/CN.4/1991/66.

16. Ibid.

17. Article 3, para. 3, of the text of the second reading, contained in Annex 1 of U.N. Doc. E/CN.4/1997/33.

18. Article 14, para. 2 of the Draft Optional Protocol, as submitted by Costa Rica, contained in U.N. Doc. E/CN.4/1991/66.

19. Article 19 of the text of the first reading, contained in U.N. Doc. E/CN.4/1996/28.

20. Article 16 of the text of the first reading, contained in U.N. Doc. E/CN.4/1996/28.

21. Article 16 bis of the text of the first reading, contained in U.N. Doc. E/CN.4/1996/28.

22. Article 13 of the text of the first reading, as contained in U.N. Doc. E/CN.4/1996/28.

23. Ibid.

24. Article 9 of the European Convention for the Prevention of Torture and Inhuman or Degrading Treatment or Punishment.

25. Article 4, paras 1 and 4 of the text of the second reading, contained in Annex 1 to U.N. Doc. E/CN.4/1997/33.

26. Article 4, para. 2 of the text of the second reading, contained in Annex 1 to U.N. Doc. E/CN.4/1997/33.

27. Article 5, para. 1 of the text of the second reading, contained in Annex 1 to U.N. Doc. E/CN.4/1997/33

28. Articles 5 and 6 and Article 4, para. 3 of the text of the second reading, contained in Annex 1 to U.N. Doc. E/CN.4/1997/33.

29. Article 4, paras 2 and 6* of the text of the second reading, contained in Annex 1 to U.N. Doc. E/CN. 4/1997/33.

30. Article 15 and Article 14, para. 4 of the text of the of the first reading, contained in Annex 1 to U.N. Doc E/CN.4/1996/28.

31. Article 9, para. 3 of the text of the first reading, contained in Annex 1 to U.N. Doc. E/CN.4/1996/28.

32. Article 9, para. 4 of the text of the first reading, contained in Annex 1 to U.N. Doc. E/CN.4/1996/28.

33. Article 14, para. 1 of the text of the outcome of the first reading, contained in Annex 1 to U.N. Doc. E/CN.4/1996/28.

34. Article 14, para. 3 of the text of the first reading, contained in Annex 1 to U.N. Doc. E/CN.4/1996/28.

35.   Article 14, para. 4 of the text of the first reading, contained in Annex 1 to U.N. Doc. E/CN.4/1996/28; Article 14, contained in Annex 2 to U.N. Doc. E/CN.4/1996/28.

36.   Article 7 of the text of the first reading, contained in Annex 1 to U.N. Doc. E/CN.4/1996/28.

Part II

Torture Crimes

3

Perpetrators of Torture

Eric Sottas

From the eighteenth century, torture, hitherto considered a legitimate means of investigation and punishment, came to be perceived – in the Western world first, thanks to the influence of the Enlightenment – as an unacceptable attack on the individual.

In 1948, when the Universal Declaration on Human Rights was adopted, no one spoke up against the prohibition of torture stipulated in Article 5, and this prohibition has been regularly confirmed in an absolute manner in the regional and universal instruments adopted since then. Nonetheless, torture, far from being a practice belonging to another age, continues to be daily or sporadically applied in over half of the states making up what is customarily known as the international community.

This chapter focuses on the perpetration of torture. I will discuss several sets of factors, including the idea of impunity, which are conducive to torture, a cancer which eats away the very foundations of human rights. However, I shall first address the question of perpetration from a different angle, arising from an unfortunate definitional void in the legal framework established to combat torture.

Torture: The Case of Children

Prohibition of torture features in numerous texts, among them the Convention on the Rights of the Child. Nevertheless, only two texts – the Declaration on the Protection of all Persons from being Subjected to Torture and other Cruel, Inhuman or Degrading Treatment or Punishment (the Declaration) and the Convention Against Torture and other Cruel, Inhuman or Degrading Treatment or Punishment (the Convention) – provide definitions of the crime. These are not identical, and only the definition contained in the Convention (article 1) is considered as a minimal rule for States Parties who are bound by Article 4 of the Convention Against Torture to legislate to forbid the acts referred to in Article 1 as acts of torture and punishable as such.

An examination of the reports of States Parties to the Convention discloses that many states either fail to adopt any definition as such, or define torture in terms which differ from those used in the Convention. More restrictive definitions reduce the protection of potential victims and frequently prevent the prosecution of those presumed responsible.[1]

The Convention on the Rights of the Child does not contain any definition of torture and may be explained by the structure of the instrument. However, two questions remain: first, what definition of torture is applicable and, second, is the definition given in the Convention (Against Torture) entirely appropriate to the case of minors?

Degree of pain

Both the Convention and the Declaration consider only severe pain or suffering as components of torture. This provision leaves a certain margin of interpretation, which may, in some cases, turn out to be excessive. The courts, and certain national legislators, have thus been led to clarify what exactly is meant by the term 'severe'. In the case of a child it should be noted that pain or suffering which might be considered relatively light for an adult may provoke an extremely disturbing state of anxiety or stress, resulting from the age of the victim. Moreover, it is necessary to take into account that if corporal punishment of adults is generally prohibited (with the notable exception of Islamic countries applying Sharia) the same is not true for children. Corporal punishment is still predominantly accepted within educational establishments and within the family, by law. It is important to note in this regard that certain codes make provisions for extremely lenient sanctions should the child die from a light beating.[2]

Corporal punishments are, moreover, not the only matter of concern with regard to definition. Prison sentences or periods of solitary confinement could provoke in a child suffering on a very different level than that in an adult. Furthermore, the conditions of detention – notwithstanding the provision of the Convention on the Rights of the Child, the United Nations Guidelines for the Prevention of Juvenile Delinquency (Riyadh Guidelines), and the United Nations Standard Minimum Rules for the Administration of Juvenile Justice (the Beijing Rules) – are frequently appalling. Every week sees cases registered that document extreme levels of violence involving children in detention (rape, physical abuse, food deprivation etc.). These problems are generally linked to the infrastructures of prison regimes, which are notoriously insufficient and provoke appalling levels of overpopulation.[3]

The intention of those responsible

The Convention also makes clear that pain or suffering must be inflicted intentionally to qualify as a violation. As far as children are concerned, this concept seems far too restrictive. My organization, Organisation Mondiale contre la Torture (OMCT, The World Organization Against Torture), registers every year a very high incidence of cases of violence inflicted by fellow detainees upon children, who are being held in the same cells as adult criminals.

The staff in charge of such detention centres must be aware of the grave and pressing danger to which minors are exposed, particularly the very young. The fact that those responsible may not have intentionally sought to inflict pain or suffering on these minors does not seem to be a relevant element for excluding such cases from the definition of torture. To the extent to which torture is applied to children, it is necessary to take into account not only intention but also the element of gross negligence.[4]

Status of the perpetrators of torture

The Convention provides that the term 'torture' applies only to pain or suffering 'inflicted by or at the instigation of or with the consent or acquiescence of a public official or other person acting in an official capacity'. As opposed to an adult, who is autonomous, the minor is legally subject to the authority of his/her parents or of a guardian.

At a conference in India organized by OMCT in January 1992 the issue of forced child labour (as part of payment of debt contracted by parents) was addressed in order to clarify if certain forms of it could be considered acts of torture. The severity of the violence was not called into question. We looked at two types of violence. First, violence that was a result of the harsh work and second, chastisement inflicted for attempted escape. The latter chastisement sometimes resulted in permanent handicap. Yet the perpetrators were not state agents; rather, they were the 'employers' of children whose parents had given their 'consent'. In the same vein, one can cite the violence suffered by child slaves in Sudan and children given by their parents to 'holy men' (marabouts) in Mauritania, who, in addition to forcing them into the life of a beggar, inflict serious ill-treatment; yet again, these are not agents of the state.

It is interesting to note the opinion of the Human Rights Committee, which in General Comment 20 on Article 7 of the International Covenant on Civil and Political Rights (ICCPR) would seem to consider that violence inflicted on children in the framework of educational and medical institutions falls within the ambit of prohibition of torture, as detailed within the Covenant.[5] This is undoubtedly the result of pressure exerted by NGOs. This opinion seems to suggest that pedagogical measures which employ violence and result in an acute state of stress or suffering can be considered to be torture. Second, the Committee allows for an extensive interpretation of the concept of 'public official' or 'person acting in an official capacity' because the perpetrators in this case can be anyone working in a teaching or medical institution (and having authority over the patient or child). It seems that for the Committee, the fundamental element is that the perpetrators act not *on behalf of the state*, but abuse their authority *recognized by the state*.

Exclusion of torture relating to pain arising from lawful sanctions

Article 1 of the Convention states that torture does 'not include pain or suffering arising only from inherent or incidental to lawful sanctions.' While it is obvious that one may not consider as torture the suffering resulting from legitimate sanctions, the latter should, however, be proportionate both to the crime committed and to the personal situation of the individual. There is hardly need to stress the fact that as far as minors are concerned this question is especially important, in view of the particular psychological development of children which restricts their responsibility.

A double question arises in terms of the age limit from which a minor can be held responsible for criminal acts and the age from which he or she can suffer sanctions, and of what type. Different judicial systems present an extremely diverse choice of resolutions, according to tradition, culture and so forth. Article 40.3(a) of the Convention on the Rights of the Child calls for 'the establishment of a minimum age below which children shall be presumed not to have the capacity to infringe the penal law'. Furthermore, Article 4.1 of the Beijing Rules requests: 'In those legal systems recognizing the concept of the age of criminal responsibility for juveniles, the beginning of that age shall not be fixed at too low an age level, bearing in mind the fact of emotional, mental and physical maturity.' These very general approaches do not permit the possibility of addressing certain abuses, however obvious.[6]

In conclusion, there seems to be a need for the Committee on the Rights of the Child, in general comments and during the examination of specific reports, to outline its own doctrine and jurisprudence relating to the torture of children as well as notions currently undefined in terms of cruel and other inhuman or degrading treatment or punishment.

Legalizing Torture

Unacceptable jurisprudence

In 1996, the Israeli Supreme Court, acting as a High Court of Justice, was on several occasions called upon to pass judgement on the use of physical force in interrogating prisoners suspected of belonging to movements responsible for terrorist activities. On two occasions, on 11 January 1996, in the case of Abed al-Khalim Bilbisi[7] and on 14 November 1996 in the case of Muhammad 'Abd al-'Aziz Hamdan,[8] the court annulled a temporary injunction which stipulated that the General Security Service (GSS) should not continue to use force in interrogating prisoners. In November 1996, the High Court of Justice also refused the request submitted by the lawyer of Khader Mubaraq with a view to obtaining a temporary injunction.

It is worth noting that in the three cases mentioned the 'physical pressures' brought to bear led to serious suffering, and in at least one case a prisoner complained of sleep deprivation. Nonetheless, in its reasons adduced for judgement, the court insists on its conviction that the vital information held by the prisoners – information which could save lives – justifies the pursuit of interrogations, despite the conditions in which they are being carried out. Without endorsing it explicitly, the court ratifies the position upheld by the GSS in the case of Muhammad 'Abd-al-'Aziz, according to which[9] the physical pressure exercised in this case did not constitute torture in the sense of the Convention Against Torture, but came 'under the defence of necessity stipulated in article 34 (11) of the Penal Code'. It should be noted here that the Committee Against Torture has protested against this abusive interpretation.

What is particularly worrying in the Israeli case is that the justification of acts undoubtedly constituting acts of torture stems from the highest legal authority in the land. However, to our knowledge, this example has not been followed by other supreme courts. Nevertheless, in most countries where torture is a common practice the authorities seek to hide the facts or to present them in a biased manner.

Manipulative interpretations of international instruments

In the former Soviet Union, the regime after the Stalin period expended considerable efforts towards projecting an image of itself as respectful of human rights. Within this context, the security forces showed an imaginative talent for devising torture methods which were hard to denounce. The most common consisted in subjecting recalcitrant opponents to abusive psychiatric treatments for a non-existent condition. To justify such treatments, Professor Vartanian even defined a particular form of mental illness: atypical schizophrenia, the principal symptoms of which seem to have been the inability of the subject to live within the framework of a repressive society.

Another method, which was analysed during a meeting of OMCT experts with former detainees of Soviet labour camps, consisted of combining and accumulating disciplinary measures and tasks accepted or tolerated in the Standard Minimum Rules for the Treatment of Prisoners, in such a way as to engender 'severe pain or suffering, whether physical or mental'.[10] For example, a prisoner might be sentenced for disciplinary reasons to periods of close confinement and reduction of diet, and continue to be required to do demanding outdoor work, despite intense cold. Should prisoners or their family protest, the camp authorities simply notified them that a doctor, after examining a given prisoner, had considered that they could sustain this regime, and that on the basis of this norm they were treated in conformity with the conditions stated in Articles 32(1) and 71(2) of the Standard Minimum Rules for the Treatment of Prisoners. These articles do indeed comprise major weaknesses. While Article 31 absolutely forbids corporal punishment, punishment by placing in a dark cell and all cruel, inhuman or degrading punishment for disciplinary offences, Article 32 stipulates that 'Punishment by close confinement or reduction of diet shall never be inflicted unless the medical officer has examined the prisoner and certified in writing that he is fit to sustain it.' This in fact means that the camp doctor, or in certain cases medical personnel without appropriate training, may authorize these measures, despite the fact that the medical officer does not enjoy total independence, since he is attached to the camp.

In the same way, Article 71(1) stipulates: 'Prison labour must not be of an afflictive nature'; but the same article under heading 2 specifies that 'prisoners under sentence shall be required to work, subject to their physical and mental fitness as determined by the medical officer.' The apparent conformity of measures with the standard minima meant the onus was on the prisoner to prove that abuse had taken place and that this abuse was deliberate, before he could accuse those who had carried out the torture.

The measures described above were essentially aimed at concealing torture, less by denying the forms of violence used than by justifying them on a legal basis. There is a whole range of forms of torture devised in such a way as to leave only traces which are difficult to interpret. We will not develop this aspect, which is an issue involving techniques of torture. Suffice it to say that in parallel with the progress of investigative methods, new techniques are also developing which combine physical and psychological aggressions; and that blows leading to bruises and fractures are being replaced by electric shocks, ultra-sound, sensory privations, and so on, the effects of which are just as devastating, if not more so, than those resulting from other less sophisticated methods.

Criminal offence or human rights violation?

For a little over a decade, a new technique of hiding torture has been developed in certain countries, particularly in Latin America and Asia. It does not consist of hiding the facts – on the contrary – but of creating confusion as to who is responsible. Torture, as a violation of human rights, is distinguished from common-law crime by the fact that the author is a state agent. If the prisoner is subjected to violence during an interrogation at a police station, a prison, in military barracks or another official place of detention, it is virtually impossible for the personnel of these establishments to dodge their responsibility and the authorities may be challenged in such cases.

On the other hand, when a person is taken by force by a group of 'unknown individuals' who subject the victim to serious violence, sometimes proceeding to kill their prey and leave a mutilated body in the street, it is very difficult to establish that the operation was organized by state agents. This difficulty is compounded by the fact that, in certain countries, the collapse of state structures has led to the emergence of armed groups or bands defending different vested interests (groups of sharpshooters who sell their services, extremist offshoots, etc.).

When the authorities concerned are alerted by the families of victims, by non-governmental organizations and the mechanisms established by intergovernmental institutions, they generally show an apparently co-operative attitude. Enquiries are instigated, judges are charged with the investigation, national authorities are alerted and, in most cases, these steps are communicated to competent international authorities. Unfortunately, it is only very exceptionally that this activism actually leads to the identification and punishment of those responsible for torture. No-one is taken in by this, and when the same scenario occurs week after week in the same country – or even the same region – it is necessary to admit the participation or at least culpable passivity of the security services involved. Nevertheless, on a formal basis, it is difficult to lodge an accusation individually challenging state agents, who in all probability are organizing these carefully targeted operations.

While it is important to stigmatize all the methods used to mask torture, one must not lose sight of the fact that state-controlled violence is sometimes accepted by the general public, which considers it the price to be paid for ensuring security, which is perceived as increasingly threatened. From this perspective, certain developments in industrialized countries, which sometimes claim to be paragons of respect for and promotion of human rights, are very worrying.

Since 1990, the United States has devised a variety of devices intended to maintain order; one may justifiably ask why these should not be considered as instruments of torture. They include electric-shock pistols and truncheons, electrified shields, paralysing (incapacitating) pistols and (incapacitating) stun electric belts.[11] While the electrified shields and incapacitating pistols[12] may be viewed as defensive weapons which are less dangerous than traditional arms, it is important to note that they do not offer all the guarantees vaunted by their manufacturers. In Texas, a guard died in 1995 after having accidentally activated his electric shield; while as far as the pistol is considered, a coroner reported in 1991 that a number of people had died in Los Angeles after having been hit by these arrows, and that in at least nine cases the use of this pistol was the direct cause of death.

Stun belts, which are increasingly used when certain types of defendant appear before the courts, are remote-controlled and can inflict an electric shock of 50,000 volts for a period of 8 seconds. The wearer of the belt is instantly paralysed, and defecates and urinates involuntarily under the effect of the electric shock. Given that these belts are placed on unarmed prisoners surrounded by guards, the security argument advanced for the utilization of electrified shields or incapacitating pistols is irrelevant here. Instead, the device represents a means of preventing any attempt to escape, or curbing excessive agitation on the part of the defendant. Yet this result could be obtained by means which do not involve such suffering. It is amazing that judges accept the use of such instruments on people appearing before them, and stupefying that some of them even take charge of the remote-control panel which can administer the shock to the person they are judging.

Roots of Torture

The constant concern of those involved in the struggle against torture is to find effective means of action to prevent this scourge. They are therefore naturally interested in investigating the psychological and institutional mechanisms that result in such violence, and in devising preventive strategies incorporating the results of their research.

Archaic practice or a method used in all ages?

We in the Western world tend to think of torture – which up until the Enlightenment was common legal practice both during investigation (the famous painstakingly regulated 'question') and as a punishment (some crimes were punished not just by death but included particularly atrocious practices such as drawing and quartering, boiling, or burning) – as part of an archaic cultural system which we have fortunately put behind us but which persists in less developed societies. In this regard, the study conducted by OMCT at the end of the 1980s, on the occasion of the second Conference on Least Developed Countries, confirms that there is indeed a link between socioeconomic underdevelopment and massive violation of civil and political rights.[13] Moreover, some particularly serious violations are indeed carried out by armed groups or regimes which justify their actions by reference to mystical ideology that has more in common with the culture prevailing at the time of the crusades than to that of modern times (for example, the Taliban in Afghanistan, Algerian Islamic fundamentalists, or even the regimes of Saudi Arabia and Sudan).

Be that as it may, can one fairly conclude that torturers are recruited within societies based upon a system of anachronistic values going back to before our culture, which has witnessed the blossoming of human rights? Some seem to believe so, at least implicitly, since in their view human rights only appeared at the end of the eighteenth century among a Western European intellectual elite, and were only universally recognized in the twentieth century by the Universal Declaration. Prior to that date, the argument goes, not only were human rights not codified, but they could not even be envisaged, since the philosophical basis on which they were built did not exist, and the beliefs prevailing during these times were in contradiction with the very idea of human rights.[14]

Even without resorting to such radical statements, some feel that within modern cultures one can establish fundamental differences between those which, imbued with democratic values (essentially those of Anglo-Saxon or French cultures), are respectful of human rights, and those which, profoundly influenced by the authoritarianism of the *ancien régime*, consider respect for fundamental rights to be of minor importance.

Thus, for example, some have asserted that the dictatorships which flourished in Latin America, with their trail of atrocities, as well as the states of extreme violence currently being experienced in Mexico and Colombia, can be explained by a culture of violence, specific to the subcontinent, with its roots in *caudillismo*. This system of values, inherited from the colonial empire, exalts warrior-like values of order, bravura and grandeur, as embodied in the messianic figure of the *caudillo*, to the detriment of respect for civil society and its democratic representation.

While one cannot deny that all peoples are marked by their history, it appears to us that such arguments are not only simplistic, but even dangerous in several ways. When pushed to their extreme limits, they somehow result in absolving torturers, because one implicitly recognizes that they are not transgressing their own system of values. Such arguments are grist to the mill of people who deny the universality of human rights. If these rights only appear within a given cultural framework and at a particular moment of historical development, they may not be applied to societies with other ethical and cultural references.

It appears to us that these arguments stem from certain prior conceptions implying that rights only exist once they are codified and ethically justified. In reality, both from an historical standpoint and within the framework of modern cultural diversity, it appears clear that a certain number of fundamental values such as respect for the life and integrity of others – even if they are justified in different ways – have been recognized and respected for many centuries.

Well before the Universal Declaration of 1948 such attacks on these values were considered to represent a fundamental transgression. The fact that this transgression has been and still is justified in the name of other interests considered as superior does not make it any less a transgression. Therefore the question is to determine, in the face of a system which justifies such violations in the name of superior interests, why it establishes such a hierarchy of values. In most cases, one notes that it is more for reasons of political opportunism, due to an inability to handle a crisis situation, or else to defend privileges, rather than because that society holds a drastically different philosophy on the nature of man.

Nevertheless, it is true that modernism and its concomitant philosophies have given human rights an internal consistency and theoretical foundations which continue to be deepened and enriched, yet without automatically guaranteeing absolute respect. One would like to believe that the progress made on the scientific level goes hand in hand with practice, but in the field of human rights, as in others, it is apparent that these two aspects are not necessarily linked.

The struggle against revolutionary movements, left- or right-wing political opponents, or attempts to repress crime have often led, in situations of crisis or serious tension, to programmes involving the planned and systematic use of torture, disappearances and summary executions. By way of contrast with generally isolated 'slip-ups' committed by a member of the security forces, these programmes were and are devised and implemented by academics whose training and culture, far from guaranteeing a civilized approach, became tools that enabled them to develop more sophisticated and efficient techniques to break down their adversaries. Moreover, one witnesses the same intellectual mechanisms being used to 'justify' transgression: the protection of superior interests – civilization threatened by communism or religious fundamentalism; the ideals of the socialist revolution sapped of their strength by revisionists, etc. In most cases, these so-called ideals are a screen for protecting individual vested interests and privileges.

Specific psychological features?

Most verbal or written accounts of the testimony of victims who have survived torture speak of such cruelty and sadism – most frequently exercised not in the heat of the action but in cold blood and on defence-less people completely at the mercy of their tormentors – that one cannot help wondering what kind of individual is capable of such monstrous deeds. Do these atrocities not result from some kind of mental disorder?

Many psychologists and psychiatrists have examined the issue, seeking to determine whether there is a typical psychological profile of a torturer. In other terms, would it be possible on the basis of general tests to determine what kind of people carry within them the risk of turning into torturers in given situations; and could one, moreover, from the personal history of known torturers, identify the events, motivating forces and mechanisms that explain their very distinctive attitude to the pain they inflict on others?

The conclusions reached by these studies are far from unanimously accepted by specialists, some of whom question the legitimacy of the various approaches adopted. Can one consider the issue as a problem of individual pathology, or should one not rather deal with it from the angle of a social 'disease' which affects the whole of a society in which the values and mode of operating are disturbed? In the latter case, controversy over the pathological relations established between victims and their torturers (a subject popularized by the famous film *The Night Porter*) appear in a different light.

Even though scientists do not agree in this area, their contribution is important in three respects. First of all, and we will come back to this later, their demonstration that torture presupposes and results in a deterioration of the whole set of social relations within a given country, implies a holistic approach to the phenomenon, rather than considering torturers to be acting in an aberrant manner within an otherwise healthy society.

Second, they raise certain points that are useful for the development of fundamental human rights concepts – which, if they are to offer effective protection, must not only be taught but also integrated within actual social practice. (The slogan launched by UNESCO two decades ago to support its human rights educational campaign, asserting that where rights are known they are respected, proved to have a limited impact.)

Finally, on a more technical level, by enhancing the understanding of certain psychological mechanisms – although these findings are not systematically exploited – scientists have made it possible to develop preventive action at the recruitment and promotional stages for security agents, whose aptitudes may thus be examined not only in terms of professional competence but also by taking account of their personality as a whole, and particularly their mental attitude in relation to others, to violence and to power.

However, these studies undoubtedly raise as many questions as they answer. By showing that human psychology comprises features shared by humankind as a whole, they demonstrate by implication that the psychological element cannot explain – at least not in a determining manner – the phenomenon of torture. If, as it would appear, people throughout the world have a comparable psychological structure and perception of violence; and if, as also appears to be the case, the number of people with perverse tendencies is more or less identical within two groups of a given population, the fact that torture is a systematic practice within one society, whereas it is virtually non-existent within another, must be due to other factors.

Perpetrators and organizers

Torture as a systematic or quasi-systematic system of repression pre-supposes an organization which is all the more structured because it is hidden and wishes to remain so. As mentioned earlier, in contrast with the dictatorial models prevailing from the 1960s to the 1990s, torture – often associated with forced disappearances, murders and summary executions – is now appearing in states which, on the institutional level, respect the broad outlines of democracy, including the multi-party system, frequent and open elections, and separation of powers. Under such regimes, the facts are well known – selective crimes on victims chosen according to their role in society; and victims specifically identified or even designated before perpetration of the crime; we have unfortunately observed in several cases people who, immediately before dying or disappearing, told us they knew what their fate would be. Despite this, the perpetrators are never positively identified and are often impossible to get at, with the exception of low-ranking underlings.

At the General Assembly of OMCT in 1988, there was a proposal that we should develop more information in our database concerning the authors of such violations and that, wherever possible, we should denounce them in the urgent appeals we circulate. It quickly became obvious that the task was far more complex than initially foreseen and, at the request of various associations, we decided to undertake more systematic research on one country: Colombia.

The choice of this state was linked to various factors: the particularly high level of violence, which resulted in 12,859 assassinations for political and ideological reasons during the 1980s; a clear aggravation of the situation on the threshold of the 1990s, since no fewer than 9,501 people were killed for political reasons between 1988 and July 1991; a state structure conforming to 'democratic' criteria laid down by international institutions, meaning broad political and ideological pluralism, clearly defined parties, highly active trade-union organizations both in agricultural and industrial production, frequent and very open elections both for the central state and in the provinces, with a degree of autonomy, separation of powers, and the avowed determination of the executive, legislative and judiciary to promote and respect human rights, as demonstrated in the ratification of the main international conventions.[15]

The study covered the period 1977 to 1991 and, on the basis of serious violations committed in the course of these years, was particularly concerned with identifying the perpetrators of killings, massacres and other serious breaches of physical integrity. On the basis of the information gathered, a two-part *curriculum vitae* of the perpetrators of these crimes was drawn up. On one side, the data sheets on the individuals implicated provided family names and first names, the service to which they belonged and their ID code, their rank at the time of the investigation and, if available, photographs. Under these indications which enable indisputable identification, there is a summarized account of the crimes of which the person stands accused during the given period, and of what was done by the law to follow up denunciations – meaning nothing in many cases. Opposite this information, a list of promotions obtained, commanding positions held and decorations received is given for the same period.

The volume presents 350 presumed perpetrators of extremely serious violations, of whom 248 are members of the armed forces and 102 belong to the National Police. Of the 248 soldiers implicated, only one is not an officer. All the others are high-ranking or even top-ranking officers within the military hierarchy.[16] Moreover, of the 350 cases listed, only 10 – before publication of the book – had been sanctioned or removed from office due to violations committed. The conclusions of this research are comparable to other observations which may be made by analysing our data on other national situations featuring similar characteristics.

At the start of their career, perpetrators of torture are protected by high-ranking officers, who prevent them being singled out, or at least from being sentenced, thanks to various impunity mechanisms. Their 'effectiveness' often ensures them rapid promotions and key sensitive positions of command. The higher they rise within the hierarchy, the more they extend their methods, while taking less and less part in actually committing human rights violations.

One may note that the execution of the acts which are hardest to conceal, or may risk leading to identification of perpetrators, are sometimes entrusted to people who are not even part of the security forces, but are hired killers ready to commit crimes in return for money. It even occurs that those carrying out the act are themselves eliminated in turn.

The case of Aïda Abella Esquivel, member of parliament, illustrates this phenomenon. On 7 May 1996, her armour-plated car, in which she was seated with her security guards, was attacked by anti-tank weapons on one of the main highways crossing Bogotá. Thanks to the swift reactions of the driver of the car, the projectile did not reach its target but exploded in mid-air, causing a minor explosion which nonetheless seriously wounded the occupant of another car. The bomb-disposal experts who made the first observations estimated that the weapon used, if it had gone through the armour plating of the vehicle, would have caused an explosion of such violence that it would undoubtedly have killed those responsible for the shooting, as well as the targeted individuals. Moreover, this type of arms is normally exclusively reserved for the army. Following this attack, Aïda Abella Esquivel presented a full and detailed account of events to the international institutions, and expressly accused military members of the high command of having ordered the assassination attempt.

Torture and people on the fringes of society

In addition to political violence – which tends to consist more of disappearances, summary executions and assassinations, partly in order to avoid possible subsequent identification – it is worth noting that torture is frequently used on delinquents during interrogation by police, or by the injured party, or those claiming this role. For example, we were alerted some years ago to a case of torture committed by those attending a wedding in India. Some jewellery had disappeared and the bride and groom's families and guests became suspicious of a group of young people, whom they proceeded to arrest and knock about with increasing savagery, in order to make them own up to what they had done with the jewellery. When the police arrived at the scene and noted that the case had not been settled, they allowed families and guests at the wedding to pursue their violent actions, which led to serious injury to several of the suspects thus interrogated.

Unfortunately, this type of crime, often tolerated (as was the case here) or even encouraged by the police or other members of the security forces, appears very frequently to be committed against those who are on the fringes of society and as such are unable to make their voice heard, and who, compared with politicians, arouse far less attention, let alone sympathy. Little by little, thanks to the work of local NGOs, the atrocities committed against street children are beginning to be documented and denounced. Apart from this category, which arouses interest because of the youth of the victims, there are others involving marginal individuals, often living on the fringes both of society and of the law, who are subjected to serious crimes which remain unrecognized and hence unpunished.

Current economic policies

The concept of globalization has modified the dominant discourse on development. During the 1960s, liberal economists saw development as a means of 'catching up' for 'backward' countries, through the opening of markets and international aid, to the levels reached by industrialized nations. They also placed themselves at odds with the socialist bloc's argument advocating changes in the relations of production and exchange. As we know, this latter option no longer exists.

Nowadays, the concept of globalization imposes a singular approach, the idea that in a globalized model there is one system for all. Everyone seeks integration, according to a universally applied economic rationale, which is presented as scientific, ineluctable fact. Moreover, the dominant model holds that social protection measures – notably the establishment of minimum salaries – operate as economic rigidities, and falsify the laws of supply and demand in the area of labour. Thus the model opposes social protection, which, according to its internal logic, can only slow down and delay necessary restructuring, and deprive countries of the comparative advantage to be found in low labour costs.

Is there only one route to globalization, and will it avoid social fragmentation? The UNDP Report, published on 17 July 1996, gives a mixed reply. Wealth produced by the planet has never been greater than during the last fifteen years. However, this growth has been unbalanced, inequalities have increased, both between countries and within them. The much-vaunted success of Hong Kong, Singapore, Taiwan and South Korea affects less than 2 per cent of the Third World population. Since 1980, according to the report, average incomes per head in Latin America, sub-Saharan Africa and the Arab world has substantially declined. Furthermore, inequalities are growing in developed societies, and in particular in the United States. When presenting his report, James Gustav Speth, American administrator of the UNDP, declared that 'the world is today the theatre of acute polarization in economic terms, on the national as well as the international level. If current trends are prolonged, the economic disparity between industrialized and developing countries will no longer be simply inequitable but will become inhuman.'

Inequality in terms of the distribution of wealth is unfortunately not the only worrying problem. We are increasingly witnessing the rise of social problems which degenerate into less and less controllable violence. The following cases amply demonstrate these points. In May/June 1996 in Jordan, bread price hikes, a part of the IMF-imposed restructuring, sparked waves of demonstrations across the country. The reaction of the government was to impose, in the words of the king, 'an iron fist' clampdown. On 3 August 1996, Josefino Lopez, the 45-year-old president of a peasant organization and resident of Laguna, Philippines, was on his way with a friend to take photographs of farmland to help in a peaceful protest against the building of a golf course. They were stopped by thirteen armed men. Lopez has not been seen since. In Brazil on 18 April 1996, 2,500 landless peasants gathered on the Fazenda Macacheira to protest against the non-resettlement of 1,500 families. The 4th Battalion of the military police, commanded by Colonel Pantoja, resorted to violence to break up the demonstration. During the day, twenty-three demonstrators were killed, among them a child of 3. The fact that Brazil – the country with the widest gap between the richest and the poorest 20 per cent of the population – is also the scene of the largest number of assassinations of street children by paramilitary groups (several thousand cases recorded every year by human rights organizations) is no coincidence. Exclusion, when it reaches these proportions, leads inevitably to such outcomes.

We can only agree with the findings of Mr Bengoa, expert of the United Nations Sub-Commission on Human Rights, who remarked in his thought-provoking preliminary report[17] that 'extreme inequality proves intolerable for society and triggers all kinds of violence', and further that '[e]xtreme inequality within a society ... goes hand in hand with a denial of basic human rights'. Violence in this context will not be solved by simplistic *laissez-faire* solutions.

Impunity

Today the struggle against impunity is considered by most human rights defence organizations as a major – even the main – priority in the fight for the respect and restoration of human rights. This is also the feeling of populations in various countries. A recent opinion survey showed that in Peru 70 per cent of the people questioned were against the amnesty law; in Guatemala a front has formed against the adoption of clemency measures; while in Argentina there are more and more calls for the annulment of laws protecting impunity, and the opening of exhaustive legal inquiries into forced disappearances. The same is true in Africa, where the genocides in Burundi, perpetrated by the Tutsi against the Hutu, and those in Rwanda organized by the Hutu against the Tutsi, were fostered by a whole chain of unpunished crimes.

It is important to reject spurious theories which claim to explain or even justify impunity by invoking a sociological peculiarity, according to which a culture of impunity is said to be rooted in the history of certain regions. It is equally false to claim that impunity is the price to be paid for guaranteeing national reconciliation and establishing lasting peace between different sectors of civil society.

Impunity is generally the rule when, in a country where the police force enjoys significant privileges, victims are defenceless individuals on the margins of society. I refer here particularly to the killing of street children, which is well documented in Brazil, Guatemala and Colombia, but is by no means exclusive to this region of the world. Here, too, the number of cases we have identified amounts to several thousand, at least as far as Brazil is concerned; nevertheless, there are very few condemnations due to the fact that most members of the paramilitary enjoy total impunity.

Victims' rights

In its session of August 1996, the United Nations Sub-Commission on Human Rights adopted the conclusions of the Louis Joinet report, namely that the struggle against impunity is based on the protection and promotion of the fundamental rights of victims. Particularly highlighted in this context were the right to knowledge, the right to justice and the right to reparation. To determine to what extent these rights are protected, one must first examine the scope and manner in which they are violated and, potentially, what remedies might be applicable, or constitute the most effective ways of fighting such violations.

Amnesty, or should one say auto-amnesty, is one of the commonly used elements of impunity. Amnesty within the framework of policies of national reconciliation cannot be decreed by authorities under the control of the perpetrators of gross violations. Nevertheless, this is precisely what we have witnessed in most countries of Latin America, beginning with Chile. Moreover, the perpetrators of serious crimes according to international law, as well as those responsible for massive and systematic violations, cannot enjoy amnesty until the victims have had the chance to exercise their rights and obtain an equitable decision. This principle is systematically flouted, since amnesty on the contrary tends to forbid or limit plaintiffs' access to legal authorities, and is thus in total contradiction with the set of principles defined in the Universal Declaration of Human Rights and the International Covenant on Civil and Political Rights.

A frequent bargaining tactic used in transition phases lies in the so-called reciprocal amnesty mechanisms, meaning a procedure claiming to deal in the same way with both parties concerned by placing victims and their torturers on the same level. Former prisoners, tortured for crimes of conviction, meaning victims of major breaches of human rights, are thus granted amnesty for their 'crimes' on a par with their torturers. This political pseudo-equilibrium amounts to a fresh breach of fundamental rights.

It is also essential to draw attention to the overindulgent or even conniving use of doubtful extenuating circumstances to protect perpetrators or justify abuses committed within the framework of prescription mechanisms. Human rights defence organizations and a certain number of Latin American lawyers have suggested adopting the concept of ongoing crime. They aim to avoid a situation where victims and related parties eligible for compensation are confronted with statute of limitations due to the time elapsed since the facts. Forced disappearance is probably the most interesting legal case for evaluating the consequences of this proposal.

If one considers that the crime is committed at the time when the person disappears, following an arrest/abduction, one must set the statute of limitations as from the date of commission, meaning from the day of disappearance. On the other hand, if one deems that, during the whole entire period that the person remains absent, the victim continues to be subjected to the crime, one could set the statute of limitations deadline from the moment when the crime ceases, meaning the reappearance of the person or the undisputed establishment of his or her decease.

In parallel with the effort to recognize ongoing crimes, Latin American organizations and lawyers on the subcontinent are fighting for a broader interpretation of the concept of crimes against humanity, a crime which is by definition imprescriptible!

Obstacles to legal action

Other mechanisms of impunity deserve mention. These include obstacles to legal action, particularly constituted by the monopoly granted the attorney general to decide on prosecution. The Inter-American Commission on Human Rights has on several occasions expressed its opinion on this abuse, which prevents the victims from taking action themselves and limits the competence to intervene to one authority, often itself under the control of governmental authority. However, despite remarks made by the Inter-American Commission on Human Rights, this practice is still very much the rule in many countries. Another widespread mechanism is that of special legal places of jurisdiction, which consists in referring certain crimes to military or exceptional courts, which – for political, ideological or hierarchical reasons – are not sufficiently independent to punish perpetrators or crimes.

Combating impunity

A number of ways of effectively combating impunity could be suggested, including a more systematic use of the universal competence of courts stemming either from the Convention Against Torture or from the instruments of the Red Cross (1949 conventions) and a better follow-up of resolutions and recommendations. In my view, it is demoralizing to be content with drafting new reports, while nothing is actually changing. Mechanisms should be established to ensure rigorous monitoring of states to observe what becomes of these resolutions, and to take sanctions against certain states in some cases.

Impunity should be considered as a crime in itself. Professor Cassese[18] recalled a case of jurisprudence which, in the aftermath of World War II, made it possible to condemn a Japanese general, not on the basis of the crime committed, but for not having intervened to prevent it or punish those responsible. There is thus a jurisprudential basis for making impunity a crime in itself. Nevertheless, in the past fifty years, to my knowledge, no state has legislated in this field and courts have not seen fit to base their decisions on this precedent.

I believe that it is becoming crucial to set up documentation centres on amnesties and equivalent measures, in order to challenge abuses in this field. Also, I propose that a database should be established on perpetrators of gross violations of human rights. As I outlined above, several years ago my organization took part in writing a report presenting the main individuals responsible for state violence in Colombia.[19] This publication made it possible to clarify responsibilities, for neither the army nor the police as such are made up entirely of torturers. An international centre of this type should be set up to deal with the systematic collection of all relevant information in the field. Within such a context, one should demand that European and North American states, as well as those in other continents should make archives available to the courts and official research authorities concerning people who have participated in massive human rights violations. It is scandalous that states which claim to defend human rights should conceal elements which could serve as proof before validly constituted courts.

I also would propose that an international fund be set up, based on obligatory contributions, which would examine the requests submitted in a totally independent manner, determine the harm done and compensate the victim, and, further, that an international system be established whereby the victims' right to reparation and rehabilitation is guaranteed and the burden of compensation is firmly placed on those responsible, whether on the state or directly on the actual perpetrators, provided the latter have the means to face up to their obligations and may be prosecuted.

This latter proposal is aimed at resolving a problem linked to impunity. When victims seek to obtain reparation for the wrong they have suffered, they come up against two types of difficulty. The first lies in establishing the respective responsibilities of the perpetrator and the authorities. For how can one demand reparation if, due to impunity mechanisms, the person responsible for the crime committed cannot be prosecuted or sentenced, thereby preventing legal recognition of a breach of human rights? The other obstacle which leads many victims to refuse any compensation, consists in 'offering' assistance which is conditional on their abandoning any attempt to prosecute the perpetrators of the violation.

Political Will

The last three decades have witnessed the development of a large set of international instruments intended to ensure that torture is prohibited in all countries of the globe. These mechanisms, which have been set up on both international and regional levels, were created to enable verification of the extent to which internationally recognized standards are effectively expressed in national legislation, and whether they are implemented in accordance with their underlying principles. From this standpoint, considerable progress has been made; and all the more so in that non-governmental organizations – whose voice had been somewhat muffled hitherto – are now recognized as valid partners in this work and have become the mouthpiece of the voiceless.

During the same period – as, for instance, confirmed by the urgent appeals and interventions daily circulated by OMCT at the request of a network comprising hundreds of organizations around the world – torture as a practice is far from having been eradicated. Sophisticated legal mechanisms, methods which leave few traces, as well as the systematic elimination in certain countries of human rights defenders – all too often such strategies make it possible effectively to conceal the most serious crimes. Nevertheless, it would be wrong to conclude that nothing can be done. It is possible, thanks to the courageous and serious work of reliable bodies, to identify not only the victims but also the perpetrators of torture. Too often, unfortunately, the latter escape any form of sanction and their impunity leads to fresh violence. Only the authorities, by implementing the law as defined in the international instruments, are in a position to ensure respect for the state of law, an essential prerequisite for human rights. This is a question of political will which arises in all countries of the world.

Notes

1. See OMCT periodic report on Senegal at both CAT and the CRC (November 1995) concerning the absence of a definition of torture in the legal system of the country and its consequences.

2. However, whilst section 7 of the Nepal Children's Act forbids the practice of torture, it makes an exception in the case of beating 'in the interests of the child': 'Provided that the act of scolding and minor beating to the child by his father, mother, member of the family, guardian or teacher for the interests of the child himself shall not be deemed to violate the provisions of this section.' What is meant by a 'minor beating' is not indicated. Should the beating result in serious injury, Chapter 9 of the *Muluki Ain* (on battery and assault) states that if hurt, injury or grievous hurt are caused by one of the above-mentioned persons, 'while beating his ward using simple force for the benefit of the ward [child] he *shall not be held responsible for the result of his act*' (emphasis added). Should the beating result in the death of the child, Chapter 10 of the *Muluki Ain* (on death), section 6, states: 'If death is caused while beating or doing something else for the benefit of the deceased by his teacher or guardian, *he shall be punished with a fine of up to 50 Rupees*' (emphasis added). See 'CRC Report on Nepal', OMCT, Session 12 May 1996.

3. For example, the prison of Fianarantsoa, Madagascar has space for 400 people. At the end of 1992, 1,400 adults and children were being detained there. The FEBEM detention centre (for minors), São Paulo, Brazil in 1993 had places for 90 but an actual population of 250. See 'Exactions et Enfants', OMCT, Geneva, June 1993.

4. OMCT has received information from several reliable sources expressing their concern about the continued detention of minors together with adults in Honduran prisons. The International Secretariat has repeatedly intervened in cases of detention of minors with adults (see Cases HND 040495.CC, HND 071295.CC), including three times after the Supreme Court had abolished, in January 1996, the Auto Acordado which authorized such detentions (see Cases HND 200296.CC, HND 260396.CC, HND 120396.CC).

5. 'The prohibition in article 7 relates not only to acts that cause physical pain but also to acts that cause mental suffering to the victim. In the Committee's view, moreover, the prohibition must extend to corporal punishment, including excessive

chastisement ordered as punishment for a crime or as an educative or disciplinary measure. It is appropriate to emphasise in this regard that article 7 protects, in particular, children, pupils and patients in teaching and medical institutions.'

6. See 'CRC Report on Pakistan', OMCT, January 1994, concerning the possibility opened to the courts to regard puberty as the age of criminal responsibility.

7. High Court of Justice 7964/95.

8. High Court of Justice 8049/96.

9. Reasons adduced for judgement no. 5, High Court of Justice 8049/96.

10. See article 1 of the Convention Against Torture and Other Cruel, Inhuman and Degrading Treatment or Punishment.

11. See 'Les nouvelles technologies au service des tortionnaires', Amnesty International, French section, March 1997.

12. Incapacitating pistols fire two arrows equipped with a hook which lodges in the body of the victim. Linked to the arm by an electric wire, these arrows enable the user to send electric charges.

13. 'The Least Developed Countries: Development and Human Rights', OMCT, 1990.

14. This kind of clear-cut view is voiced by Imre Szabo in the article 'Fondements historiques et développement des droits de l'homme', published in *Les dimensions internationales des droits de l'homme*, UNESCO, 1978. The author states on page 12: 'The Middle Ages were not favourable to the idea of human rights nor to human rights as such. Today we would say that such thinking is not open to a concept centred upon man.'

15. Colombia fulfilled the criteria of international institutions so well that the UNDP, in its first report on human development in which it classified countries, gave it one of the leading places.

16. *El Terrorismo de Estado en Colombia*, published by OMCT and other organizations, NCOS, Brussels, 1992.

17. U.N. Doc. E/CN.4/Sub.2/1995/14.

18. Public Hearing on 'Impunity: The Need for an International Response', European Parliament, Brussels, 30–31 October 1996.

19. U.N. Doc. E/CN.4/Sub.2/1995/14.

4

'Dance, Sister, Dance!'

Lisa M. Kois

M, a 25-year-old mother of two, was startled awake at 3 a.m. by the sound of a man's voice shouting and pounding at her front door. Quickly, she got out of bed, took her two children to the bathroom, quieted them, and locked the door behind her. As she placed the key in her pocket and turned toward the front door, it smashed open with a loud bang. She could hear her two-year-old call out for her.

The man rushed toward her, grabbed her arm, knocking her down as he did, and dragged her into her bedroom, throwing her against the wall. Standing over her, he started firing questions at her, about her whereabouts during the last two days, about the friend she had been seen meeting with, about the man from the school who had come frequently to her house. She tried unsuccessfully to give answers to the questions. Repeatedly, he kicked and beat her. She could not breathe and was unable to respond to the questions that kept coming. Suddenly, the man disappeared. Hopeful, she listened for the door to close and felt herself sink into a relieved unconsciousness.

Waking some time later, M dragged herself to an upright position against the bed. From somewhere behind her, she heard the familiar click of a lighter and then a heavy booted walk approaching her, stopping close to her. She could not raise her head to look at him. She could only stare at his feet. He began to pace slowly back and forth in front of her. Again, he asked for the details of her whereabouts during the last two days. She could remember very little. Trying to speak, she coughed blood instead. At one point, her interrogator's mood seemed to change and he helped her onto the bed. Her thoughts were of her children.

After what seemed like hours of beatings, questions, and more beatings, he left the room once again, and then returned with a kitchen knife. Slowly, he cut her clothes as he repeated his angry request for cooperation. The knife was cold as it touched her skin, ran over her breasts, down her stomach, and then her thighs. She regretted letting him help her onto the bed. She tried to sit up but couldn't. Instead, she found herself floating somewhere high above, looking down at herself and this man as he took the knife and raped her.

For anyone familiar with the tactics of official torture, the incident described by M may be clear; it is a typical scene of state-sponsored torture.
It is the scenario of the state agent sent to extract information from the
suspected collaborator. Although he knows that she may or may not, in
fact, be involved in any illegal activities, she has been spotted too often
with those who are. She has information the state wants. It is his duty
to get that information and more importantly to send a message – a
message to those he is looking for, another message to those who might
contemplate joining the opposition. Her tortured body will send that
message clearly.

Undeniably, the description of the violence perpetrated against M that
night fits the profile of a fairly typical incident of state-sponsored violence
against women. The documentation efforts of human rights activists
throughout the world have made such stories all too easily recognizable.
The scenario described, however, is not that of state-sponsored torture.
Rather, it is the story of any equally typical case of domestic violence –
of the jealous soon-to-be-ex husband who stalks his wife and then con-
fronts her with the evidence of her 'crime' – in this case, her alleged
infidelity. The details of M's experience that night are startling for their
unmistakable similarities to the experiences of so many victims and survivors of state-sponsored violence. The tactics are, inescapably, the same.
And yet the official story is that she was not 'tortured'. In some countries,
she was not even 'raped'.

Despite the fact that, for centuries, women have been both the victims
and the survivors of torture as it is understood by the Convention Against
Torture and Other Cruel, Inhuman or Degrading Treatment or Punishment ('the Convention') – as well as torture as it is understood by women
irrespective of conventional definitions – there is little evidence of this
fact, and fewer provisions attesting to this reality, within the Convention
itself. The Convention speaks to neither the experiences nor the needs of
women, except inasmuch as those experiences and those needs fit neatly
into the, at best, androgynous and, at worst, gender specific (i.e. male),
model of the torture victim portrayed by the Convention.[1]

This chapter will first look at the ways in which torture has been
socially constructed and understood both through psycho-medical models and through the law, and how such models have excluded women's
experiences of torture. It will then go on to discuss those experiences –
using, whenever possible, women's narratives. Not only does the chapter
endeavour to look at women's experiences of torture, as it is traditionally
understood under international law; it will also explore the ways in which
state violence intersects with domestic violence, and how domestic torture
mirrors political torture. The nature of state-sponsored torture has com-

pelled the international community to develop a complex legal regime on torture. The chapter will assess the ways in which international mechanisms established specifically to address torture, including the Special Rapporteur on Torture, the Committee Against Torture, and the Special Rapporteur on Violence against Women have – or have not – dealt with the torture of women.

Legal Framework

Resolution 1994/45 of the UN Commission on Human Rights, 'The question of integrating the rights of women into the human rights mechanisms of the United Nations and the elimination of violence against women', 'calls for [an] intensified effort at the international level to integrate the equal status of women and the human rights of women into the mainstream of United Nations system-wide activity and to address these issues regularly and systematically throughout relevant United Nations bodies and mechanisms.'[2] An apparent consequence of the strategic campaign by the international women's movement leading up to the 1993 World Conference on Human Rights, resolution 1994/45 explicitly acknowledged 'the long-standing failure' of the United Nations' mainstream human rights mechanisms to protect and promote the human rights and fundamental freedoms of women in relation to violence against women.[3] Despite the supposed gender-neutrality of traditional human rights discourse and law, symbolized most markedly by its ethos of non-discrimination, notions of human rights have developed in a gendered manner. Women's experiences with violence, repression and abuse have been interpreted to exist outside the purview of international human rights protections.

Feminist analyses of human rights have focused heavily on the dichotomy of public versus private that characterizes liberal social paradigms, including conceptualizations of human rights. The public/private dichotomy distinguishes and ascribes value and import based on the perceived 'public-ness' of roles and actions. The state exists as quintessentially 'public', set against the intrinsically 'private' realm of the home. Overwhelmingly, women have been and continue to be the denizens of the private sphere, while their male counterparts have dominated the public. International human rights law, a response to overt forms of state violence against, and repression of, actors within the political – and hence public – sphere, has developed along similar fault lines. Consequently, women have not derived the same benefits from human rights law; their experiences with violence and repression have been, until recently, omitted from the annals of human rights discourse and jurisprudence.

Overwhelmingly, international definitions of torture have been interpreted narrowly and, consequently, have led to a profoundly gendered portrait of the torture victim as a male prisoner of conscience; it is the male who pervades the political/public sphere and, thus, it is the male who serves as the likely target of state violence and repression. Such portrayals, however, fail to represent adequately women's experiences as victims and survivors of torture.

An elemental component in attempting to articulate women's experiences with torture is definitional, specifically identifying how torture has come to be and is understood. The literature on torture, which represents a varied and multi-disciplinary approach, provides numerous examples of the attempts made to qualify, quantify and, ultimately, comprehend torture.[4] Definitions have been formulated and lists enumerated in an attempt to understand better the scope, significance and consequences of torture. From the minute details of the acts committed in the torture chamber to broad socio-political theories of the reasons why, torture has been dissected under a powerful lens.

Gonsalves et al. conceptualize torture as a sophisticated institution that targets and undermines the individual as well as social structures through a systematic and deliberate campaign. Methods utilized in such policies include 'illegal house searches, kidnappings, domestic secrecy and disinformation abroad, threats against one's life, disappearances, imprisonment, social isolation, physical and psychological abuse, psychological warfare, ongoing systematic disinformation, violation of basic human rights, massacres, selective executions, and the exile of specific sectors of the population.'[5] Thus torture, highly individualistic in its application, extends far beyond the individual experience and attacks also the community.

At the micro-level, the list of known torture techniques is vast. Although it is easy to imagine this list growing as governments' desire for power and control unites insidiously with the human capacity for evil, there is a high level of consistency and uniformity among the torture techniques utilized throughout the world. Such uniformity serves as the basis for attempts theoretically to situate torture as universal. The universality of torture, in turn, contributes to attempts to develop appropriate treatment and counselling modalities.

According to psychologists, torturers frequently concentrate torture on bodily functions important for somatic as well as psychological well-being.[6] Thus, common loci of torture are the brain and the sexual organs. Much torture is perpetrated when the victim is naked, and thus highly vulnerable.

Like all other crimes, torture has been socially constructed and named. Legally, torture is understood and articulated as an aggregation of acts, intentionality and motive. According to the Convention (Article 1.1), torture combines the following elements:

1. intentional infliction;
2. of severe pain and suffering, whether physical or mental;
3. for such purposes as obtaining information or a confession, punishing, intimidating or coercing, or for any reason based on discrimination of any kind;
4. inflicted by or at the instigation of or with the consent or acquiescence of a public official or other person acting in an official capacity.

Although international definitions of torture have developed almost exclusively in terms of overt state violence, the UN definition was indisputably broadened in the time that lapsed, and through the debates that transpired in that time, between the drafting of the Declaration on Torture and Other Cruel, Inhuman or Degrading Treatment or Punishment ('The Declaration') and the Convention.[7] Whereas the Declaration confines the definition of torture to intentional and purposeful acts solely 'inflicted by or at the instigation of a public official', the Torture Convention (Article 1.1) expands the protection to include not only acts inflicted by or at the instigation of a public official but also those inflicted 'with the consent or acquiescence of a public official or other person acting in an official capacity'.

The broadening of the definition creates an opening through which states could, depending on the interpretation of the Committe Against Torture, be held accountable for private acts of torture, whether such acts are committed by paramilitary groups, armed opposition groups, or private individuals in the context of domestic violence. State responsibility for such acts is based upon the state's responsibility to exercise due diligence in protecting against and punishing violations of human rights wherever they occur. A failure to exercise due diligence may result in a finding of state 'acquiescence' in otherwise private acts of violence.

Having said that, it is important to recognize that the Convention was clearly meant to address a very particular human rights abuse: politically motivated violence directed against an individual by an official state actor. Individuals are seen as needing heightened protection from such violence. The argument is clear: when the state, through one of its actors or agents, perpetrates violence in an overt and purposeful way, the state cannot then be relied upon to provide adequate remedies or redress for victims. Torture, symptomatic of the breakdown in the rule of law, is unlikely to be fairly or effectively redressed through national legal systems. Thus the international system intervenes, not only by providing an alternative mechanism of redress through international human rights law, but also by treating torture as a violation of the highest order, subject to universal jurisdiction.[8]

There is no question that the Convention was never intended to be a convention on violence against women. However, it was also never intended to be a convention on violence against men. Nevertheless, that is essentially what – like so many other 'gender neutral' human rights instruments – it became. Irrespective of its use of non gender-neutral language, which is at least partially a consequence of the historical context in which the Declaration and then the Convention were drafted, the protections afforded by the Convention have developed in a highly gendered manner. Mirroring the socially prescribed division of male and female roles in the public and private spheres respectively, it is men in their public roles that have traditionally been the benefactors of such protection. The concomitant 'privatization' of women, their concerns and the violence perpetrated against them has further increased this divide.

Consequently, even when women's roles cross over into the overtly public – when they assume political roles and become public actors – the violence perpetrated against them has not been deemed to reach the level of torture. It has not been granted the same significance in human rights discourse or law. The most egregious example of this is the failure by the international community to view rape as a form of torture. This has even been the case when rape is perpetrated in circumstances that would typically be construed as torture – for example, when a woman is in the custody of the state, jailed for overtly political reasons and is raped to elicit information or a confession.

If the soles of her feet are beaten, it will be called torture. If she is given electric shocks, it will be called torture. If she is tied, beaten, burned, deprived of her basic needs or forced to stand for hours, it will be called torture. However, if she is raped once by one prison guard or repeatedly by many guards, it has until recently been called something else.[9]

Quickly dismissed as the aberrant acts of a few bad eggs, rape by state actors has, as has rape in all other circumstances, been privatized. Like other forms of sexual violence against women, there has been a tendency to understand custodial rape and sexual violence as the private acts of sexually depraved men. Although sexual torture has been repeatedly identified as a distinct form of torture, the rape of women has rarely fallen within definitions of sexual torture. Consequently, women's experiences with torture often have been understood not as torture, but as rape or sexual harassment and have, at best, been treated as a distinct category and, at worst, completely ignored.

Like all forms of violence against women, allegations of rape arise within the context of patriarchal constructions of female sexuality. Thus an allegation of rape – even if the rape is perpetrated by state agents while the woman is being detained under the state's power (or abuse of such power) – is likely to become little more than an allegation of rape. Rape charges against the police, military or prison officials must generally be investigated and prosecuted under the same, at best faulty and at worst archaic, laws encoded in the state's penal code and rules of evidentiary procedure. Thus the question is quickly focused – and in many cases solely focused – on whether or not the woman was raped or, indeed, whether the victim is lying. Rarely are accusations of torture treated with the same scepticism.[10]

Classifying custodial rape as rape rather than as torture subjects the denunciation to the gender stereotypes and victim-blaming characteristic of the criminal justice system in dealing with cases of violence against women. Although characterizing the act as 'torture' rather than rape is unlikely to result in swifter or surer prosecution, allegations of torture carry with them strong normative force. Furthermore, at least to some degree, a denunciation of torture rather than rape may protect the survivor from the anti-woman rhetoric that has universally developed in reaction to formal complaints of rape. Unlike in cases of rape, few would question whether the victims consented to torture.

The traditional treatment of rape as something other than torture is particularly questionable in light of the justifications underpinning the very creation of an international legal regime on torture. Rape, by private or public actors, more than any other crime has been systematically dismissed by national legal systems; prosecution rates have been, and continue to be, appallingly low in cases of rape. Even when rape is prosecuted, rapists have given disproportionately low sentences. Thus, if the Convention is supposed to provide a remedy in cases perceived to be otherwise outside the law, rape clearly qualifies. Even in the best of circumstances, rapists are not prosecuted for their crimes against women. In the worst of circumstances, when the perpetrator is acting on behalf of the state or with the colour of the state, there is even less hope for prosecution.

Although legal definitions of torture, found in and arising from regional and universal treaties and declarations, have done much to shape modern concepts of torture, personal understandings of 'torturous' acts do not necessarily conform with such legal definitions. Looking at a comprehensive list of torture techniques, one finds that methods of torture are not only replicated throughout the world by state actors, but also by private and definitely non-state actors.[11] Those who have worked with victim-survivors of domestic violence recognize in such lists the myriad techniques utilized by male domestic partners against their female counterparts.[12]

While the violence perpetrated against women in the home is not wholly analogous with the official torture of women, it nonetheless exists on the same continuum of violence against women as a powerful tool in the systems that keep women oppressed and deny them their rights to full participation in their own societies. The techniques employed in the perpetration of official torture and domestic torture are analogous, as are the objectives. Increasingly, parallels have been drawn between official torture and domestic violence. As demonstrated by this chapter's opening narrative, the violence perpetrated by public and private actors against women is alarmingly similar.

> Like the act of torture, batterers use an often debilitating combination of physical and psychological violence in a process of domination and the exertion of control meant to destabilize and victimize the woman, rendering her powerless. Psychological abuse resulting from the spoken word, limitations on and the control of social mobility, and deprivation of economic resources generally accompanies physical battering. The physical violence is used, 'as a pathway to the mind and spirit' which is intended to invoke fear and break the will of not just the victim, herself, but also the group with whom the victim is associated. In the case of domestic violence, that group is women. The mere existence of violence against women, in general, and domestic violence, in particular, spreads fear among women, often restricting the way in which they must lead their lives.[13]

Furthermore, similarly to torture victims who are forced into exile, many victim-survivors of woman battering, fearful for their lives, are likewise exiled from their homes.

Despite these similarities, victim-survivors of domestic violence do not have available to them the same human rights mechanisms as do victim-survivors of torture. Because of the non-official nature of domestic violence, the connection between the state and the violence is more tenuous. Nevertheless, the Torture Convention does not entirely exempt the state from responsibility for domestic torture. The definition provides for state culpability in cases where the acts are committed, and the pain or suffering inflicted, with the acquiescence of the state. Thus a state's failure to act with due diligence to protect against and punish acts of domestic torture may in fact leave the state vulnerable to accusations of complicity and/or acquiescence.

While many commentators may argue that the difference lies in the official nature of state violence and the consequent unreliability of the state in providing a remedy for violence for which it is overtly responsible, victims of domestic violence, like rape and all other forms of violence against women, have few if any legal recourses and little state protection from the violence. The Special Rapporteur on Violence against

Women has documented a persistent pattern of state complicity in domestic violence through states' non-prosecution.[14] Thus the same argument may apply if a pattern of non-prosecution can be demonstrated. But does this mean domestic torture should fall within the purview of the Convention? Traditionalists would say not. Women's human rights activists would argue otherwise.

Women's Experiences in the Torture Chamber

On 17 May 1997, Mrs Murugesapillai Koneswary was allegedly raped and murdered by police personnel in one of the conflict zones of Sri Lanka.

According to neighbors, Mrs Koneswary had numerous problems with the police at Central Camp, including frequent and persistent harassment at the Central Camp checkpoint. Two months prior to her murder, police allegedly came to Mrs Koneswary's home, cut down and took a tree from her yard. Although she quickly filed a complaint with the head of the police post, nothing was done. Subsequently, Mrs Koneswary traveled to the capital of the district and complained to the DIG who intervened on her behalf, instructing the Central Camp police to return the timber to the family. It was after this incident that the verbal abuse and sexual harassment of Mrs Koneswary began.

On the afternoon of 17 May 1997, one such incident occurred. As Mrs Koneswary was passing through the check point at Central Camp, she was allegedly verbally assaulted and sexually harassed by four police officers on duty at the time. Mrs Koneswary responded, demanding that they leave her alone.

At approximately 11:00 p.m. that night, an unknown number of armed men in uniforms entered Mrs Koneswary's home. By 11:30 p.m., she was dead. Reportedly, she was killed instantly when a hand grenade was exploded on her abdomen. There has been speculation that the grenade was used to destroy all evidence of gang rape.

There has been no discussion in the press, by the government, or by activists of Mrs Koneswary's torture. All inquiries and questions have centered around the allegations of rape – was she or was she not raped.

The story of women and torture is one of pain and terror, strength and survival. Overwhelmingly, however, it is a story that has been, and continues to be, shrouded in silence, scepticism and shame.

Undoubtedly, women are targeted not only by gender-neutral forms of torture, but also by gender-specific forms of torture, including rape, sexual abuse and harassment, forced impregnation, virginity testing, forced abortion, forced prostitution, and forced miscarriage. Rape and other forms of sexual violence have been clearly documented as manifest forms of state terror against women. Consistent with conventional definitions of torture, rape and other forms of sexual violence – or the threat of such violence – are utilized by public officials or persons acting in their official capacity in order to obtain information or a confession, or to punish or intimidate. There can be little doubt that, at the very least, intimidation is implicit in the act of rape. Therefore, there can be no question that rape by a state actor or agent is torture; state-sponsored rape unequivocally conforms to the Torture Convention's definition.

The most particularized element in the torture of women is the sexualization of torture. Although the sexual anatomy of men as well as of women is targeted in the physical stages of torture, rape and the threat of rape, as well as other forms of sexual violence, are perpetrated more consistently against women detainees.

The body, viewed as the way of access to the mind and spirit, plays a prominent role in torture. Both within and outside the confines of the torture room, the body is perceived through a socially constructed lens of sameness and difference. The male torture victim's body is nothing more than his body, a body likely replicating the body of the torturer. The female body, however, has the added burden of the sex implicit in that body. It is the 'difference' of that body that leads to its increased vulnerability; that leads the woman's body to become a particularly vicious weapon against the woman herself. The female body in the torture chamber epitomizes the female body as it exists anywhere outside that room. It is sexualized, objectified, commodified. Thus, as the woman's body is sexualized, the torture of the woman is sexualized. So much so, in fact, that individual acts of torture on a woman's body cannot be divorced from such sexualization.

Certain torturous acts, when perpetrated against women as opposed to men, often assume disparate significance. Take, for example, A – a Muslim Bosnian tortured during the war in the former Yugoslavia – who described how she was beaten and her thighs were burned prior to being repeatedly gang raped.[15] The significance of the thighs and the exposure of the thighs, which is likely exacerbated for Muslim women, is imbued with sexual danger in a way that, for example, *falanga* is not. Arguably, it is the proximity of the vagina to the thigh, and thus the implication of sex in the representation of the exposed thigh, that has made the female thigh a social taboo to which shame is attached. Thus the forced exposure to the torturer of the thigh is forced exposure of the woman's sexuality, within which there is danger and violence implicit.

Rape is used as a form of torture not only directly against the rape victim but also against male family members who are forced to witness the rape of their wives, sisters, partners, daughters or mothers. In some cases, rape is used to punish the witness for allegedly failing to produce adequate answers during interrogation. Thus, for the witness, such rapes assume a distinctly psychological character, for he (or, less likely, she) is burdened with the apparent responsibility for 'causing' the rape. A typical strategy in which this technique is applied is through the 'impossible choice' scenario, whereby a detainee is presented with an impossible choice between two equally horrifying alternatives: for example, either tell 'us' (the state, through the torturer) where 'your' (the political prisoner) partners are hiding or we will rape your wife. Such choices presume knowledge that the detainee often does not possess. Nevertheless, the framing of the interrogation in such a fashion shifts culpability for the act – at least in the mind of the detainee – from the torturer to the tortured, giving the detainee a false sense of control over outcome. In the end, whether or not the information is forthcoming or, indeed, whether or not the detainee has the information, is irrelevant.

The technique of the impossible choice has long been recognized as a distinctly psychological form of torture. Likewise, the act of being forced to watch the rape of another has been recognized as such. Surprisingly, however, in such scenarios, the rape itself often has not qualified as torture. Rather, like the electric shock, the shackles or the police baton, the rape of women was viewed as one of the torturer's tools – a tool not against the rape victim herself, but against he who is forced to stand by and helplessly witness the rape. Although forcing a detainee to witness the rape or torture of another detainee is used in many cases irrespective of the relationship between the two detainees, it is likewise common to force a detainee to watch the rape of a woman with whom the detainee shares an intimate or domestic relationship. The woman's body is seen as little more than a possessory interest of the detainee or an object in which the detainee has a proprietary interest. As has been the case throughout history, the attack on the woman's body is perpetrated as an attack on the male – his honour, his dignity, his property.[16]

Similarly, women's bodies have been strategically usurped and violently tortured to further the aims of militaries in times of armed conflict. Sexual torture has been used in genocidal campaigns against warring communities and, more generally, as a weapon of war. The rape of a woman of one community by a member of another community is not only perpetrated but also perceived as an attack on the community more than as an attack on the individual woman – except, that is, by the woman herself.

The former Yugoslavia and Rwanda present the most notorious examples of the way in which mass and systematic rape has been used to perpetrate genocide through 'ethnic cleansing'. In such cases, rape is not the sole form of torture. In order to ensure forced impregnation, the sexual torture is systematized. Women in the former Yugoslavia, for example, were detained in rape camps where daily they were repeatedly gang-raped. If the perpetrators are 'successful', the torture will be sustained for up to nine months (or even longer, if the victim-survivor raises the child). With every bout of morning sickness, every kick, and every back pain, the survivor of sexual torture will be forced to relive her rape.

In many communities, victim-survivors of rape continue to be viewed with shame and threatened with expulsion from their home or their community. Victim-survivors are forced to relive the torture through the suspicious and condemning eyes of community members. If forcibly impregnated, with no desire for or access to abortion, the victim-survivor will have little choice about whether to go public with her story; her growing belly will speak for her. In many communities, unmarried women will find themselves unmarriageable as a consequence of rape. Married women may be forced out of their homes and face the prospect of divorce. Dictates on marriageability and divorceability are further exacerbated when the rapist was a communal enemy. Thus women are tortured and then tortured again – once by the state and then again by their family or community members.

When women are forcibly impregnated, it is the woman as womb that is co-opted for the purposes of the opposition force – for the cause of communal slaughter. Long after arms have been set aside and peace accords signed, the consequences of these attempts to destroy the community will reverberate throughout the community, particularly in communities that harbour shame and condemnation for victim-survivors of rape. The rape of the woman, which many will see as the symbolic rape of the community, will be relived through pregnancies and births of children of rape. The community will thereby be challenged to accept and incorporate the children – who are likely in the eyes of many to embody the enemy – into the community itself.

Although rape by members of security forces or opposition groups is a commonly utilized weapon of war – recognized and prohibited as such by the Geneva Conventions on the Rules of War[17] – it is only recently that rape during armed conflict is beginning to gain recognition as a distinct form of torture, most notably through the work of the War Crimes Tribunal on the Former Yugoslavia. Traditionally, rape in wartime has been quickly dismissed as one of the spoils of war. Once the men – that is, the protectorates – have been successfully slaughtered, the women's bodies are little more than wartime booty. Likewise, the rape of women is a direct affront to both man and military machine, revealing the weakness of their position.

It is because of the link between militarism and sexual violence against women that local prostitution tends to flourish, and is in fact often officially encouraged, in proximity to military bases. Conventional military wisdom, which links rape solely with sexuality but not with violence, in fact equates prostitution with rape.[18] According to such wisdom, the troops will have no *need* to rape if prostitutes are readily available to the troops. Thus, again, the woman's body is seen as little more than a sexual object – as something to buy, steal or kill for.

Women as Targets of the State

Women are targeted by the state in their numerous and varied public and private roles. In fact, in many ways, the rigid distinctions embedded in the public/private dichotomy are not so clear when looking at state abuses against women. The state does not refrain from intruding upon the private sphere or attacking women because of the private roles.

Like men, women are targeted by the state because of their public personae. Increasingly, for a myriad of political, economic and social reasons, women throughout the world are venturing out of their socially prescribed place – the home – and taking on significant roles in the public sphere. Women are entering public spaces from which they have previously been denied access, at least some of which remain – or in some cases become upon women's entry – politically contentious. In many cases, the apparent increased power and autonomy of women is perceived as a threat to or assault on communal values and morality. Consequently, seeking to put women back in their place, as defined by traditional, religious or cultural norms, women are targeted by the state or opposition groups.

The Taliban's torture of women in the public sphere, generally by beatings or flogging, is the most notable contemporary example of violence against women perpetrated by state, or in the case of the Taliban, pseudo-state actors for such reasons. The torture of women is used by the Taliban to enforce physically their anti-woman edicts, paramount among which is the prohibition on women in public spaces. Perpetrated in the streets, the torture of women by the Taliban takes on a distinctly public character and serves as an even more potent example to other women.

Increasingly, women are assuming overtly political roles and consequently are similarly being targeted by the state for such roles. The political torture of women as political actors has been documented throughout the world. Human rights workers have always been a favourite target for state repression. As women become more visible as activists for women's human rights, they are similarly targeted. One of the ways in which the lines between public and private are blurred is when women become distinct political actors because of their private, domestic roles as mothers, daughters, grandmothers and wives. The Argentinian organization Madres de la Plaza Cinco de Mayo was the first group of mothers, or other family members, to organize around the disappearance of their children. Similar groups exists in, among other places, Chile, Uruguay, Guatemala and Sri Lanka. Public and private roles thus converge; women have entered the public sphere because of their domestic relations and, in turn, states have concentrated their violent tactics against women. María Rumalda Camery, for example, was 'disappeared' in Guatemala in 1989 allegedly in retaliation for her activities with Grupo de Apoyo Mutuo por el Apareci-miento con Vida de Nuestros Familiares (Mutual Support Group for the Appearance of our Relatives Alive).

Women are targeted for torture not only as political actors in their own right but also as the mothers, sisters, wives, partners and daughters of political activists. As described above, rape of female domestic partners or relations is used as a way of torturing male political detainees. Women are also targeted by the state in the search for male political activists wanted by the state. Thus the distinction of public and private crumbles as the state intrudes upon the private sphere and targets women in their private roles, torturing them in their homes because of their domestic relationships. In Egypt, Human Rights Watch has documented the 'hostage taking' of family members of suspected Islamist militants by government security forces. In numerous cases, female family relatives are arrested, detained and tortured as a way to coerce the surrender of male suspects. The threat of sexual violence against female family members is a particu-larly powerful mechanism of coercion in Egypt, like many other countries, where '[t]he threat of rape and the sexually degrading treatment of women are perceived to be profound offences against a woman's individual honour as well as the honour of her family and male relatives.'[19] Thus women's bodies are again used to target their male counterparts.

Women are often forced to experience the violence associated with the arrest of their male counterparts. Wives, mothers, sisters and daughters not only experience the arrest of their husbands, sons, brothers or fathers under violent circumstances but are themselves also, during the course of the arrest, subjected to torture in the form of beatings, rape or sexual violence. The direct violence experienced in the course of the arrest is compounded by the psychological violence perpetrated through witnessing the event and from the uncertainty that often ensues.

> Everything was abnormal, our existence was shattered, and we were not told what had happened to our husbands. The rumours were incredible but were little by little confirmed: our husbands had disappeared, dead under torture, killed trying to escape, executed by firing squad etc. In thousands, we woman

stood every day outside the prisons or detention centres hoping in vain to see our husbands or to know if they were still alive. The uncertainty tormented us to such an extent, that each day it was more difficult to control the accumulated tension. Life became a true nightmare for us and forced us slowly into a condition of incredible mental torture.[20]

The experience described by the wife of a former prisoner and torture survivor is that of psychological torture itself. If they are not primary targets of state torture, female family members in particular are secondary targets of torture. State violence seeks not only to destroy individuals but, more broadly, to destroy community, the centre of which is the family unit.

International Human Rights Mechanisms

UN Special Rapporteur on Torture

The torture of women has not been treated by the UN Special Rapporteur on Torture as a particularly distinct or unique phenomenon compared with the torture of men. With the possible exception of rape and other forms of sexual torture, which is increasingly recognized as a gender-specific form of torture that differently targets and impacts women, the torture of women has been treated as the feminized version of the torture of men. So while there is gender-disaggregated information provided in the Special Rapporteur's reports – a notable improvement on prior reports – there is little gender analysis. Since the inception of the post, the UN Special Rapporteur on Torture has included sexual violence within the purview of his mandate, thus defining rape and other forms of sexual violence as a form – at least in some cases – of torture. On the whole, however, the Special Rapporteur on Torture has failed to demonstrate an acute understanding of the distinct issues impacting women as victims and survivors of torture.

The first Special Rapporteur on Torture classified 'sexual aggression', including rape and the 'insertion of objects into the orifices of the body', as a form of torture in his initial report to the UN Commission on Human Rights, thereby identifying rape and other forms of sexual violence as potential forms of torture.[21] However, the distinction made by the Special Rapporteur between rape and the 'insertion of objects into the orifices of the body' exemplifies the traditional definition of rape as nonconsensual penile penetration of the vagina, thereby 'reinforc[ing] misapprehensions that rape is primarily an expression of sexual desire or that it is an inevitable, if reprehensible, aspect of sexual relations between men and women.'[22]

It is, therefore, not entirely surprising to note that, even when the Rapporteur did address rape, he neglected to discuss its gender-specific character or the link between sexual violence against women and the oppression of women. Only occasionally did he note particular patterns of rape against women.[23] In what was his strongest statement regarding the issue, in 1992, the Special Rapportur recognized 'that [since] rape or other forms of sexual assault against women in detention were a particularly ignominious violation of the inherent dignity and the right to physical integrity of the human being, they accordingly constituted an act of torture',[24] thereby providing a clear framework for his successor to approach the issue of sexual violence against women in detention.

Notably, the first Rapporteur did at least contemplate an expansive interpretation of the definition of torture, arguing that the state may be held accountable for failing to protect its citizens against torture by private individuals such as paramilitary groups. His argument relied upon both the ICCPR's and the Convention's prohibition on torture not only committed 'by or at the instigation of' a state actor but also perpetrated 'with the consent or acquiescence of a public official or other person acting in an official capacity'.[25] Similarly, Professor Kooijmans included 'sexual mutilation' as a form of torture for which the state could be held responsible if the state fails to act with due diligence to prevent and punish such violations. While including discussions of such potentially broadening conceptualizations, however, Professor Kooijmans did not rigorously apply these interpretations to his reporting. He did not, for example, include in his reports information about torture perpetrated by private actors.

The second Special Rapporteur on Torture continues to assume a fairly, albeit not wholly, gender-insensitive perspective in his reports on torture. Although his report to the Commission of 1995 contained a fairly comprehensive analysis of the forms, reasons and consequences of the torture of women, his country reporting has consistently failed to reflect such insights. So while, for example, he categorizes rape as an overwhelmingly gender-specific form of torture likely to have 'dire consequences for the private and public life of the woman',[26] his case-specific reporting fails to provide elucidating examples of such consequences. Additionally, although the Special Rapporteur has noted the increased risk of impunity for torturers when rape is used as a form of torture,[27] he has not documented the way in which this phenomenon plays out in any given country context.

The Special Rapporteur, in general restricting himself to a brief recitation of the allegations of what, when, where and who, has at times failed to make important links between violence against women and torture or ill-treatment. For example, in 1996, although he reported on the commutation of Sarah Balabagan's death sentence and the flogging sentence that was imposed instead, he did not include any information on the nature of her alleged offence,[28] which many argue was self-defence after she was raped.[29] Although the Special Rapporteur has made attempts to identify the gender of victims, it is only women whose gender is noted in his reports, thereby emphasizing the 'otherness' of women and their experiences with torture. Such otherness has historically been linked with the devaluation of woman's experiences and thus raises questions about the Rapporteur's approach to gender disaggregation. Furthermore, since the reports have not been fully gender-disaggregated, the gender of the victim in many cases is unclear.

Perhaps the most notable example of the Special Rapporteur's apparent lack of a strong gender perspective can be found in his field report to Pakistan,[30] a country known for state violence against women, including torture and ill-treatment of women. Although he notes that he 'received numerous allegations of women being held in police custody and raped' he did not investigate these allegations during the mission, claiming only that he was 'unable'.[31] Furthermore, although the Special Rapporteur did note that the offence of *zina*, as articulated in the Hudood Ordinances, 'has been alleged to deter denunciations of rape' due to the threat that the alleged victim may be prosecuted under the ordinance if the perpetrator is acquitted, he failed to include any of the numerous examples in which this has indeed been the case. These omissions are coupled with one incidental visit to the women's section of Lahore Central Jail where he spoke with women detainees, who – except for two foreign women who had allegedly been ill-treated during police custody – 'indicated that they had been treated well within the prison itself'.[32] The Special Rapporteur also noted the 'far superior' conditions of the women's cells compared to the men's cells. Thus, in the end, we are left with an, at best, incomplete and, at worst, misrepresentative picture of the torture and ill-treatment of women in Pakistan.

Lastly, the Special Rapporteur provoked the ire of many women's human rights experts through the statement in his 1996 report that '[i]n his report to the Commission in 1995, the Special Rapporteur addresses the issue of torture as it pertains to women', thus clearly implying that he was not going to address it again.[33] Instead, he writes, 'the issue of torture and children is considered'. Although this perspective may be at least partially engendered by resolution 1994/37 B, in which the Commission invited the Special Rapporteur to examine torture against women and children, resolution 1994/45 called for the human rights of women to be addressed 'regularly and systematically'. Thus, the Special Rapporteur's stance that women and torture has already been covered and thus needs no further comment is provocative, flying in the face of repeated calls for gender integration in the work all human rights mechanisms.

UN Special Rapporteur on Violence against Women

Unlike other thematic or country mechanisms that address one particular human rights violation or one particular country, the UN Special Rapporteur on Violence against Women is responsible for investigating and reporting on all forms of violence against women throughout the world. Thus her mandate reaches not only traditional human rights violations directed against women such as torture, 'disappearances' and arbitrary executions,[34] but also non-traditional human rights violations such as those that occur in the domestic sphere or in the community. The latter have, until now, been largely excluded from the international human rights agenda. The unifying link between all violations for which she is responsible is female gender specificity. Although there has been some confusion in her office about how 'gender-specific' the violation must be to qualify under the mandate, the Special Rapporteur has now settled on a broad interpretation of the requisite level of gender specificity. Thus, for classification within the Special Rapporteur's mandate, it may be enough that the victim is a woman. The issue will be more clearly defined through her upcoming report on violence against women by the state, which is the gravest area in terms of what constitutes gender-specific violence.

Reflecting the UN Declaration on the Elimination of Violence against Women,[35] the broad mandate of the Special Rapporteur on Violence against Women is broken down into three substantive areas:

(a) Violence in the family (including domestic violence, traditional practices, infanticide, incest, etc.).

(b) Violence in the community (including rape, sexual assault, sexual harassment, commercialized violence such as trafficking in women, prostitution, labour exploitation, pornography, women migrant workers, etc.).

(c) Violence by the state (including violence against women in detention and custodial violence, as well as violence against women in situations of armed conflict and against refugee women).

The torture of women by the state is thus treated by the Special Rapporteur under (c), violence by the state, including violence against women in detention and custodial violence.

Thus far, the Special Rapporteur has presented three main reports to the Commission on Human Rights and four accompanying mission reports.[36] The Special Rapporteur took the opportunity, in her preliminary report, to outline the topics under each of the three substantive categories – violence in the family, violence in the community, and violence by the state – that were to be more fully addressed in the coming years of her three-year mandate. Thus far, it is the only place in which she has addressed state violence against women. The two subsequent reports to the Commission focused on violence in the family and violence in the community in 1995 and 1996, respectively. Field missions have additionally taken her to, and resulted in reports on: (1) Democratic People's Republic of Korea, the Republic of Korea and Japan, to investigate war-time sexual slavery; (2) Poland, to investigate trafficking in women and forced prostitution; (3) Brazil, to investigate domestic violence; and (4) South Africa, to investigate rape and other forms of sexual violence in the community. The Special Rapporteur's fourth report, subsequent to the renewal of her mandate in 1997, will deal exclusively with state violence against women, including during times of armed conflict. The report will thus address women and torture.

In her preliminary report, the Special Rapporteur clearly defined rape as a form of torture that 'is used as an instrument of torture by States against women in detention'.[37] Additionally, the Special Rapporteur identified '[c]ustodial violence against women [as] a widespread and troubling phenomenon'.[38] The areas identified in her initial report for further consideration in her eventual report on state violations against women include: (1) rape and other forms of sexual violence as torture; (2) prolonged illegal detentions and deprivation of food, sleep and water; (3) disappearances and extrajudicial killings; (4) the emergence of 'special laws' such as Pakistan's Hudood Ordinance; (5) preventive detention laws; and (6) police complicity in prostitution and trafficking in women. Additionally, the report will explore the ways in which rape as a form of torture is used during armed conflict and consider recent legal developments to address rape as torture.

In her second report to the Commission, devoted entirely to issues of domestic violence, the Special Rapporteur unequivocally declared that some forms of domestic violence do rise to the level of torture. The report included an entire section on '[t]orture and cruel, inhuman and degrading treatment', in which the Special Rapporteur stated that 'domestic violence can constitute torture or cruel, inhuman and degrading treatment or punishment under the International Covenant on Civil and Political Rights and the Convention Against Torture and Other Cruel, Inhuman or Degrading Treatment or Punishment.'[39] Included in this section is an in-depth analysis of the *de facto* and *de jure* ways in which domestic violence should be classified under international law as a form of torture, for which states are responsible.

The approach of the Special Rapporteur has thus far reflected the developmental nature of international law in respect to violence against women generally, and the rape and torture of women specifically. Thus, while she has not yet devoted an entire report to the subject, all indications are that when she does she will be instrumental in clearly articulating the international norms that have been developing regarding the torture of women, as well as pushing the limits of such norms.

UN Committee Against Torture

The Committee Against Torture (CAT) has done little to incorporate a gender perspective into its work. CAT's position as the treaty body for the Torture Convention places it in a highly strategic position to impact and broaden interpretations of torture. Although largely confined to questioning and commenting on State Parties' reports, the Committee has the capacity to steer content through consistent and targeted questioning on violence against women and through its ability to promulgate general recommendations regarding interpretations of the treaty. Thus far, CAT has utilized neither of these strategies to impact State Parties' reporting regarding violence against women. Consequently, such reports fail to provide an adequate assessment of gender-specific forms of torture, as well as failing to provide information on state remedial measures.

Additionally, CAT has continuously failed to utilize its role as a treaty-monitoring mechanism to incorporate arguments being put forth in the international arena regarding non-traditional forms of torture, such as that which has been made by the Special Rapporteur on Violence against Women. As noted above, the Torture Convention itself maintained a certain level of ambiguity in respect to non-traditional forms of torture. Although it does not specifically define, for example, domestic violence as a form of torture under the purview of the Convention, the language of the Convention leaves room to interpret it as such. In outlining the trigger mechanisms for obtaining state responsibility for acts of torture, the Convention includes state 'acquiescence' as a mechanism of state responsibility. Not only does such language grant the Committee licence to consider information about domestic violence in which state acquiescence has been persuasively demonstrated; it compels the Committee to do so.

Conclusion

Despite the fact that women have been both the victims and survivors of torture through the centuries, it is only recently that women's experiences as such have begun to be understood as distinct and equally egregious violations of international law. Inasmuch as international definitions of torture have been narrowly interpreted – leading to a profoundly gendered portrait of the torture victim as a male prisoner of conscience – women have been denied equal protection under both international and national law.

Noting this disparity is not, and should not be, a question of who has 'got it' worse or who is more or less victimized by torture. Such questioning would be absurdly pedantic, and the answer painfully clear: the tortured – whether male or female – are nonetheless the tortured. There is no competition when it comes to the nefarious nature of torture. Nevertheless, it is imperative to reconstruct and differently 'gender' the portrait of the victim, the perpetrator, and the institution of torture itself – which is what this chapter has endeavoured to do.

Notes

Special thanks go to Radhika Coomaraswamy, Nigel S. Rodley and Ameena Hussein-Uvais for their comments, critiques and general intellectual inspiration and input along the way.

1. Feminist scholarship has exposed the universally gendered nature of the socially constructed 'norm'. As demonstrated by words such as hu*man*, *man*kind, and wo*men*, male gender, in fact, informs much of the English language. The visual image associated with norms are inherently gendered, based on social constructions of what is properly female as opposed to properly male (and, notably, that which is female is just that, opposed to that which is male). The female is the other. Mental images accompanying words such as 'policeman', 'doctor', 'judge', or 'mailman' are generally male, whereas images associated with 'nurse' or 'teacher' are more likely to be female. There can be little doubt that the drafters of the Torture Convention had a male model in mind, particularly considering the Convention's silence on rape as torture.

2. U.N. Doc. E/CN.4/1994/L.11/Add.5, at 7.

3. Ibid., at 3.

4. Ibid.

5. Carlos J. Gonslaves, Tato A. Torres, Yael Fischman, Jaime Ross and Maria O. Vargas, 'The Theory of Torture and the Treatment of Its Survivors: An Intervention Model' in *Journal of Traumatic Stress*, vol. 6, no. 3, 1993, p. 352.

6. See, for example, Peter Vesti, Finn Somnier and Marianne Kastrup, *Psychotherapy with Torture Survivors: A Report of Practice from the Rehabilitation and Research Centre*, RCT, Copenhagen, 1992; Allan Staehr and Mia Stehr, *Counselling Torture Survivors*, International Rehabilitation Council for Torture Victims, IRCT, Copenhagen, 1995.

7. See U.N. Doc. E/1979/36, paras. 17–18.

8. Universal jurisdiction provides all states with both the jurisdiction and the obligation to investigate, arrest and prosecute perpetrators of certain crimes, such as torture, through their national criminal justice systems, regardless of the nationality of the perpetrator or the site of the violation or to extradite the perpetrator.

9. It was, for example, only in 1991, in their publication *Rape and Sexual Abuse:*

Torture and Ill-treatment of Women in Detention, that Amnesty International character-ized the rape of women by government officials – whether the women are in actual or effective custody – as torture. See *Rape and Sexual Abuse: Torture and Ill-treatment of Women in Detention*, Amnesty International, AI Index: ACT 77/11/91, December 1991 ('When a policeman or a soldier rapes a woman in his custody, that rape is no longer an act of private violence, but an act of torture or ill-treatment for which the state bears responsibility.')

10. Rape allegations against state actors fall prey to the same practical impedi-ments that all rape prosecutions face, the biggest of which is the issue of consent. Consent in the context of custody is a misnomer. Where there exists such inher-ently unequal power dynamics such as those that exist between the jailer and jailee or detainor and detainee, there can be no *de facto* consent. 'In prison, correctional employees have nearly absolute power over the well-being of prisoners and a corresponding obligation to ensure this power is never abused. When an officer has sexual contact with a person, even without any overt pressure or exchange, he commits a gross violation of his professional duty.' See *All Too Familiar, Sexual Abuse of Women in U.S. Prisons*, Human Rights Watch, Women's Rights Project, 1996, p. 4.

11. As identified by the Centre for the Victims of Torture, Nepal, torture techniques include: (1) beating; (2) *falanga* or *falaka* (the beating of the soles of the feet); (3) finger torture; (4) suspensions; (5) cold torture; (6) heat torture; (7) irritant torture (using chilli powder, table salts, etc.); (8) forced walking or sitting on sharp objects; (9) dental torture; (10) ear torture; (11) hair torture; (12) scratch-ing with knife; (13) being tied down; (14) forced positions; (15) chepuwa (victims legs clamped very tightly with bamboo sticks or similar objects causing severe pain); (16) twisting of body parts; (17) poking; (18) electrical torture; (19) suffo-cation; (20) sham execution; (21) enforced physical exhaustion; (22) forced labour; (23) *telefono* (simultaneous beating on both ears); (24) mutilation; (25) disfigure-ment; (26) sensory deprivation; (27) perceptual deprivation; (28) social deprivation; (29) deprivation of basic needs; (30) forced, impossible choices (disclose the loca-tion of a friend or have a family member tortured); (31) incongruent actions (being forced to sign false statements, disclose information, commit blasphemous acts, violate social taboos, witness the torture of others); (32) threats and humiliation; (33) misinformation; (34) conditioning techniques; (35) double-binding techniques (victim is tortured followed by seemingly human and sympathetic treatment); (36) reverse-effect techniques (torture is continued in spite of submission to every demand of the torturer); (37) pharmacological torture; (38) sexual torture using instruments, without instruments, and by animals. Dr Nirakar Man Shrestha and Dr Bhogendra Sharma, *Torture and Torture Victims: A Manual for Medical Professionals*, Centre for the Victims of Torture, Nepal, 1995.

12. It must also be noted, however, that domestic violence also occurs between homosexual domestic partners.

13. Lisa M. Kois, 'Working Paper on Domestic Violence, Prepared for the UN Special Rapporteur on Violence against Women', 29 September 1995, p. 9. See also Dorothy Q. Thomas and Michele E. Beasley, 'Domestic Violence as a Human Rights Issue', *Human Rights Quarterly*, vol. 15, no. 1, February 1993, pp. 36–62.

14. *Report of the UN Special Rapporteur on Violence against Women: Its Causes and Consequences*, U.N. Doc. E/CN.4/1996/53, 5 February 1996.

15. Dragica Kozaric-Kovacic, Vera Folnegovic-Smalc, Jrmila Skrinjaric, Nathan M. Szajnberg and Ana Marusic, 'Rape, Torture, and Traumitization of Bosnian and

Croatian Women: Psychological Sequelae', *American Journal of Orthopsychiatry*, vol. 65, no. 3, July 1995, pp. 428–33.

16.   The perception of the torturer is replicated through scholarship on torture, which likewise fails to define the victim of rape as the victim of torture.

17.   Although the Geneva Conventions include explicit prohibitions on rape, it is conceptualized not as a crime against personal integrity but as a crime against honour. According to Article 27 of the Fourth Geneva Convention, '[w]omen shall be especially protected against any attack on their honour, in particular against rape, enforced prostitution, or any form of indecent assault' against women, who are 'protected persons' under Article 4. Additionally, Article 76(1) of Protocol I and Article 4(2)(e) of Protocol II also prohibit rape, enforced prostitution and indecent assault. Article 4(2)(e) also includes 'outrages upon personal dignity, in paticular humiliating and degrading treatment'.

18.   See, Addendum, *Report of the Special Rapporteur on Violence against Women, its Causes and Consequences, Ms. Radhika Coomaraswamy, in accordance with Commission on Human Rights resolution 1994/45; Report on the mission to the Democratic People's Republic of Korea, the Republic of Korea and Japan on the issue of military sexual slavery in wartime*, U.N. Doc. E/CN.4/1996/53/Add. 1, 4 January 1996.

19.   *Human Rights Watch Women's Rights Project*, The Human Rights Watch Global Report on Women's Human Rights, 1995, p. 188.

20.   Lone Jacobsen and Peter Vesti, *Torture Survivors – A New Group of Patients*, The Danish Nurses' Organization, Copenhagen, 1990.

21.   *Torture and Other Cruel, Inhuman or Degrading Punishments*, Report by the UN Special Rapporteur, U.N. Doc. E/CN.4/1986/15, para. 119.

22.   International Human Rights Law Group, *Token Gestures, Women's Rights and UN Reporting*, p. 1; The UN Special Rapporteur on Torture, June 1993.

23.   For example, according to the 1993 report of the Special Rapporteur on Torture, in India '[r]ape and ill-treatment of women by the police seems to be widespread throughout the country. In the northeast states and Jammu and Kashmir, there is a pattern of rape of women by the army and paramilitary forces'; in Myanmar, '[r]ape of women while their husbands are taken away for porter duties seems also to be a common practice'. In Pakistan, 'female prisoners held for political reasons are frequently raped in police custody'; in Peru, '[i]n the areas where a state of emergency was in effect the military frequently resorted to rape'; and, lastly, in Turkey, '[i]t was also reported that almost every woman submitted to torture is sexually harassed and sometimes even raped' (paras. 257, 336, 352, 355, 479, respectively). This pattern of reporting has continued under the present second Rapporteur. See U.N. Doc. E/CN.4/1995/34, para 334 (noting that in Jammu and Kashmir 'the practise [of custodial rape] was reported to be systematic'), para 544 (noting that 'the substantial majority of women held in police custody [in Pakistan] were subjected to some form of sexual assault'). See also U.N. Doc. E/CN.4/ 1996/35/add.1, para 243 (noting again that in Jammu and Kashmir '[r]ape was said to be carried out frequently to punish women suspected of being sympathetic or related to alleged militants and to intimidate the local population').

24.   Oral statement to the UN Commission on Human Rights, E/CN.4/1992/ SR.21, para. 35.

25.   Notably, this is the same language utilized by many women's human rights advocates to argue for state responsibility for private acts of domestic torture.

26.   *Report of the Special Rapporteur, Mr. Nigel S. Rodley, submitted pursuant to Commission on Human Rights resolution 1992/32*, U.N. Doc. E/CN.4/1995/34, 12 January

1995, para. 19.

27.   Ibid.

28.   *Summary of communications transmitted to Governments and replies received (Addendum)*, U.N. Doc. E/CN.4/1996/35/Add. 1, para. 784.

29.   Amnesty International, for example, in the urgent action it issued after the flogging sentence was given, made the connection between Sarah Balabagan's crime and her rape. Urgent Action, AI Index: MDE 25/02/96.

30.   See *Report of the Special Rapporteur, Mr. Nigel S. Rodley, submitted pursuant to Commission on Human Rights resolution 1995/37 (Addendum, Visit by the Special Rapporteur to Pakistan)*.

31.   Ibid., para. 48.

32.   Ibid., para. 75.

33.   *Report of the Special Rapporteur, Mr. Nigel S. Rodley, submitted pursuant to Commission on Human Rights resolution 1995/37*, U.N. Doc. E/CN.4/1996/35, 9 January 1996, para. 9.

34.   Notably, the UN Commission on Human Rights has created mechanisms to address each of these human rights violations: a Special Rapporteur on torture; a working group on disappearances; and a Special Rapporteur on summary and arbitrary executions. Thus, while each thematic mechanism should have been, throughout the years, investigating and reporting on gender-specific violations as well, the position of the Special Rapporteur on Violence against Women was largely a response to the failure of mainstream human rights mechanisms, such as the ones listed here, to take into account the situation of women.

35.   *United Nations Declaration on the Elimination of Violence against Women*, adopted 20 December 1993, U.N. Doc. A/48/29, reprinted in 33 ILM 1049 (1994). Although there are slight discrepancies between the mandate and the Declaration, the Special Rapporteur interprets her mandate according to the Declaration.

36.   In chronological order: *Preliminary Report submitted by the Special Rapporteur on violence against women*, U.N. Doc. E/CN.4/1995/42, 22 November 1994; *Report of the Special Rapporteur on violence against women*, U.N. Doc. E/CN.4/1996/53, 5 February 1996; *Report on the mission to the Democratic People's Republic of Korea, the Republic of Korea and Japan on the issue of miliary sexual slavery in wartime (Addendum)*, U.N. Doc. E/CN.4/1996/53/Add.1, 4 January 1996; *Report of the Special Rapporeur on violence against women*, U.N. Doc. E/CN.4/1997/47, 12 February 1997; *Report on the mission of the Special Rapporteur to Poland on the issue of trafficking and forced prostitution of women (Addendum)*, U.N. Doc. E/CN.4/1997/47/Add.1, 10 December 1996; *Report on the mission of the Special Rapporteur to Brazil on the issue of domestic violence (Addendum)*, U.N. Doc. E/CN.4/1997/47/Add.2, 21 January 1997; *Report on the mission of the Special Rapporteur to South Africa on the issue of rape in the community (Addendum)*, U.N. Doc. E/CN.4/1997/47/Add. 3, 24 February 1997.

37.   *Preliminary Report on the Special Rapporteur on violence against women, its causes and consequences, Ms. Radhika Coomaraswamy, in accordance with Commission on Human Rights resolution 1994/45*, U.N. Doc. E/CN.4/1995/42, 22 November 1994, para. 51 (stating that '[r]ape is an instrument of torture') and para. 173.

38.   Ibid., para. 248.

39.   *Report of the Special Rapporteur on violence against women, its causes and consequences, Ms. Radhika Coomaraswamy, submitted in accordance with Commission on Human Rights resolution 1995/85*, UN Doc. E/CN.4/1996/53, 5 February 1996, para. 42.

5

Atrocities by Non-state Actors

Bertil Dunér

In the early 1990s the Algerian military annulled the general elections and banned the Islamic party, which was set to win. This prompted a wave of extremist violence. Massacres of villagers were continually reported, and every method seems to have been employed, including beheading of victims with chainsaws. Members of a family which fled killings only 25 kilometres from the capital reported in March 1997 that an armed group began killing villagers because they refused to collaborate. One member of the family added: 'We have no more to give. They've already taken everything.'[1]

Encouraged by the independence of the Asian republics after the fall of the Soviet Union, Uighur nationalists started to resist the Chinese policy of strengthening the Han Chinese presence in Xinjiang province. In recent years bombs have been exploded on buses in the capital of Xinjiang as well as in Beijing. After a bomb went off on bus in Beijing during rush hour, the Organization for Turkestan Freedom was quoted by the Central News Agency of Taiwan as maintaining that the explosion was 'the only way for the Xinjiang Uighur people to take revenge against Communist China's oppression'.[2]

In January 1996 news media reported that at least eighty people died and more than 1,400 were injured in an explosion which wrecked the main commercial district of Colombo, Sri Lanka. The blast happened when a lorry packed with explosives rammed the Central Bank building, setting fire to adjacent buildings and cars. The attack was attributed to members of the Liberation Tigers of Tamil Eelam.[3]

Tragedies such as these seem to repeat themselves incessantly all over the globe. They are typically not discussed in human rights terms, however, since internationally recognized human rights are defined by international law, which fundamentally addresses the responsibilities of governments. From a moral point of view, of course, atrocities carried out by non-governmental actors, as in these examples, appear just as objectionable as similar actions carried out under government protection. And, of course, situations of the former kind are also, as a rule, the object of juridical attention and castigation, albeit under national law. However, it might be relevant to incorporate non-state atrocities in human rights discussions, to the extent that these are linked to governmental cruelties and the focus of this chapter is precisely on such links.

Some clarifications are needed here. By 'non-state' is meant organized groups which are not merely temporary constellations and which conduct activities that are directed against the state, its policies or its authority. The kind of activities intended cannot, of course, be defined by reference to national legislation, since this varies considerably. We need to find a common standard. To be practical, I suggest that we are referring to torture or similar cruelties – in short, torture in the sense intended in international (human rights) law, particularly when the victims thereof are unrelated to ongoing conflicts. In order to emphasize that NGO actors rather than states are intended, I shall use the term 'atrocities'.

We are well aware that the chosen point of reference is not applicable to most of the actors we will be focusing on here.[4] Again, this is just a practical solution; this chapter does not aim to contribute to the discussion about the juridical status of non-state actors. Rather, it sets out to explore the possible (empirical) relations between non-state and state atrocities (torture) and consider whether the fight against torture could be refocused in a more effective way.

External Targets

The non-state actors are primarily involved in events in their 'home' country but sometimes they also carry out violent actions abroad. A number of West European countries have been external targets for non-state brutality. For instance, Kurdish organizations have carried out attacks in France, the United Kingdom, Germany and Switzerland and the Provisional Irish Republican Army has attacked targets in Germany. France has been hit by the Basque Fatherland and Liberty organization as well as by Algerian militants. In 1995, for instance, a number of attacks took place, including a bomb explosion in an underground station in Paris, killing seven people and injuring eighty-four. The French police concluded that the attacks were the work of an organization which operated directly on the orders of the Armed Islamic Groups with leaders based outside France.[5]

Several Palestinian organizations have struck against targets outside their 'mother' (primary) target – that is, Israel and territories controlled by Israel. The Abu Nidal organization is frequently thought to have the most widespread external targets. Actions by NGOs in other parts of the world (Asia and Latin America) can also be mentioned in this context.

It may be instructive to discuss one of these cases in more detail. The Kurdistan Workers' Party (PKK) has fought for self-rule in southeast Turkey since the mid-1980s. The insurgency escalated in the 1990s, when the situation in Northern Iraq after the Gulf War had made it easier to carry out armed operations. The PKK also started violent operations in Germany, which houses a Turkish population of about two million, including half a million Kurds. In 1993 it staged a series of attacks against Turkish consulates and businesses, including one in which a person died. In 1995 there was a spate of arson and other attacks on Turkish travel agencies, mosques and other property across Germany.[6]

The PKK holds Germany co-responsible for the 'Turkish genocide against Kurds' in Turkey because it supports Turkey economically and otherwise, and Germany is also criticized for its treatment of Kurdish activists in the country. In 1996 the PKK leader made a drastic move, which attracted much attention, when he threatened to hit Germany even harder, including attacking German holidaymakers in Turkey.[7] Germany has found this situation difficult to handle. In 1993 the government issued a ban on the PKK, after blaming it for a series of attacks. This action was very much welcomed by Turkey and seen as a vindication of its demands that Germany end its tolerance towards the organization. However, Germany has advocated that Turkey seek a peaceful solution to the Kurdish question and that the Kurds be given cultural autonomy.

It is natural for Germany to sell military equipment to her partner in the NATO alliance, and it has done so since the mid-1960s, but it has also shown its discomfort over Turkish anti-insurgency policy in a very pointed way. In 1995 for instance it protested Ankara's incursions into northern Iraq to operate against rebel Kurds there, by suspending a shipment of hardware.[8] Subsequently, however, German sympathy for the Turkish position seemed to increase, probably under the influence of the PKK threats mentioned above (which in some circles were understood as practically a declaration of war) and Bonn appeared willing to cooperate with the Turkish authorities concerning Kurdish violence in Germany.[9]

External target states are obviously concerned about conflicts in the 'mother' country, and it seems a perfectly reasonable policy to discuss a conflict with the mother country and urge resolution by peaceful means so that it will not spill over to other countries. Ordinary foreign-policy measures, such as various diplomatic approaches and the manipulation of transaction flows can be used to this end (as they were by Germany).

However, a slightly different approach may be taken, the possible merits of which I will try to make clear. Ending the conflict could be relegated to being a goal of lesser prominence; the primary and more explicit goal would be for all parties to the conflict to work for the end of torture and similar brutal activities. If successful, this approach would further the target state's national interests just as effectively as the peace-oriented approach would, albeit perhaps in a less clear-cut way. What is more, it seems easier to pursue, since the focus is more restricted.

Pressing a state to lay down arms and negotiate with rebels may frequently appear a rather onerous demand, particularly if the latter are pushing for autonomy or even a separate state, as in the case of Turkey – the PKK leader advocates independence, and has also spoken in favour of uniting the Kurdistan populations from four countries into a separate federation. The state, as a sovereign and internationally recognized unit, considers itself perfectly within its rights to use violence whenever necessary to combat separatism, and to count on considerable support for such a position. Even extending such activity outside its own territory may be considered perfectly legitimate. When Turkey was criticized for invading northern Iraq to hunt for PKK guerrillas, the Turkish foreign minister said: 'Imagine if there were a no-man's-land in Europe where only terrorists held sway.... Months pass and the terrorists use it as a base to attack villages and kill people. Can you imagine that Europe would just look on? Would Europe say, that is not our territory and we cannot go in?'[10] This view is certainly widely accepted in the international community, as well as inside the country. It is often thought that the army's excessive influence in Turkey thwarts non-military solutions to the Kurdish unrest. However, the truth seems to be that neither the politicians nor public opinion is prepared to grant concessions.[11]

When it comes to torture and similar brutal treatment, however, neither Turkey nor any other state could claim to be within its rights to use such methods in its dealings with its opponents, since it is bound by international conventions. Therefore a target state would be in a strong position if it linked the behaviour of both parties, pressing each to stop its atrocities, and drew parallels between certain of their actions.

It should be relatively easy to mount a campaign for humane behaviour on the part of both the mother state and a rebellious NGO, and on that basis a comparatively simple task to win strong international support. Interestingly, the PKK has shown some sensitivity toward public opinion. In 1996, apparently influenced by negative reactions in Germany, the PKK leader promised to halt further incidents in the country.[12]

Proxy Organizations

Let us now take a completely different perspective and consider NGOs hostile to national governments, whose actions may be influenced by external governments. It is well known that rebellious and armed NGOs frequently rely on outside support in some way or another. The key question here is what happens when an external state's *responsibility* for atrocities is raised.

This kind of relationship is closely related to a more general phenomenon, which is typically discussed under the heading of international terrorism and which we shall now consider. However, since 'terrorism' is a highly contentious word, a note on terminology is in order. Terrorism is frequently seen as NGO-biased. Leonard Weinberg, an expert in the field, notes that 'we ordinarily think of terrorism as a type of violence carried out by clandestine groups.'[13]

The negative connotations of the term are so strong that enemies of the state tend vehemently to resist the label and are at pains to show that in fact it applies to their enemies, those that repress them. This is in contrast to earlier times, when the term was less reviled by revolutionaries. 'In the nineteenth century, for example, Anarchists proudly called themselves terrorists, traced their lineage at least back to the French Revolution, and sometimes to the Order of Assassins in medieval Islam. Later, Trotsky was not embarrassed to speak of the benefits of the Red Terror. The last group to speak of *itself* as a terrorist organization was the one widely known as "The Stern Gang"...'[14]

By implication, the concept of terrorism is frequently chided for being pro-Western, whereas, according to Alexander George '[t]he plain and painful truth is that on any reasonable definition of terrorism, taken literally, the United States and its friends are the major supporters, sponsors, and perpetrators of terrorist incidents in the world today.'[15] Questions about the 'proper' use of the term are irrelevant here and the NGO perspective is, of course, implied in the title of this chapter.

International terrorism is one of the many concepts referring to important social phenomena that does not have a generally accepted definition. Dr Cees Visser discusses this in a conference report published a decade ago: 'I do not know how many definitions of terrorism there are, but the number could very well correspond with the number of terrorism researchers all over the world.'[16] Nevertheless, he believes that all share the view that terrorism has something special which distinguishes it from other types of political violence. The term is frequently used by news media and independent analysts who report and analyse atrocities by individuals and NGOs that have connections with foreign states.

Examples abound of contacts between violent NGOs and external states, covering the whole range of possible support, from low-key verbal support and provision of material resources to direct plotting. A dozen or so states have frequently been singled out as being particularly involved, including several Middle Eastern and African countries. Syria, for instance, is generally perceived as having had a prominent role historically in this connection. During the Cold War, Edgar O'Ballance points out, Syria

> sheltered and sponsored terrorists, providing them with training facilities, and in this sphere liaised closely with the Soviet KGB. This was revealed later, when secret East European files were unearthed. With KGB assistance, international terrorists sheltering in Iran, Iraq, Libya, Syria and South Yemen were able to penetrate into Western Europe, often through the (then) divided city of Berlin. The governments of these countries were able to assist the spread of international terrorism westwards to embarrass states hostile to them, while blandly denying any involvement.[17]

Our primary interest here lies with those situations when a state is *indirectly* implicated in atrocities abroad, because of its relationship with an NGO perpetrator, here called proxy. These relations are in contrast to atrocities abroad in which the state is *directly* involved. It is, however, writes Richard Clutterbuck, 'less common for government agents to carry out individual international terrorist attacks, presumably because these are counterproductive if they are found out'.[18] Such acts certainly have been carried out, however; for instance Iran, Iraq and Libya are imputed to have ruthlessly persecuted dissidents abroad. Iranian dissident organizations have claimed that more than ninety nationals have been killed abroad by the theocratic regime in Tehran.[19]

In 1997 a landmark event occurred in Germany when a Western court for the first time explicitly linked the Iranian state to such a crime. Two people were sentenced for the murder of three Iranian dissidents and their translator in Germany. The presiding judge declared that the perpetrators harboured no personal motives but were fulfilling an assassination decree issued by Tehran's Committee for Special Operations, on which the country's top authorities are represented. The judge also said the court was struck by the incidence of boasts by Iran's leaders whenever they wanted to silence a dissident voice.[20]

Fighting international terrorism is a matter of national policy for targeted states, but for a long time there have been efforts to internationalize the response to international terrorism. The USA has assumed a high profile in this connection, and has, generally, adopted a forceful attitude toward international terrorism. The Department of State is the leading agency for the formulation and implementation of American counter-terrorism policy, and an Office of the Coordinator for Counter-terrorism has been set up. An important task of this office is to provide Congress with an annual report, in which terrorist events in the world are listed and analysed.

For the purposes of the report terrorism means 'premeditated, politically motivated violence perpetrated against noncombatant targets by subnational groups or clandestine agents, usually intended to influence an audience', whereas international terrorism 'means terrorism involving citizens of the territory of more than one country'.[21] An important function of this report is to identify states which have 'repeatedly provided state support' for international terrorism – that is, supporting, training, supplying or providing safe haven to known terrorists. At the time of writing, this so-called terrorism list comprises seven countries: Cuba, Iran, Iraq, Libya, North Korea, Sudan and Syria.

It is an aim of US foreign policy to bring maximum pressure to bear on countries that are on the terrorism list, by imposing sanctions of various kinds (political and diplomatic, as well as economic – for example, against foreign trade) and urging other states to do likewise. American success in getting others to rally behind its punishment drives has in fact been rather limited, but the USA maintains bilateral consultations with a large number of other governments, and cooperates by, for instance, sharing expertise, intelligence and information with them as well as supporting anti-terrorism training.

The USA is working multilaterally within a number of settings and is particularly striving to tighten cooperation within the major industrial countries. Since 1978 it has worked with the so-called Group of Seven to develop practical measures to counter terrorism. In 1996 an extension of the group (including Russia) agreed on a large number of recommendations, concerning among other things the safety of mass transportation (standards for more complete and accurate passenger and cargo manifests; marking and tracing of explosives and the like), the decoding of communications transmitted by terrorists, the prevention of terrorist fund-raising, and the expansion of international treaties outlawing terrorism.[22]

The most notable international treaties and conventions are the following (exempting regional, European, conventions): Tokyo Convention on Offences and Certain other Acts Committed on Board Aircraft, 1963; Hague Convention for the Suppression of Unlawful Seizure of Aircraft, 1970; Montreal Convention for the Suppression of Unlawful Acts against the Safety of Civil Aviation, 1971; Convention on the Prevention and Punishment of Crimes against Internationally Protected Persons, Including Diplomatic Agents, 1973; Convention on the Physical Protection of Nuclear Material, 1979; International Convention against the Taking of

Hostages, 1979; Montreal Protocol for the Suppression of Unlawful Acts of Violence at Airports Serving International Civil Aviation, 1988; Convention for the Suppression of Unlawful Acts Against the Safety of Maritime Navigation, 1988; Protocol for the Suppression of Unlawful Acts Against the Safety of Fixed Platforms Located on the Continental Shelf, 1988; Convention on the Marking of Plastic Explosives for the Purpose of Identification, 1991.

Obviously the anti-terrorism regime has developed considerably over the years. However, the regime has been criticized for its weakness and its loopholes. It has been pointed out, for instance, that progress has been achieved primarily with respect to areas for which consensus is rather easily achieved, such as hijacking and safety of diplomatic personnel. This may be so, but in a certain respect this fact is rather trivial, since any law, national and international alike, is the manifestation of negotiations and consensus achieved.

Certainly some states would prefer a regime which is harder and covers a wider range of crimes, including state sponsorship of terrorism; this is the view particularly of the USA, which sees itself as leading the way in ratifying and bringing into effect these treaties and taking a much higher profile than its allies. A national security advisor to President Clinton has stated the following:

> Well, there's no question that, in this constellation of issues that are involved in terrorism, state sponsorship of terrorism is one very important dimension of it. We have been, and the President in particular has been, very, very firm and forceful from the very beginning about the need for the United States and our allies to take stronger measures with respect to ... countries that are engaged in state-sponsored terrorism.... We expect our allies to do more, and we have pressed them – there is almost no meeting that takes place with this President and a foreign leader in which this subject does not come up.[23]

The point I wish to make here is not that the regime is defective with respect to state-sponsored terrorism (of NGOs), but rather that this aspect could be approached as an issue of *human rights* of (all) citizens who run the risk of being hurt by terrorist atrocities. A consistent approach along such lines has not been pursued; nevertheless it does seem natural and has many advantages. It is true that the human rights concept has not been completely absent in these contexts. However, its role has not been more than marginal – for instance being conceived as a restriction in international anti-terrorist cooperation[24] and focusing upon the treatment of perpetrators of violations rather than victims thereof.[25]

For reasons of logic and effectiveness, the atrocities under discussion here could be included as human rights issues. They relate to the violation of values that are recognized as fundamental human rights, such as the right to life and freedom from torture or cruel, inhuman or degrading treatment or punishment. Furthermore, they are inserted in an optimal framework for raising questions about the responsibilities of states; it is precisely the limits of states' responsibility for violations that lie at the heart of human rights law.

This is not necessarily to say that these atrocities already have a firm place in human rights law, implicitly. To the extent that they have, however, the task seems relatively easy; this connection could be made explicit and stressed in some kind of document, for instance an additional protocol. To the extent that they have not, the need for more fundamental work would, of course, be implied. This touches upon the issue of new rights versus synthetic rights, which we need not go into here.

The human rights approach would also facilitate linkages with the UN human rights system. It is the UN Human Rights Commission which is generally seen as the foremost of all the bodies that make up this system and it should be recalled that this body over the years has extended its mandate, abandoning its earlier cautious profile and adopting increasingly effective procedures to investigate human rights crimes, including the so called 'thematic' procedures.

It would certainly be expedient to develop a linkage with appropriate structures, in spite of the fact that resources for investigations are rather modest at present. On the other hand, the level of resources that are put at their disposal are, of course, contingent upon the will of the member states to contribute. It seems that for states which take a strong interest in terrorist issues there would be a golden opportunity here to contribute to the growth of the investigative resources of the secretariat (or the Center for Human Rights), for instance by setting up voluntary funds, which is an established technique used for raising money within the UN. It would also provide an opportunity to discuss the mandate of the secretariat, particularly its freedom to carry out fact-finding on its own initiative, not being bound by assignments from political bodies.[26]

While recognizing a link between human rights and anti-terrorism, some would perhaps want to demur that there nevertheless seems to be a contradiction between the two, perhaps of an ideological nature: whereas the latter is animated by lofty ideals – such as stated in the Vienna Declaration and Programme of Action: 'The World Conference on Human Rights ... recognizing and affirming that all human rights derive from the dignity and worth inherent in the human person...' – the former is motivated by a more earthly concern for security.

However, this, if anything, points to a semantic rather than a substantive disagreement. There is no question that the anti-terrorism regime has been propelled by national interests. The USA, for instance, has not denied this. The Coordinator for Counterterrorism has stated the following:

> It is a paradox that although terrorism kills relatively few people, compared to other forms of violence, and although the statistical probability of any of us being killed by terrorists is minuscule, we are preoccupied by terrorism, and our government and others pay extraordinary attention to combating it. Let me suggest some reasons why.... One can argue that terrorism has failed historically, as a strategic weapon. But that is no cause for comfort. There is no doubt that it has caused great damage to American interests and those of our friends around the world. For example it has prolonged the Israeli–Palestinian conflict, and the Northern Ireland conflict for decades. Real progress toward peacemaking in these struggles has come only when terrorism has been renounced and its practitioners marginalized.... Terrorism also has a high economic cost. The US Government alone spends about $5 billion a year to guard against terrorism, at home and abroad, and these costs will doubtless rise.[27]

The fact that the national interests of states are involved in a given issue, however, is not a valid argument against taking it up as a human rights issue; historically, this has not been important. In fact, the most basic of all modern human rights instruments, the Universal Declaration of Human Rights (in its preamble) makes a connection between human rights and security, and this linkage has frequently been dwelt upon by states ever since.

Some years ago the Swedish foreign minister addressed the UN General Assembly, listing a number of challenges of a global nature. After mentioning globalization in the environmental field, she addressed human rights and concluded: 'Working for respect for fundamental human rights in all countries is an important aspect of efforts to achieve international peace and security.'[28]

The example of development is perhaps even more pertinent to the present discussion. At the end of the 1960s developing countries started to call for a new international economic order (NIEO). The thrust of this idea was to give the developing countries more influence in the world economy and for the industrial countries to provide resources. The Group of 77 pursued this idea, which was recognized by the UN some years later. Using the NIEO catchword they also started to push for the recognition of development as a human right. This battle became much more protracted, however. Western states expressed reservations, for conceptual reasons (this right being one of the questioned 'peoples' rights') and for fear of the unspecified means that might be required of them. In spite of the fact that a Declaration of the Right to Development was adopted by the General Assembly in 1986, this right did not gain complete recognition until 1993 (at the 2nd World Conference on Human Rights).

The concept of proxy (indirect) atrocities used here has, of course, rather vague contours. However, using other terms instead, such as state-sponsored terrorism, would not change much in that respect. A process of defining its meaning would be likely to generate a great deal of controversy. This, however, would be nothing new – vagueness and conflict have long gone hand in hand in the process of human rights norm-setting.

The consideration of minority rights is an example in point. The existence of 'minorities' is recognized in the International Covenant on Civil and Political Rights of 1966 (article 27). Yet, notwithstanding strenuous efforts over the years, no definition has emerged within the UN (not even in the UN declaration of 1992 on the rights of persons belonging to minorities).[29]

In spite of the long voyage of development towards recognition as a human right, the content of this right has not been clarified. The conflict about means remains. However, the issue has now passed from higher levels in the UN structure to a permanent working group established by the Commission on Human Rights subsequent to the World Conference.

When integrating proxy atrocities into the framework of human rights a number of intricate questions will have to be addressed. Is state responsibility involved just in cases of active NGO encouragement (as perhaps primarily indicated by the term 'proxy') or should a state be held responsible also if it is giving only passive backing? An awkward version of this question is the following: should restrictions be placed on states to prevent them allowing NGOs (or their affiliates) that have committed atrocities to open offices on their territories?[30]

Even more problematic is the definition of active encouragement. Should a distinction be made between a state which actually encourages an NGO to commit atrocities, and a state which in one way or another supports the NGO (supplying material resources, funds, training, advice on strategy and so on), short of encouraging its torture and other such abuse – much as the US government agencies did in Nicaragua.[31]

This example, furthermore, makes it clear that questions of sovereignty and intervention, themselves rather complicated matters, will have to be brought into the discussion.

Vicious Circle

In the study of conflict the notion of escalation is central. Disputes may turn into violent conflict, more and more parties may be brought in, different stages may be reached and so on. Conflict dynamics of these kinds are generally described as escalation, although this term is less frequently used than one might think, given the volume of conflict research that is produced. For example, it is not to be found in the subject index of many prominent studies of international relations, including such a monumental work as Henry Kissinger's on diplomacy.[32] Can one conceive of escalation in the specific sense that the use of torture (atrocities) by one party is somehow connected to its use by the opposing party? Such a hypothesis seems quite reasonable in view of Donatella Della Porta's comparative study of political violence in Italy and Germany. She finds that there is a dimension involved of tactical adaptation, including harshness of means used, both between movements and against the police.[33]

In his second report to the UN Commission on Human Rights the Special Rapporteur on torture draws attention to the danger of governments being caught up in escalatory behaviour. In situations of civil strife, he says,

> [v]iolence, fed by mutual hatred, becomes the predominant feature of everyday life. Especially where civil strife has taken the form of guerilla tactics, military and security personnel feel threatened and may gradually fall into the practice of physical abuse and torture to extract information about their opponents. Every person living within the guerilla area may be seen as a potential enemy who withholds information and may, therefore, be forced to disclose it by all available means. Although in many cases the victims of such abuse are completely innocent, the inevitable effect of such practices is that mutual hatred increases and life becomes ever more violent.[34]

In what follows I use the concept of vicious circle. By this I mean that one party's practice of torture fosters the other party's practice of torture – that is, it prompts the latter to use (more) torture or makes it easier for him to use it, and so on, in a circular logic.

A number of different mechanisms can be conceived that make for a vicious circle. First of all, torture is likely to produce sorrow and anger, which in turn risk triggering an aggressive response. Such an impulse may be described in terms of retribution (tit-for-tat), punishment, and the like, and is hardly that strange a way of thinking and acting, given that for centuries torture was widely practised and even accepted as a legal sanction by state authorities and the like in order to give the culprit condign punishment.[35] Moreover, torture is likely to be practised for instrumental purposes. Several uses to help the waging of conflict may be mooted, including the seeking of intelligence. Torture is supposedly effective for gaining information and extracting confessions.

It has repeatedly been pointed out that intelligence gained by coercion is of doubtful trustworthiness. Yasar Kemal has brought this fact absurdly to life in his novel about the revolutionary hero Ince Mehmed (Book 3). A peasant boy wanting to disclose Ince Mehmed's whereabouts and defencelessness to the police was not believed. He was subsequently tortured, whereupon the truth he tells becomes distorted into untruth to the detriment of the torturers.

It is reasonable to assume that torture is likely to be functional in certain circumstances. In a recent letter to the *New York Times* a lawyer gave examples of how the application of physical pressure ('moderate physical force') on people suspected of involvement in bombings in Israel has decreased the random murder of civilians.[36] In fact, interrogation practices amounting to torture by Israeli security officials seem to be permitted by official sanction and have given rise to considerable international concern.[37]

Torture could certainly also be functional in causing horror and producing submissiveness within a recalcitrant group of people, or inducing passivity within possible opponents. It could also be utilized for raising funds – blackmail – or gaining other resources, such as recruits. Such a perspective based on utility implies that the actors would build this means into the balance-of-power calculus, which they are likely to do constantly, and thus if one party makes more use of it, it is likely that the opposing party will think in terms of compensatory tactics along the same lines.

Other instrumental purposes for torture come to mind, the circular logic of which tends not to be so clearly visible. David Rapoport, for example, has pointed out that in original Anarchist doctrine, atrocities were a means of enabling the terrorist to gain self-respect.[38]

Apart from mechanisms that generate (more) atrocities, one may also consider a 'weaker', *facilitation* mechanism involved. If one party makes use of torture and similar methods, or increases the use of it, his opponent could feel, or at least maintain, that he is justified in responding in kind. This is of course, strictly speaking, one of the well known fallacies of relevance known to logicians.[39] However, a fallacy of logical reasoning is one thing, a tense conflict situation quite another.

This self-exoneration mechanism might seem irrational, even counterproductive, in the long run. Nigel Rodley has pointed out that when a state uses this strategy to minimize the negative public impact of human rights violations committed by its own agents, it may have the effect of encouraging those agents to pursue tactics that rely on extreme violations, and such a recourse may have an effect opposite to that intended. Far from putting down an insurgency, the tactic might well engender hatred and thereby deprive the state of the legitimacy it seeks to protect.[40] Of course, the balance between perceived short- and long-term gains and losses could only be struck by the actors involved and the paucity of theory and research on gross violations prevents us from forming a judgement on the amount and kind of rationality that inspires the decisionmakers at different levels.

A variant of this is the feeling and/or claim that outsiders unfairly concentrate their attention on and hence blame one party's atrocities (e.g. the state, since the state is responsible before international monitoring bodies), and unfairness is thus taken as an excuse for continuation of the behaviour in question.

It is difficult to verify the operation of vicious circles, let alone their frequency, without conducting case studies specifically designed for such purposes. However, some clear indications may be obtained by means of readily available sources. Suffice it here to give a few examples.

In Myanmar/Burma, both the military regime and opposition groups have committed atrocities, although apparently on a larger scale on the government side. The present situation in the country goes back to 1988 when a military junta seized power after having crushed nationwide demonstrations demanding freedom and democracy; in the wake of the coup several new armed opposition groups were set up.

The governments's atrocities over the years are well documented (e.g. by the US Department of State, the UN Commission on Human Rights and human rights NGOs). It seems, for instance, that interrogation of detainees is usually carried out under cruel conditions intended to intimidate and disorient. In addition, ordinary citizens have been subjected to harassment and physical abuse. It is more difficult to document the abuse committed by opposition groups, but there is no doubt that this has taken place, and some atrocities have even been admitted by the movement responsible. As news agencies, human rights organizations and others have reported, anti-government groups have used forced labour and subjected prisoners to harsh treatment. Groups have used violence to obtain confessions and prisoners who were allegedly government spies have been executed following summary procedures.

In the culture of violence that has developed in the country, outrageous acts do not appear wholly independent of each other. For instance, the main organization of dissenting Burmese students admitted in early 1997 that alleged government spies had been executed and tortured using electric shocks, and beating seems to have been used to extract confessions. A principal secretary of the organization's central committee stated the following: 'Torture is a very strong word. It wasn't done to all the accused. It is not right to torture people, but it is right if the enemy is very cruel and brutal.'[41] It should be noted that the government, for its part, denies wrongdoing and maintains that allegations of gross violations are unfounded and frequently reflect political motives.[42]

Let us consider another case. About one-seventh of the population in Turkey is Kurdish, half or more residing in the western part of the country. In the east the PKK, or Kurdish Workers' Party, has launched an armed campaign for independence from the central government. Both parties to this conflict have committed grave human rights crimes. The government's failure to abide by international rules on torture and other cruel, inhuman or degrading behaviour is amply documented by both international and national organizations. The Human Rights Foundation of Turkey states that it has information about more than five thousand cases of torture since 1980. It is alleged that children also have been abused.[43] It should be noted that not all atrocities have been carried out in the east.

The PKK ambushes security forces, but it also targets civilians.[44] Local Kurdish families have been intimidated, particularly in villages known to be sympathetic to the government. The PKK has been involved in murders of civilian state employees and their family members, including such non-offensive officials as schoolteachers. It has, furthermore, targeted foreigners, industrialists and tourist resorts. According to a highly placed PKK leader, tourists can come when there is a free Kurdistan. In the meantime, 'Tourists should know that every dollar they spend becomes a bullet against our people.'[45]

Some analysts have stressed the interdependence of atrocities in Turkey: for example, Bozarslan, who makes the point that '[t]he state's repressive policy ... is undoubtedly the principal element feeding the armed struggle, which, in its turn gives rise to other social or political violence'; and he means to suggest that most analysts would share this assessment.[46]

It seems that the state, in a roundabout way, acknowledges the relation of some state atrocities committed at lower levels to PKK atrocities. In a US report on human rights in Turkey (in a section on 'Torture and Other Cruel, Inhuman, or Degrading Treatment or Punishment') it is stated that government officials admit the occurrence of torture, though denying that it is systematic. They explain that it is closely tied to the state's fight against what it calls terrorism and the opportunities for harsh treatment that exist during lengthy detention periods.[47]

Representatives of the Kurdish opposition, for their part, appear willing to verify the interdependence of atrocities. The PKK's chief spokesman in Europe was asked about PKK atrocities, the existence of which he denied, and then asked whether the organization intended to destroy Turkey. His answer, that 'I have every right to destroy a country which destroys mine', seems to reflect a *tu quoque* attitude.[48]

Many examples could be given, from countries of different types. It is often maintained that democratic rule is a strong impediment to torture, and hence escalatory behaviour. But it is certainly not a sufficient condition. Antonio Cassese writes that torture thrives in all illiberal states and is a pathological deviation in essentially democratic states.[49] One of the examples given above, Turkey, of course constitutes such a 'deviation'.

To the extent that a vicious circle mechanism is operating, some conclusions may be drawn. Recently, the Swedish foreign minister appeared before the UN Commission on Human Rights. In a passage on torture, the minister explicitly mentioned a couple of culprits and then said: 'Also, I would call on the Government of Turkey, as a member of both the United Nations and the Council of Europe, to show its determination to eradicate the practice of torture and ill-treatment in Turkish prisons once and for all.'[50] She refrained from saying anything further about the country, although the occasion presented a good opportunity to touch on the issue of feedback mechanisms. Such an approach may indeed have been beneficial, since it could have provided an increased understanding of the problem. Also, the Turkish state apparatus is known to be divided with respect to the use of torture and thus any denouncement of PKK atrocities would have been likely to strengthen the hand of the moderates.

Though it might have been politically wise for the activities of the PKK to be raised, states often only want to point the finger at other states in this kind of forum, due to the 'sovereignty reflex'[51] – that is, the fear of undermining the status of the state. This traditional attitude may represent a disinterested, principled belief, but in fact it is also a power resource of great significance for many states that are fearful of separatism, which is what many non-state groups fight for. Not only do states command greater means of coercion, writes Bozarslan, but they can also appeal to international law.

> These factors may appear 'minor' at first sight. Nevertheless, they explain the fate of almost all national disputes in the Third World; even though they are capable of maintaining themselves sometimes for decades, no movement of national liberation that is opposed to a state that was born out of decolonization or of a war of independence against a Western power has ever succeeded in achieving its ends. The only two exceptions that we know only confirm the rule: Bangladesh succeeded in proclaiming its independence because the 'mother country' was far removed and because India intervened militarily. Eritrea formerly colonized by Italy achieved independence from an Ethiopia which was never colonized and which was itself undergoing a transition from Empire to nation-state.[52]

In fact, it seems that the risk of endangering the sovereignty of states in the present context is rather slight; at any rate this could be considerably reduced or even eliminated. Any discussion of vicious circles, such as within the Commission of Human Rights, could be accompanied by a strong disclaimer to the effect that no juridical status whatsoever will be conferred on rebels, and the state under scrutiny is, according to international law, entitled to keep its territory intact. Such a disclaimer could be issued without explicit mention of the movement in question.

Links

Since World War II we have witnessed an increase in cooperative efforts among states. International Relations experts now use the faddish word 'regime'[53] to denote the framework of rules, expectations and procedures in such areas as economic interaction, natural resources, security, environment and so on. Human rights are also a regime in this sense, or rather a set of regimes, including that of torture.

Strong regimes have developed in many fields, for instance in a number of economic issue areas, but this is not the case with respect to torture, despite the fact that freedom from the fear of torture is among the most valued of human rights. Why is this so? To provide an explanation using regime theory, which considers inter-state conformity in terms of mutual benefits,[54] one would venture to state that in this 'issue area' the national interests (of states) are not sufficiently at stake; nor is a state's goal achievement contingent upon the behaviour of others. On the contrary, as was noted above, some, such as Israel, might pursue their own ends in blatant opposition to internationally recognized rules. This interest vacuum will probably remain wanting: one would have to engage in 'piecemeal social engineering', in Popperian terms[55] rather than utopian thinking to strengthen the regime. Perhaps consideration of connections between state and non-state responsibilities could carry us one small step further.

Three connections have been identified here. These are not necessarily the only ones but perhaps they are the most conspicuous. Taking them into account would imply various problems, including the need for a fresh attitude towards international law. However, to the extent that extant international law is a real hurdle it is certainly more important with respect to intergovernmental organizational (IGO) settings than in bilateral politics, and so any government ought to feel able beyond the intergovernmental corridors to communicate its rejection of atrocities by nongovernmental agents, wherever these take place, including being able to denounce external support whenever relevant.

The whole array of direct and indirect signals can be used for such purposes. Bilateral action seems the more expedient since no attention is concentrated in the UN on NGO atrocities, and the world organization's lack of resources represents a severe restriction on all information-gathering. In his 1996 report to the Commission on Human Rights on the situation of human rights in Myanmar, the Special Rapporteur lamented that the UN's financial crisis had caused 'great difficulties to him and seriously impeded his activities'.[56]

However, even within a restricted interpretation of the rules, there may be some room for manoeuvre within IGOs. Preparatory functions such as the collection and analysis of information could systematically incorporate NGO atrocities and focus on feedback loops, external targets, proxy relations and so on. This may be done without conferring any legitimacy on NGOs, or indeed incorporate explicit denials of any such implication. A similarly expanded outlook might also be applied when state representatives are involved in debates, as argued above. None of this would necessarily imply that the same perspective should be applied in subsequent resolutions, in which, of course, only states would be held responsible.

Notes

1. *International Herald Tribune*, 23 April 1997.

2. *International Herald Tribune*, 10 March 1997.

3. *Keesing's Record of World Events*, vol. 40, p. 906.

4. However, cf. the *Declaration of Minimum Humanitarian Standards*, adopted by an expert meeting convened by the Institute for Human Rights, Åbo Academy University, in Turku/Åbo, Finland, in 1990. The Declaration is to a large extent meant to be a codification of minimum standards which may already be in force today. 'Torture' is among the acts which, according to the declaration, are prohibited in all situations and this prohibition is applicable for all actors. Allan Rosas, 'Human Rights at Risk in Situations of Internal Violence and Public Emergency: Towards Common Minimum Standards', in Asbjörn Eide and Jan Helgesen, eds, *The Future of Human Rights Protection in a Changing World. Fifty Years since the Four Freedoms Address*, Norwegian University Press, Oslo, 1991, pp. 165–81.

5. *Keesing's Record of World Events*, vol. 40, pp. 656, 743, 791, 917ff.

6. *Keesing's Record of World Events*, vol. 39, p. 756; vol. 40, p. 469.

7. *International Herald Tribune*, 30–31 March 1996.

8. *International Herald Tribune*, 4 April 1995.

9. 'Central Europe and Balkans', Business Briefing, BBC Monitoring Service, 15 April 1996.

10. *International Herald Tribune*, 4 April 1995.

11. Cf. Carol Migdalovitz, 'Turkey's Kurdish Imbroglio and U.S. Policy', *CRS Report for Congress*, Congressional Research Service, Library of Congress, Washington DC, 18 March 1994, p. 12.

12. 'Patterns of Global Terrorism, 1996', US Department of State, Washington DC, 1997.

13. Leonard Weinberg, ed., *Political Parties and Terrorist Groups*, Frank Cass, London, 1992, editor's introduction, p. 3.

14. David Rapoport, 'The Politics of Atrocity', in Yona Alexander and Seymor Maxwell Finger, eds, *Terrorism: Interdisciplinary Perspectives*, The John Day Press, New York, 1977, pp. 46–61 (stress in original).

15. George Alexander, ed., *Western State Terrorism*, Polity Press, Cambridge, 1991, editor's introduction, p. 1.

16. *International Aspects of Terrorism*, proceedings of the 11th Conference of Directors and Representatives of Institutes of International Affairs, 2–5 June 1987, The Netherlands Institute of International Relations, Clingendael, The Hague, July 1987, p. 3.

17. Edgar O'Ballance, *Islamic Fundamentalist Terrorism, 1979–95: The Iranian Connection*, Macmillan, London, 1997, p. 59.

18. Richard Clutterbuck, *Terrorism in an Unstable World*, 2nd revised edn, Routledge, London, 1994, p. 156.

19. Ganji Manouchehr, 'The West Must Stop Its Failed "Critical Dialogue" with Iran', *International Herald Tribune*, 30 April 1997.

20. *International Herald Tribune*, 10 April 1997.

21. 'Patterns of Global Terrorism 1995: Introduction', US Department of State, Washington DC, April 1996.

22. See, for example, US Department of State, International; Policy; Countries; Issues; Embassies [http://www.state.gov/www/global/terrorism/index.html], 1 May 1997.

23. Press Briefing by Deputy Assistant to the President for National Security Affairs, Samuel Berger; Ambassador-at-Large for Counterterrorism, Philip Wilcox; and Deputy Assistant Attorney General for International Enforcement in the Criminal Division, Mark Richard; The White House, Office of the Press Secretary, for immediate release, 29 July 1996.

24. See the Recommendation No. R.(82)1 by the Committee of Ministers of the Council of Europe, 'Concerning International Cooperation in the Prosecution and Punishment of Terrorism', *International Co-operation in the Prosecution and Punishment of Acts of Terrorism*, Strasbourg, 1983, p. 6: 'Emphasizing that any measure of international cooperation must be fully compatible with the protection of human rights.'

25. Cf. Patrice Jean, 'The Jurisprudence of the European Commission and Court of Human Rights with Regard to Terrorism', in Rosalyn Higgins and Maurice Flory, eds, *Terrorism and International Law*, Routledge, London, 1977, ch. 12, pp. 217–50.

26. It has been suggested that systematic review activity should be structured on a country-by-country basis following the model of Amnesty International. See Manfred Nowak, 'Future Strategies for the International Protection and Realization of Human Rights', in Asbjörn Eide and Jan Helgesen, eds, *The Future of Human Right Protection in a Changing World*, Universitetsforlaget, Oslo, 1991, pp. 59–78.

27. Remarks by Coordinator for Counterterrorism, Ambassador Philip Wilcox Jr, before the Denver Council on Foreign Relations, Denver, Colorado, 12 September 1996.

28. Statement by the Minister for Foreign Affairs, Mrs Margaretha af Ugglas, in the General Debate of the Forty-Sixth Session of the UN General Assembly, 10 October 1991.

29. Nor within the Council of Europe; see Geoff Gilbert, 'The Council of Europe and Minority Rights', *Human Rights Quarterly*, vol. 18, 1966, pp. 160–89.

30. Greece has long been criticized for allowing Turkish front organizations to establish themselves in Athens.

31. It should be noted that the International Court of Justice held the USA responsible for breaking international law by assisting the Contras, but not on the grounds discussed here. See Michael Akehurst, *A Modern Introduction to International Law*, 6th edn, Routledge, London and New York, 1987, pp. 282ff.

32. Henry A. Kissinger, *Diplomacy*, Simon & Schuster, New York, 1994.

33. Donatella Della Porta, *Social Movements, Political Violence and the State: A Comparative Analysis of Italy and Germany*, Cambridge University Press, Cambridge, New York and Melbourne, 1995.

34. U.N. Doc. E/CN.4/1987/13, ch. VI, para. 73.

35. Antonio Cassese, *Human Rights in a Changing World*, Polity Press, Cambridge, 1990, p. 89.

36. Stephen Flatow, 'Interrogation Methods in Israel Are Justified', *International Herald Tribune*, 20 May 1997.

37. See *Report on the situation of human rights in the Palestinian territories occupied since 1967, submitted by Mr Hannu Halinen, Special Rapporter, pursuant to Commission on Human Rights resolution 1993/2 A*, U.N. Doc. E/CN.4/1997/16, 19 February 1997, pp. 7f., 10.

38. Rapoport, 'The Politics of Atrocity', p. 54.

39. See James D. Carney and Richard K. Scheer, *Fundamentals of Logic*, 3rd edn, Macmillan, New York, 1980, ch. 2, in which all fallacies are considered. That in question is the *tu quoque* fallacy.

40. Nigel Rodley, 'Can Armed Opposition Groups Violate Human Rights?', in Kathleen E. Mahoney and Paul Mahoney, eds, *Human Rights in the Twenty-first Century: A Global Challenge*, Martinus Nijhoff Publishers, Dordrecht, Boston and London, 1993, pp. 297–318; 316.

41. Reuter News Service, Bangkok, 1 March 1997.

42. Letter dated 18 March 1996 from the Permanent Representative of Myanmar to the United Nations Office at Geneva addressed to the Assistant Secretary-General for Human Rights, U.N. Doc. E/CN.4/1996/139.

43. *File of Torture*, HRFT Publications 5, Human Rights Foundation of Turkey (Ankara, March 1996), p. 69.

44. Migdalovitz, 'Turkey's Kurdish Imbroglio and US Policy', pp. 6ff.

45. Jonathan Rugman and Roger Hutchings, *Atatürk's Children: Turkey and the Kurds*, Cassell, London and New York, 1996, p. 93.

46. Hamit Bozarslan, 'Kurds: States, Marginality and Security', in Sam C. Nolutshungu, ed., *Margins of Insecurity: Minorities and International Security*, University of Rochester Press, New York, 1996, pp. 118, 120. Cf. Baskin Oran in *Conflict Dynamics and Human Right Problems, 22–25 September 1995. Report of the Oslo seminar on the human rights situation in areas inhabited by Kurdish groups in Turkey, Iran, Iraq and Syria*, edited by Gunnar M. Karlsen, Norwegian Institute of Human Rights, Human Rights Report No. 6, Oslo, May 1996, pp. 71f.

47. 'Turkey Country Report on Human Rights Practices for 1996', State Department, Washington DC, 1997.

48. Rugman and Hutchings, *Atatürk's Children*, p. 94.

49. *Human Rights in a Changing World*, pp. 90f.

50. Address by the Swedish minister for foreign affairs, Mrs Lena Hjelm-Wallén, at the United Nations Commission on Human Rights, Geneva, 11 March 1997.

51. This expression is borrowed from Georges Abu-Saab, 'Non-International Armed Conflicts', in *International Dimensions of Humanitarian Law*, Henry Dunant Institute, UNESCO, Martinus Nijhoff Publishers, Dordrecht, Boston and London, 1988, ch. 14, p. 217.

52. Bozarslan, 'Kurds', p. 128n.

53. 'The concept of a regime itself is often used so loosely that critics have reasonably questioned whether the concept is anything but a woolly notion likely to produce more confusion than illumination.' Oran R. Young, *International Co-operation. Building Regimes for Natural Resources and the Environment*, Cornell University Press, Ithaca NY and London, 1989, p. 1.

54. See Robert O. Keohane, 'The Analysis of International Regimes: Towards a European–American Research Programme', in Volker Rittberger and Peter Mayer,

eds, *Regime Theory and International Relations*, Clarendon Press, Oxford, 1993, p. 23: 'The concept of international regimes ... defined as co-ordinated mutual adjustment of states' policies yielding benefits to participants.'

55.   This expression is from Karl R. Popper, *The Poverty of Historicism*, Routledge & Kegan Paul, London and Henley, 1957, section III, p. 21.

56.   *Report on the situation of human rights in Myanmar, prepared by Mr Yozo Yokota, Special Rapporteur of the Commission on Human Rights, in accordance with Commission resolution 1995/72*, U.N. Doc. E/CN.4/1996/65, p. 6.

Part III

Victims of Torture

6

Treatment of Victims of Torture

Lone Jacobsen and Edith Montgomery

This chapter considers the after-effects of torture for individuals and their families and the methods of rehabilitating those who survive torture. Torture has been defined in various ways. The definition of torture used here follows that adopted by the World Medical Association in 1975:

> Torture is the deliberate, systematic, or wanton infliction of physical or mental suffering by one or more persons acting alone or on the orders of any authority, to force another person to yield information, to make a confession or for any other reason.[1]

Since the passage of the Tokyo Declaration, it has become clear that the objective of torture is to break down a person's integrity and personality. When released back into the community, his broken state of health will keep others from opposing the suppressing regime. His private and social life after torture will not be the same. The torturers have achieved their goal when the will of the victim has been broken.

When we talk about torture, we refer to government-sanctioned torture. Survivors of this type of torture and oppression came to Europe and North America in the 1970s and 1980s, where they were granted asylum. Health-care personnel were then faced with the challenge of examining and treating a new group of patients. At the newly established rehabilitation centres the torture survivors, with their knowledge and experiences, were the basis for the development of rehabilitation methods for torture survivors and their families. One of the first rehabilitation centres in the world was the Rehabilitation and Research Centre for Torture Victims (RCT) in Copenhagen, Denmark, where the authors have worked for many years. Our experiences with families who have survived torture form the background of this chapter.

In the chapter, the torture victim is referred to as 'he', because the majority of clients at the rehabilitation centres are men. However, it is emphasized that women also experience torture. Often the assaults take place in the home, either in connection with the arrest of the husband or when the police or the military break in while the husband is under arrest and, as part of their harassment of the family, commit serious assaults against the wife and children. These assaults are often not covered by the definition of government-sanctioned torture. In addition to that, the women are more hesitant than men in seeking treatment for the after-effects of torture because they are afraid of stigmatization and disgrace if the assaults, which often include rape, become known to the rest of the family.

After-effects of Torture

The after-effects of torture are mental, physical and social. They are often so incapacitating as to require interdisciplinary management. The whole family, not only the torture victim, is severely affected when one or more members have been tortured.

This section on the after-effects of torture describes the mental and physical reactions of the torture victim and his family. Some specific problems related to the victim's existence in exile will be mentioned later.

Mental reactions

The victims describe the mental reactions after torture as the most disabling by giving them a feeling of having changed their personality. Before the torture, many of the victims were extrovert and active persons, but afterwards they prefer to isolate themselves from their surroundings. They have lost their self-respect and confidence in other people, and they avoid contact. *The feeling of having a changed identity* is one of the most characteristic effects of torture.[2]

Other serious symptoms include *anxiety, sleep disturbances, and nightmares*, often combined. The anxiety is often chronic, and may be present even during sleep. Torture victims try to suppress their anxiety, but they are seldom successful; it is easily aroused and increased by associations with torture. People who have been isolated in small rooms during torture become very anxious and afraid when they are enclosed in small spaces, such as hospital examination rooms, lifts, and so on. The same anxiety is provoked when they have to meet authorities, especially uniformed ones, to the extent that they fail to come for appointments because of fear. Their very low self-respect and their suspicion, coupled with fear, make it almost impossible for them to explain themselves vis-à-vis the authorities. In particularly stressful situations, their fear may lead to panic so that they suddenly have to leave the room.

Torture victims usually only sleep for a few hours at a time. They wake up because of nightmares about torture that make them relive their extreme anxiety, and several hours may pass before they dare to go back to sleep. Their sleep is thus superficial, adding to the tiredness and irritability. When awake, victims may relate how memories of the torture can overwhelm them in the form of flashbacks, and that they can do nothing to prevent them. A flashback is often provoked by everyday events that produce associations with their torture experiences (the sight of medical equipment, personnel in uniforms, etc.). Van der Veer[3] defines a flashback as 'an intrusive memory, that results in a reexperience of a traumatic situation of the past, so that the individual for a restricted period (varying from a few seconds to a few hours) partly or totally loses contact with the present reality'. Torture victims do not share their painful memories with others. They are alone with them and afraid of becoming insane. Nightmares and flashbacks, however, are normal reactions to what they have gone through.

Torture victims almost always suffer from a severe feeling of *guilt*, such as the so-called survivor- or death-guilt, in which they blame themselves for having survived while others died. Torture victims have often been forced to witness the execution of comrades, friends and family members. In this meeting with death, they were not capable even of feeling appropriate emotions (overwhelming rage against the torturers, profound compassion for victims).[4] Their feeling of guilt may also have been provoked by situations in which the torturers have forced them to perform unacceptable acts or express opinions contrary to their own convictions and ideals – possibly even in public (on television). Family members of victims are often at great risk of being harassed and arrested – even tortured or killed – because of the torture victims' ideological views. This is, of course, a great burden on the victim and gives him a feeling of guilt, which can be increased if family members are forced into exile against their will.

Many torture victims have a *negative self-image*, characterized by shame, feelings of guilt and loss of dignity. This self-image often stems from deep humiliation, for example during sexual torture, which is very common, but often not mentioned by the victims. On top of that, there is decreased memory and lack of concentration. All this makes the victims afraid that their brains have been destroyed by the torturers, as they were told during the torture. However, these symptoms can be ascribed to the long-lasting mental pressure to which they have been exposed.

Finally, torture victims may find it difficult to manage their feelings of aggression. They become easily excited and angry in stressful or noisy situations, and later feel depressed and guilty because of their loss of control. Depressive conditions, together with a feeling of guilt for having survived their murdered friends, increase the risk of suicide. Other factors associated with suicide include social isolation and loneliness. Torture survivors in exile without their families are especially at risk.

Physical reactions

Immediately after the torture victims naturally have many serious physical pains – from nails that have been torn off, broken teeth, ruptured ear drums. They have wounds, haemorrhages, fractures, and so forth. No treatment was given in prison, or it was wrong or insufficient. In addition, the physical conditions were extremely bad. The cell was either very cold or very hot, and too small for a prisoner to stand upright or to sleep in a normal position. Access to toilets was very limited, or nonexistent, and in any case controlled by the guards. The nutrition was insufficient, lacking in proteins and vitamins – and perhaps even polluted. The level of noise prevented sleep. These conditions together, combined with the torture, greatly decreased the natural resistance to infections, often causing death.

The acute effects of torture are not seen at RCT, because the survivors reach here only after several years. By contrast, we see the late physical after-effects, which mainly depend on the kind of physical torture used. In 1992–93, Juhler and Smidt-Nielsen systematically registered late after-effects in fifty torture victims at RCT.[5] They showed that up to 90 per cent had symptoms from damage to the musculo-skeletal system, which has been confirmed by others. The severe beatings cause chronic muscle pain. If the victims have been suspended by their arms they have shoulder pain, radiating to the arms and accompanied by sensitivity disturbances including tiredness. A special form of suspension is the 'Palestinian hanging' in which the entire body weight is supported behind the back by the extended and internally rotated shoulder joints. This is very damaging to the shoulders, inducing painful limitation of shoulder movements and sometimes recurrent dislocation.[6]

Falanga is a very common form of torture in which the soles of the feet are beaten with sticks, cables and similar tools. The tissue of the soles is destroyed, with resultant pain in the feet and legs, often burning in character.

Juhler and Smidt-Nielsen also found that up to 85 per cent of the torture victims had symptoms from the central and peripheral nervous systems, and that about half of these had corresponding physical findings. The victims complained of headache, poor concentration, inadequate memory, dizziness and fatigue, which may have been caused by the many direct blows to the head. Consequently, some survivors suffer chronic pain in the face and head, and also on their bodies because of nerve injury from beating. The pains are severe, shooting or burning, but this chronic state of pain may improve in time.

Approximately 75 per cent of the torture victims have short-term shooting pains around the heart, palpitations and difficulty with breathing. Abnormal physical findings are rare. Furthermore, about 75 per cent of survivors have gastro-intestinal symptoms; only 30 per cent have abnormal findings. Ulcer symptoms are common – for example, epigastric pain (hunger pain relieved by food).

There may be visible scars and marks from torture on the skin (cigarette burns, etc.). These marks are a constant reminder to the victim of his ordeal and thus further the mental pain. The scars may also cause itching.

Children in families that have survived torture

Children in families that have suffered torture are affected by experiences from three qualitatively different sources: the children's own *direct experiences* of violence (such as assaults, beatings, witnessing violent events), *the loss of and separation from* important family members (e.g. during parental imprisonment or hiding), and the impact of torture and other traumatic experiences on *parental responsiveness and role function.*

Children depend on their parents' ability to project a sense of stability, permanence and competence, and several studies have focused on the buffering role of parents in situations in which children are confronted with violence.[7] A direct impact of traumatic experiences on family functioning may, however, include parental loss and subsequent impaired care and/or separation of children from family members. Post-trauma disturbances of parental responsiveness and impairment in parental role function are major sources of secondary stress in children.[8] In chronically violent environments, child-rearing practices may become more authoritarian and restrictive, thus altering parent–child interactions, decreasing opportunities for play, and disturbing family communication. It may compromise the parental roles of discipliner, affection-giver, and role model, which may influence long-term moral development in children.[9]

Studies of children of torture survivors seem to indicate that they suffer from various mental symptoms of an emotional, psychosomatic and behavioural nature. Anxiety, sleeping problems, including nightmares, and psychosomatic symptoms such as stomach pain or headache are frequent symptoms among these children.[10] A follow-up study of a group of children from torture-surviving families from Chile, whose parents had been treated at the RCT between three and four years previously,[11] indicated that the symptoms do not disappear by themselves. On the contrary, more children had symptoms of emotional imbalance, and the amount of symptoms for each child had increased significantly during this period.

Factual information seems to help children to cope with a stressful situation.[12] Lack of information makes the child a victim of his own imagination. Many torture survivors are not able to tell their wives and children what happened to them, and the torture experience can become a barrier between the survivor and his family. In some families, however, the torture-surviving parents tend to overburden the children with descriptions of traumatic experiences in order to relieve themselves of the pressure. Too-detailed information of torture, however, can have negative consequences for the child, if the parents do not manage to take care of the child's anxiety, but rather overwhelm it with their own.

Being witness to the father's inability to care for his family's needs, and experiencing his inability to adapt to the new life in exile, changes the child's image of his father. This hitherto powerful figure is, in the eyes of the child, reduced to a weak and vulnerable person, unable to provide the security that the child needs. The process of identification is complicated, and the child's development of a feeling of personal identity is thus impeded. Living in exile without a firm link to the cultural values of his homeland complicates the development of identity even more.

A structural change takes place within the family, both at the time when the father or mother is taken away and imprisoned and at the time of his or her return. Often it is the father who is imprisoned, and his wife is left to provide for the children, normally without support from the authorities and stigmatized on account of the husband's activities. Later, when the family is reunited, possibly in exile, the father has to be reintroduced in the family, reclaiming his previous role in child upbringing and family life. Due to his own emotional instability, it can be difficult for him to cope with that challenge. The wife might have difficulties supporting her husband, partly due to personal traumatization, and partly because she holds him responsible for the situation of the family. In some cases she will have developed new and previously unknown capacities during the time of her husband's imprisonment; when he returns, she does not want to return to a more subordinate role in the family. This might contribute even more to the low self-esteem of the torture victim.

Living in exile

People who have been tortured and later sought asylum in a country of exile have been forced to flee because of circumstances. This fact will influence their integration in the new country. A hasty flight has meant that the torture survivors were often unable to say goodbye to family members, near friends, or even spouses. They often continue to be emotionally involved in the situation and problems of their home country, such as the political struggle they took part in, and they may be haunted by fantasies about the fate of those they left behind. Are they persecuted, imprisoned, or even tortured? Is an ill father left behind still alive? Does the family have money to cover the most basic needs of food, clothing, and so on? On the one hand the tortured refugee experiences a feeling of liberation from persecution and torture, but on the other a need, perhaps almost an inner demand, to return to the home country.[13] This conflict can cause great suffering.

Countries of exile sometimes show a negative, perhaps even hostile, attitude to refugees and may thus consider the torture survivors as immigrants who are trying to obtain economic advantages – to take jobs away from Danes, for example – and as the cause of unemployment, and so on. As a consequence, torture survivors may isolate themselves vis-à-vis the people of the country of exile. It is the experience of the authors that survivors genuinely want to make contact with their new fellow citizens, but that they are hesitant because they feel themselves misunderstood for the above-mentioned reasons. Because of poor memory and reduced ability to concentrate, it is difficult for them to learn a new language, which is often very different from their own. This makes it even more difficult to make contact with their new countrymen.

Torture victims in exile have suffered many and massive losses: friends and family who were left behind, or died during the flight, loss of homeland, language, job, property and status, and other physical conditions, including the home landscape and climate.

Rehabilitation of Victims of Torture

Rehabilitation of torture victims is best planned and coordinated by a multidisciplinary team with knowledge of torture victims and their reactions. When the victims and their families feel that professional staff have a deep insight into torture and its methods and after-effects, confidence is more easily established. Not all survivors need such extensive care as is described in the following section, but they may benefit from rehabilitation outside the framework of the Rehabilitation Centre.

Special considerations

The principles of rehabilitation of torture victims and their families at RCT were formulated in 1974. They are still being developed, for instance in collaboration with RCT's international, professional contacts.[14] The following principles form the basis for the treatment:

- Procedures that remind the victim about the torture may provoke unrest and anxiety. Therefore these must be completely avoided in certain situations, or special precautions must be taken.
- Treatment must cover physical and mental aspects, and these must be coordinated.
- Physiotherapy is an important part of physical treatment.
- Nursing care serves a coordinating and health educational function.
- Social conditions must be considered and followed up by social counselling and guidance.
- Treatment must include not only the victim but also his family. Partners and children are offered appropriate examination and treatment.

It is important to stress that torture survivors are reluctant to tell others that they have been tortured. There is a silence about the trauma: not even family or close friends know what happened. The survivors are often convinced that nobody will believe them if they say they have been tortured, just as they were told by their torturers. The professionals may hesitate to ask because they feel uncertain about the client's reactions, or for other reasons. A *conspiracy of silence*[15] may ensue in which both client and professional are silent about the trauma. If this pattern continues, the victim continues to feel alone, isolated with his memories and feelings, and will not receive the correct treatment. Today, especially in our part of the world, with the available knowledge about torture, professionals within the social and health sectors are obliged to learn about torture, its methods, after-effects, and the possibilities for rehabilitation as prescribed in the UN Convention Against Torture. When good contact has been established between the professional and the client, it may be time to ask about the client's traumatic background, and this is often a relief for the victim.

Torture survivors' suspicion of other people is also directed at doctors, since prison doctors often help the torturers rather than the prisoners. The health personnel must therefore pay special attention to gaining further confidence, for instance by spending a lot of time in listening to the client's own version of his problems, and what he is wanting help for. The professional should explain all available options for help.

Interpretation

An interpreter is usually needed for work with torture victims. If the client has lived in the country of exile for some years and speaks the language to some extent, it is tempting to dispense with an interpreter. However, this limits communication, especially with respect to the expression of feelings. Important information may be lost, which may have a negative influence on the course of treatment. It cannot therefore be sufficiently stressed that professionals in the health and social services must have an interpreter when talking with clients who have not mastered the new language. This is, of course, also a requirement in other professional situations.

Professional secrecy is a fundamental principle when interpreters are used. It applies to interpreters in the same way as to other therapeutic personnel. This is an important point to get across to the torture victim.

Another principle is the observation of neutrality: that is, impartiality on the part of the interpreter. The interpreter must be as true as possible to the exact meaning of the spoken message; he must not let his own sympathies or antipathies colour the interpretation. This neutrality should not make the interpreter deny his own identity. He must show an interest in the client as a person and have a clear attitude against torture.

Preliminary examinations

Most torture survivors who are treated at RCT today (1997) are referred by their own general practitioner or by the social services. Treatment is not started before residence status is granted. The treatment, paid for by the Danish state, is free for the client and the referring institution.

Before the start of treatment, the client is invited to a preliminary talk with the aim of assessing the mental and physical problems, the social situation, and the motivation for and expectations of the treatment. The situation of family members is also discussed.

Due to the torture victim's preoccupation with his physical condition, the rehabilitation begins with a thorough *physical examination*. Since the torture, which often took place many years previously, the victim has suffered physical pains and other symptoms that have taken away any joy with respect to his own body. The daily pains have made him fear that his torturers have destroyed his organs and caused chronic disease.

The examination must take place in surroundings in which the survivor is not exposed to situations that can be associated with previous torture experiences. At the Rehabilitation Centre, the doctors and nurses avoid wearing uniform, and it is possible to avoid periods of waiting, which might remind the client of the time he was waiting for his own torture. Many victims have been tortured naked, and the mere act of undressing in connection with an examination may provoke fear and unease. Otoscopy, examination of the ear, may recall electrical torture to the ear, and so on. This does not mean, however, that such examinations cannot be performed. The victim wants to go through them to get an explanation of his pains. The most important thing is to explain how the examinations take place, and what their aim is. But of course, if the client does not want to be examined, this must be respected. However, some examinations are so distressing that general anaesthetic may have to be used (for example, in the cases of gastroscopy, rectoscopy, and cystoscopy).

When precautions as described above are taken, the victims are reassured that other people respect their bodies, without aiming to cause pain and injury. Such care also helps to create confidence between client and doctor, confidence that can be transferred to the other members of the professional team.

The physical examination programme at RCT currently consists of clinical examinations by a nurse; a general practitioner; a rheumatologist; an ear, nose and throat specialist; and a dentist. The *rheumatological examination* may include an X-ray of the spine. The nurse's examination includes taking blood specimens to test for haemoglobin and liver and kidney function, a urine examination, and other relevant examinations. Today, all clients are offered an examination for HIV and hepatitis-B infection. The heart is examined by electrocardiography. For the sake of the clients, as many examinations as possible should take place at the rehabilitation centre – that is, RCT. When examinations take place outside the centre, for instance at a specialist in private practice or in a special hospital laboratory, it is necessary for the interpreter to accompany the client, and, for examinations particularly likely to provoke anxiety, also the nurse.

The *nurse* evaluates the client's need for health education and offers follow-up training and guidance. The coordination of further physical examinations and treatment remains the task of the nurse during the whole rehabilitation course. As a rule, it is important to involve the *social worker* at an early stage to evaluate the social situation together with client and family, and to plan subsequent actions in collaboration with the client's social worker in his local municipality.

When the victim has completed the preliminary examinations and assessments, an individual treatment plan is developed by the multidisciplinary team. This plan is followed up and revised at regular team conferences during the whole treatment period. The various forms of treatment will now be described briefly.

Somatic treatment

Somatic treatment of torture victims, medical and surgical, does not differ fundamentally from treatment of other patients. *Drug treatment* is used particularly in connection with chronic pain affecting the musculoskeletal system. Mild analgesics such as paracetamol or NSAID preparations (for arthritis) may be tried. Morphine is used only exceptionally because of the risk of addiction. Sleeping tablets are rarely used, partly because of side-effects, partly because, in our experience, they are ineffective against the serious sleeping disturbances of torture victims.[16]

The mental after-effects of torture are usually not treated with drugs. However, antidepressants may be used during depressive phases, and neuroleptics and antidepressants in small doses may be used during anxi-ety-dominated crisis situations.[17]

In some cases it may be obvious that disfiguring scars on the skin should be removed by *plastic surgery*. In surgical interventions it is necessary to admit the client to hospital. In such cases it is important to inform the staff of the department about the victims's possible reactions.

Finally, *dental treatment* is important. Muscular tension in the chewing muscles may produce headache, and the dentist may help by adapting occlusal splints and re-establishing the biting and chewing function. It should be remembered that many victims have suffered electric torture to the gums and teeth, and have therefore resisted consulting a dentist because of associations with this violent form of torture.[18]

It has gradually been realized that torture victims have a low *compliance*: that is, they often do not adhere to medically prescribed treatment, guidance, prophylactic activity, or examination.[19] It may be that side-effects from drugs produce associations with previous torture trauma – for example, palpitations in connection with sham executions, and dry-ness of the mouth from enforced thirst.[20]

There may also be biological reasons for the high non-compliance. It has been shown that some ethnic groups – for example, from the Middle East – metabolize drugs differently from previously examined population groups. This means, among other things, that the drug dose should be reduced. Finally, it should not be forgotten that torture survivors in general mistrust the authorities. This mistrust may be directed particularly to-wards doctors if the clients have experienced doctor-torturers in the prisons.

In order to obtain good compliance it is therefore very important to spend a long time on introduction and instruction concerning the pre-scribed drug, especially with respect to effects and side-effects, and when an effect is expected to occur.

Physiotherapy

The rheumatological examination is the basis for the examination and treatment of the client by a physiotherapist. The musculoskeletal pains of torture victims are often associated with daily routine; they may be present both at rest and during movement, and may be severe enough to disturb sleep. Physical torture, depending on its form, leaves tissue injury in muscles, joints and nerves.

The physiotherapist tries to map out the pain, by marking it on a drawing of the human body, and the degree of pain is evaluated. The victims's body carriage is influenced by fear and restrained feelings. The carriage may be characterized by slight collapse of the back and by a pulling forward of the shoulders – a pattern that may be fixed – leading to muscular tension and painful movement.[21] Most of the victims at RCT have been exposed to *falanga* (systematic beating of the soles of the feet). This gives pain when walking, even a short distance. At the same time, damage to the nerve supply of the feet gives impaired balance while walking and standing.[22] Almost all the victims have been beaten on the chest and restrained in awkward positions, which may lead to impaired and painful respiration. At the same time, the situation of continuous anxiety and stress leads to fast, superficial breathing.

Physiotherapy includes massage and careful muscle extension to relieve tissue pain. Training in warm water makes muscles and joints move more easily and gives rise to a feeling of bodily well-being. It should be re-membered that training in water must be done with great care, or per-haps completely omitted, if the client has been exposed to *submarino* – that is, has had his head submerged in water almost to the point of suffocation. It may be necessary to supply the client with various aids. After *falanga* torture, he should be provided with special footwear with shock-absorbing, flexible soles, often with additional orthopaedic sup-port. Woollen underwear helps to keep muscles and joints warm, and a back support may relieve back pain.

With respect to physiotherapy, confidence and safety are essential preconditions, which also means that the suggested treatment cannot begin until the client accepts it.

Nursing care

At an early stage, the nurse will discuss the examinations with the client and arrange appointments. As mentioned, some of the examinations may be so stressful that they will have to be carried out under general anaesthetic at a hospital. In this case it is important for a nurse to accompany the client and advise the hospital staff about special precautions, in particular in the department of anaesthetics. At the start of the anaesthetic, for instance, the client should never be constrained or have his nose and mouth covered by the mask before he is fully asleep, since this can cause panic from associations with previous torture while lying constrained and defenceless. It is our experience that torture victims often relive part of their torture while falling asleep, and therefore become afraid. To hear a well-known voice or see the familiar face of his nurse will reduce fear and pain.

As mentioned before, torture victims often experience physical symptoms for which there is no obvious organic basis. This is possibly due to somatization, a reaction against the massive and violent attack of the torture. These symptoms should not be ignored; on the other hand, endless investigations may not further the therapy. When examination results are normal, this should be stressed as something very positive by the nurse, doctor and psychotherapist.

In connection with the drug treatment of chronic pain in particular, the client must regularly visit the nurse for adjustment of the dose and to report how the pains influence daily routines – a useful yardstick to measure the effect of painkillers in chronic conditions. The treatment of chronic pain is difficult, but the best precondition for success is to include the whole therapeutic team in the planning.

In addition, the nurse can offer health education at a stage during the treatment when client and family feel ready for it. Many clients are well motivated in discussing subjects related to their health, especially those concerning nutrition and sexuality.

A large number of torture victims have suffered sexual torture, including violation of their sexual organs, and they have been told that they would never have a normal sex life again, or normal children. If they are worried about this, it may help to tell them that there is no evidence that torture has such after-effects. This fear is probably much stronger than they admit, and it is therefore important that the need for such discussions is considered at an early stage of the treatment.

Social counselling

Torture victims in exile usually experience social problems. An important task for the social worker is to inform the client about the rights and obligations of, in this case, Danish citizens, and if possible help the client and his family to become independent of social support. Many refugees have a good education and find it humiliating not to be able to take care of themselves and their family.

In order to fend for themselves in Danish society, refugees must have a working knowledge of the language. However, some feel so unwell and are so afraid of being together with other people that they are unable to take courses in Danish. These therefore have to be postponed; special support can be given in the form of individual teaching until they again feel strong enough to be in a group.

The situation of the children must also be discussed, especially the importance of contact with Danish children. For the youngest children it is often a question of making sure that they are found a kindergarten. They must learn to speak Danish to prepare them for later schooling.

If there are problems at school for one or more of a family's children, the social worker can arrange a meeting between the parents and teachers. The parents may feel that they are not being listened to, and the teachers that the parents are not taking problems seriously. Misunderstandings may occur, for instance because of lack of an interpreter. Such contacts are, of course, only arranged with the agreement of the parents.

A source of great worry may be family members left behind in the home country. If it is not possible to contact them, it may be that they are in a refugee camp in the home country or a neighbouring country. The social adviser can arrange contact with the Red Cross in the country of exile, and they will start a search for the disappeared persons via the International Red Cross in Geneva.

Psychotherapy

The aim of the psychotherapy is to help the torture victim deal with the mental effects of traumatic experiences and so reduce his distress and help him to regain mastery of his own life. He feels incompetent and unable to cope with the challenges in his life situation, a state of mind that has been termed 'demoralization'.[23] Feelings of guilt and shame, alienation, isolation from and resentment towards the surroundings are part of this state of mind, restricting the way the individual perceives himself and his possibilities in life. Symptoms of anxiety and depression are direct expressions of this state of mind.

Psychotherapy takes place within a professional context. It is conducted by trained professionals, and the activity is systematically guided by an articulated theory that explains the sources of the clients' suffering and prescribes methods for alleviating them.[24] In this it differs from more informal kinds of psychological help, often sought and received from family members or others.

The establishment of a confiding relationship with a helping person is a first step towards healing and a prerequisite for psychotherapy. With torture victims the establishment of this therapeutic relationship may take a long time. The psychotherapist can facilitate the process by maintaining a listening and respectful attitude towards the client. The client's sense of isolation is gradually reduced through this attitude.

Many torture victims find it difficult to understand how talking about personal problems with an unknown person can be helpful. They often present their problems to the expert, and expect the correct cure to be prescribed. The psychotherapist must introduce the thinking behind psychotherapy, and its procedures, in an understandable and convincing way. The actual therapeutic school of the therapist has proved to be of less importance for healing than the personal skills of the individual psychotherapist and his/her ability to create an atmosphere of confidence and trustworthiness. When this is established, the client's ability and willingness to trust others is strengthened.

At an early stage, therapist and client agree on a therapeutic collaboration, a contract.[25] The therapist commits him/herself to making available his/her knowledge and professional skills, the client to contributing with his history, thoughts and reflections. The therapist outlines the frequency and length of the sessions, and a 'setting' is agreed on, usually individual talks on an out-patient basis once or twice a week.

When the client regards the therapy sessions as a safe place, he gradually dares to express thoughts and feelings that have previously been avoided. When strong emotions are expressed, the therapist provides a sense of security by his/her ability to listen calmly and by directly expressing his/her understanding and reassurance. This reawakens the client's hope for a better life in the future.

Often the client has had a narrow understanding of his problems, leaving little possibility for change. He might have lost faith in the values he once treasured and completely lost all meaning in his life. When client and therapist together explore the client's life, relationships and worldview, attention is drawn to new ways of understanding and dealing with his problems, and room for change is created. This can result in a growing sense of mastery and control over his own life and eventually in improved self-confidence.

During imprisonment and torture, most torture victims are told by the torturers that no one will believe them, should they later speak about their experiences. Talking about the traumatic events proves the torturers wrong, and strengthens the client's faith in himself. This reconstruction of the past must be done with great sensitivity and at a time and a pace that respect the client's need to feel safe.[26] By exploring together his ideals and dreams, fights and conflicts before and after imprisonment, a connection between past and present is established, helping the client to

re-create a meaning in life.[27] Dealing with massive loss is another important theme in psychotherapy. Loss of family and friends, of home country,
social position and material possessions, loss of health and abilities, loss
of self-confidence and of confidence in others, and loss of personal identity – all are important subjects that must be discussed within the context
of psychotherapy, with particular attention paid to the meaning of the
losses in the present life of the torture victim.

Most torture victims feel that they will never become what they were
before. They will continue to be vulnerable in future stress situations,
and major changes in life such as childbirth, death of relatives, disease
and ageing can reactivate the traumatic memories and cause symptoms of
anxiety and depression to recur. With sufficient support, however, many
torture victims will be able to regain mastery of their life and to create
a meaningful future life with their family.

Family-oriented rehabilitation

As mentioned, children in torture-surviving families are stressed by their
own traumatic experiences, loss of and separation from important family
members, and changes in parental responsiveness and role function. Such
experiences may have long-lasting consequences for their development.
Any rehabilitation programme for torture victims must therefore also
attend to the needs of the family, particularly the children.

Three levels of intervention must take place simultaneously: preventive community intervention, adequate parent and family support, and
specialized medical and psychological treatment of children with severe,
prolonged traumatic reactions. Important features of any *preventive community intervention programme* are summarized in the STOP model:[28]

S = Structure   A child who is experiencing inner chaos needs an outer
structure in order to avoid becoming overwhelmed. School and kindergarten activities are very valuable: the school becomes an oasis in
the middle of war or war-like conditions.

T = Talking and Time   All children who have had traumatic experiences need to be able to talk about them, supported by a grown-up
who is able to listen and give them enough time. By talking, the child
structures what has happened. Small children often express themselves
better in drawings or play. The grown-up should listen and show an
empathic and accepting attitude without interpreting.

O = Organized play   Children learn through play, but many traumatized children are not able to play by themselves; they have to be
taught. During play the child can forget his terrors for a while. Also

during play his hope for a better future is strengthened. A grown-up must be present to help the children organize their play in a healthy and meaningful way.

P = Parent support Any programme for children should include support for parents in their role as caretakers. Parents must be informed of children's reactions to traumatic experiences and supported in their attempts to cope both with their own problems and with those of their children.

Parent support at RCT is often given in sessions, with the parents alone or the whole family together. The sessions are based on the family system's own strength and capacity for healing. The family's own attempts at solving its problems are pointed out to them, very often to their great surprise, because they are usually preoccupied with their defeats. The therapist draws the family's attention to the dilemmas they are experiencing, without suggesting concrete solutions.

Since a general feature in families that have survived torture is silence about the torture and imprisonment, an important issue during the family sessions is the re-establishment of open and accepting communication between the family members. Just how much torture is mentioned depends on the composition of the individual family, but some explanation is necessary, even for small children. At times the children's imaginings can be worse than reality, and some children feel that they carry the responsibility for the difficult family situation.

Another important issue is the shift in roles within the family before, during and after imprisonment. The oldest children have often had to assume the role of caregiver for their younger brothers and sisters during their father's absence; return to their earlier roles as children is complicated by their parents' poor emotional states. Questions to the family members about differences in role expectations and behaviour now and previously make them aware of the effects of these role shifts, and they help to make future changes possible. Questions concerning the family's ideas and thoughts about the future help them to realize the possibility for change.

Children who are severely affected by their experiences need *specialized treatment*, often in the form of individual psychotherapy. Psychotherapy is a long journey and demands trained professionals; otherwise damage instead of cure can result. A prerequisite for psychotherapy is a stable and accepting environment. To conduct psychotherapy during war-like conditions is not appropriate. In such environments the child should instead be supported and helped to build up defences in order to cope.

The Effect of Treatment

During the years 1993–94 information on treatment activities and mental symptom profiles in clients receiving treatment at RCT were systematically collected as part of the general RCT monitoring system.[29] In 1993, 40 clients were discharged from the RCT after a mean treatment period of 8.4 months (0–22 months), in 1994 the 48 clients discharged had been in treatment for a mean period of 14.5 months (0–29 months). The mean number of psychotherapeutic sessions during these years was 20.1 (1–71) and 21.9 (0–78), respectively.

The mean total anxiety score (Hamilton Anxiety Scale, HAS)[30] at pre-examination (75 clients), admission (83 clients) and discharge (36 clients) during 1993–94 was 27.1 (range 5–40), 26.7 (10–39) and 12.4 (3–28), respectively. The corresponding depression scores (Hamilton Depression Scala, HDS, which has three types of total scale scores) were HDS a–f: 9.5, 9.4 and 4.5; HDS mes: 18.1, 18.3 and 9.8 and HDS 1–17: 15.5, 15.2 and 6.9.

The findings from the 23 clients who were rated at all three points in time during this period and the 36 clients who were rated at admission and discharge followed the same pattern: no change during the period between pre-examination and admission, and a reduction of approximately 50 per cent at discharge. The reduction in mean scale scores at discharge were found to be statistically significant (t-test for paired observations) concerning both anxiety and depression (change in HAS total scale score in 36 clients rated at admission and discharge: −14.1, P < 0.001; and in HDS total scale scores: −5.0 to −8.7, P < 0.001).

While there was no change in symptoms during the period between pre-examination and admission, the clients seemed to experience a reduction in symptoms of anxiety and depression during the period of treatment. Controlled studies are needed, however, to establish this reduction as an effect of the treatment given at the RCT.

A qualitative investigation of the course of psychotherapy in twenty torture survivors carried out at RCT in the early 1990s focused on how clients and psychotherapists experienced the progression in treatment.[31] While the professionals focused much more on the content of treatment and the psychodynamic process (changes), the clients focused on form (regularity, time, setting) and extra-therapeutical factors (political subjects, situation in home country) when discussing the importance of the talks. Both clients and professionals, however, found the psychotherapeutical process meaningful and helpful.

In the future, there is an urgent need for systematic follow-up investigations of torture survivors who participate in multidisciplinary rehabilitation programmes as described in this chapter.

Secondary Traumatization of the Professionals

To listen to torture victims' accounts of their torture makes a deep impression on the professionals. Indirectly, they become witnesses of human evil through the victims' sufferings. The professionals may react to this with trauma symptoms, also called secondary traumatization. At the personal level, the professionals may experience changes in their perception of themselves, their fellow human beings, and the surroundings. Their basic confidence in others disappears, and some develop depression and cynicism such as lack of interest and concern for the problems of others outside the therapeutic sphere. They may lose their belief in basic justice and in being able to influence the world for the better.

These changes may show in the professionals' work; they may try to avoid their clients, or overidentify with them. Mistrust and lack of confidence may develop in relation to their colleagues, leading to deep conflicts.

It is essential to point out that the attitude of the larger society to professionals and institutions working with traumatized refugees is of great importance for the development of secondary traumatization.[32] Understanding for the work, and the necessary financial contributions from society, help to prevent secondary traumatization. The institutions concerned must pay attention to how this traumatization manifests itself, and take precautions to prevent it. Regular supervision should be available from an experienced supervisor.

It must be stressed, however, that the work with survivors of torture is also very rewarding. When sadness, depression and perhaps despair are transformed to hope, and the client regains his belief in the meaning of life, the work, with all the joy it gives, feels very meaningful.

Notes

1. 'World Medical Association, 1975: The Declaration of Tokyo', reproduced in *Ethical Codes and Declarations Relevant to the Health Professions*, Amnesty International Publications, London, 1994.

2. F.E. Somnier and I.K. Genefke, 'Psychotherapy for Victims of Torture', *British Journal of Psychiatry* 149, 1986, pp. 323–9.

3. G. van der Veer, *Counselling and Therapy with Refugees*, John Wiley and Sons, Chichester, 1992, p. 132.

4. R.J. Lifton, 'The Concept of the Survivor' in I.J.E. Dimsdale, ed., *Survivors, Victims and Perpetrators: Essays on the Nazi Holocaust*, Hemisphere, Washington DC, 1980.

5. L. Jacobsen and K. Smidt-Nielsen, *Torture Survivor – Trauma and Rehabilitation*, IRCT, Copenhagen, forthcoming.

6. D. Forrest, 'The Physical After-effects of Torture', *Forensic Science International* 76, 1995, pp. 77–84.

7. F. Allodi, 'The Children of Victims of Political Persecution and Torture: A Psychological Study of a Latin American Refugee Community', *International Journal of Mental Health* 18, 1989, pp. 3–15; J.D. Kinzie, W.H. Sack, R.H. Angell, S. Manson and B. Rath, 'The Psychiatric Effects of Massive Trauma on Cambodian Children: 1. The Children', *Journal of the American Academy of Child Psychiatry* 25, 1986, pp. 370–76.

8. R.S. Pynoos, A.M. Steinberg, and R. Wraith, 'A Developmental Model of Childhood Traumatic Stress', in D. Cicchetti and D.J. Cohen, eds, *Developmental Psychopathology*, John Wiley and Sons, New York, 1995.

9. Ibid.; J. Garbarino and F.M. Stott, *What Children Can Tell Us*, Jossey-Bass, San Francisco, 1989.

10. J. Cohn, L. Danielsen, K.I.M. Holzer, L. Koch, B. Severin, S. Thøgersen and O. Aalund, 'A Study of Chilean Refugee Children in Denmark', *The Lancet*, 1985, pp. 437–8; B. Lukman and N. Bach-Mortensen, 'Symptoms in Children of Torture Victims: Post-traumatic Stress Disorders?', *World Pediatrics and Child Care* 5, 1995, 32–42; E. Montgomery, Y. Krogh, A. Jacobsen and B. Lukman, 'Children of Torture Victims: Reactions and Coping', *Child Abuse and Neglect* 16, 1992, pp. 797–805.

11. B. Weile, L.B. Wingender, P. Busch, B. Lukman and K.I.M. Holzer, 'Behavioral Problems in Children of Torture Victims: A Sequel to Cultural Maladaptation or to Parental Torture?', *Journal of Developmental and Behavioral Pediatrics* 11, 1990, pp. 79–80.

12. A. Carli, 'Psychological Consequences of Political Persecution: The Effects on Children of the Imprisonment or Disappearance of their Parents', *Tidsskrift for Norsk Psykologforening* 24, 1987, 82–93; Montgomery et al., 'Children of Torture Victims', pp. 797–805.

13. C. Westin, *Torture and Existence*, Center for Research in International Migration and Ethnic Relations, Stockholm University, Stockholm, 1991.

14. S. Bøjholm and P. Vesti, 'Multidisciplinary Approach in the Treatment of Torture Survivors', in M. Basoglu, ed., *Torture and Its Consequences: Current Treatment Approaches*, Cambridge University Press, Cambridge, 1992.

15. Y. Danieli, 'Psychotherapists' Participation in the Conspiracy of Silence about the Holocaust', *Psychoanalytic Psychology* 1, 1984, pp. 23–42.

16. Jacobsen and Smidt-Nielsen, *Torture Survivor*.

17. Ibid.

18. B. Jerlang, J. Orloff and P. Jerlang 'Torture Survivors, Dental and Psychological Aspects: Illustrated by Two Case Stories', *Torture* 7, 1997, pp. 43–5.

19. M. Morgan, M. Calnan and N. Manning, *Sociological Approaches to Health and Medicine*, Croom Helm, London, 1985.

20. V.V. Rivero, 'The Use of Psychotropic Medication', in Van der Veer, ed., *Counselling and Therapy with Refugees*.

21. K. Prip, L. Tived, and N. Holten, eds, *Physiotherapy for Torture Survivors: a Basic Introduction*, IRCT, Copenhagen, 1995.

22. G. Skylv, 'The Physical Sequelae of Torture', in M. Basoglu, ed., *Torture and Its Consequences: Current Treatment Approaches*, Cambridge University Press, Cambridge, 1992.

23. J. Frank, 'What is Psychotherapy?', in S. Bloch, ed., *An Introduction to the Psychotherapies*, Oxford University Press, Oxford, 1996.

24. Ibid.

25. Jacobsen and Smidt-Nielsen, *Torture Survivor*.

26. J. Herman, *Trauma and Recovery: The Aftermath of Violence*, Basic Books, New York, 1997.

27. Y. Danieli, 'Treating Survivors and Children of Survivors of the Nazi Holocaust', in F.M. Ochberg, ed., *Post-Traumatic Therapy and Victims of Violence*, Brunner/Mazel, New York, 1988.

28. L.H. Gustafsson, 'The STOP Sign – A Model for Intervention to Assist Children in War', in Raedda Barnen, ed., *Children in Emergencies*, Raedda Barnen, New York, 1986.

29. S. Bøjholm and A. Foldspang, unpublished data, RCT.

30. P. Bech, *Rating Scales for Psychopathology, Health Status and Quality of Life*, Springer Verlag, Berlin, 1993.

31. P. Elsass, *Tortur overleveren*, Gyldendal, Copenhagen 1995; English translation forthcoming.

32. C.R. Figley, ed., *Compassion Fatigue: Coping with Secondary Traumatic Stress Disorder in Those Who Treat the Traumatized*, Brunner/Mazel, New York, 1995.

7

Treatment Centres in Torturing States

Ingrid Ask, Juan Almendares Bonilla,
Terence Dowdall, Ümit Erkol
and Selim Ölçer

Introduction
Ingrid Ask

International attempts to assist victims of torture often turn out to be
unsuccessful due to political interests striving to hush the echo of the
victims' evidences. Likewise, the means to verify and prevent the practice
of torture in a specific state are scarce, particularly so when the government concerned denies such violations. An increasingly important role in
the struggle against torture and its consequences is therefore fulfilled by
non-governmental organizations and centres of treatment for torture
victims, sited within repressive states. In this chapter we will look at case
studies of centres operating in three such 'torturing states': Honduras,
South Africa and Turkey.

On a general level, the activities carried out by centres for victims of
torture focus on medical, physical and psychosocial therapy, but may also
imply research on treatment methods, documentation, education and
information, and, as far as feasible, advocacy. Most of the centres are
externally financed – the European Commission and the United Nations
Voluntary Fund for Victims of Torture are the principal contributors.[1] In
1997 the number of centres and programmes for torture victims was
estimated at 173: 60 in developing countries, 20 in Central and Eastern
Europe and 93 in OECD countries. This total is anticipated to grow by
1999 to around 212 centres.[2]

Yet it is only recently that the effects of torture have been understood
to need specialized treatment. The matter was brought to light in the
early 1970s, primarily as a result of a campaign launched by Amnesty

International. The campaign coincided with an awakening demand for appropriate rehabilitation for torture victims in many Western countries, where flows of refugees from totalitarian states had revealed imperfections in the ordinary healthcarer's knowledge of the psychosocial aftermaths of torture. In 1982, the world's first treatment centre for torture victims was established in Copenhagen: Rehabilitation and Research Centre for Torture Victims (RCT). This centre initiated a multidisciplinary rehabilitation programme, which in the years to come inspired the establishment of similar centres in many countries worldwide.

However, the increased number of centres has inevitably highlighted issues apart from the rehabilitation programmes *per se*. Centres operating in 'torturing states' are widely considered to be politically compromising and therefore compelled to struggle on two fronts: on one hand, against the consequences of torture for the individual, and on the other, against unfavourably disposed public authorities. This characterization is valid not only for centres within states where torture is practised by a repressive regime but also for those operating in states with a *previous* repressive regime – newly democratized states tend to inherit the practice of torture – as well as for those cases where torture is due to internal or external conflict. Whereas centres in OECD countries are able to give their full attention to the humanitarian and professional task of treating torture survivors, centres in repressive states are constantly forced to make political choices; for example, to what extent they should publicly condemn governmental violations. Health workers in such countries have to cope with the fear of personal harassment, the arbitrary closing down of their centres and the re-arrest of their patients on political grounds – dangers that do not exist in countries without major problems regarding political support.

What are the distinctive features of centres for treatment of torture survivors located within states that practise torture? Perhaps the most important common denominator is the salience of the political dimension, impossible to separate from medical and therapeutic rehabilitation activities. For instance, obtaining judicial redress against public authorities responsible for torture is a crucial component in restoring the victim's self-esteem, as well as putting pressure on the government. In many newly democratized states, the judicial aspect is linked to the fact that former torturers enjoy protection from prosecution by amnesty laws granting them impunity – a tremendous obstacle to centres' efforts to bring legal proceedings against violators, not to mention the attempts to encourage torture victims to regain confidence in society.

In many states with a previous repressive regime, torture remains a common practice in police stations and prisons, which – specifically regarding centres in Latin America – necessarily entails organizing visits as well as education of public officials, documentation of torture practice and systematic denunciation of government officials, partly through international channels. These kinds of activities are obviously delicate matters for states striving to maintain the correct façade in the eyes of the international community. Hence, governmental efforts *explicitly* to counteract activities of centres for torture victims are rarely observed, even though the hostile attitude may be a reality for staff members. For instance, the absence of governmental financial support for torture care is easily justifiable with respect to the state's stretched economy, even though the true reason is an unwillingness to support activities seen as compromising.

Even in cases when a solution to governmental opposition to torture treatment activities can be reached, other kinds of difficulties remain. One is the question of exactly who you will treat: what about torture victims who may themselves have been torturers? And do you treat people who have carried out acts of terror as a part of their opposition to state repression? Where, if at all, do you draw the line? Moreover, when physical violence has been practised under circumstances of war, defining the nature of violations can turn out to be tricky. An example: should guerrilla violence be considered in the same way as torture inflicted by a public official? And should the injured be treated by public hospitals or by private centres for torture victims?

On a more tangible level, centres in torturing states must overcome the crucial obstacle of reaching those in need of treatment – a problem that also has a social dimension. Centres are often confronted with scepticism regarding psychosocial care, challenging traditional belief systems that prescribe very different ways of treating psychical problems, frequently within the family or by a traditional healer. Therapeutic care is taboo in many cultures, where it raises a fear of being diagnosed with mental illness. This has proved to be an impediment to the establishment of rehabilitation programmes in some African states, where health workers have stressed the need to transform Western treatment models so that what is done meshes with traditional beliefs well enough to have credibility.

In conclusion, the activities of the world's centres for torture victims, particularly in torturing states, can be summarized as highly pragmatic: rehabilitation programmes cannot be isolated from political and social context. Therefore rehabilitation services are rarely restricted to torture victims only. They habitually include closely related target groups, such as victims of rape, child abuse, domestic violence and drug abuse. This characterization particularly embraces centres operating in states with insufficient public medical service, relying upon non-governmental organizations to assume part of the burden. Nevertheless, the centres' main focus – appropriate treatment of torture victims – continues to be a most urgent issue, the importance of which cannot be overestimated, specifically when implemented in an unfavourable political climate.

Honduras
Juan Almendares Bonilla

In the last decade, Honduras has been converted into a scene of violence where the security forces, both military and the military-controlled police, use police-state methods, torture, organized violence and death-squad activities as the instruments to fight crime and break down the opposition. There has been a rapid increase in the use of high-calibre arms by the military, and civilian paramilitary groups are increasingly being organized in urban and rural areas. Such groups carry out their own 'justice' outside the law.

Private security companies have become big business and comprise a 'parallel army' with an even larger number of 'soldiers' than the armed forces. The owners of this parallel army are the military leaders themselves. As a consequence, the population lives in a situation of constant fear, terror and insecurity.

Bombs are frequently used to influence constituent democratic components of society, such as the National Congress, the Ministry of the Economy, local courts, as well as human rights organizations. The kidnapping, extortion and hired assassination of business people are very common in the country and the violent removal of rural workers' (*campesinos*) families from land that they have lived on for years while cultivating their corn and beans has become routine.

Recent events are blatant illustration of the grave situation that exists in Honduras with regard to violence, injustice and lack of respect for human life. Military fugitives responsible for 184 disappearances and acts of torture continue to act with total impunity. In spite of a court order for their capture, these fugitives from justice organized a press conference, and the authorities were not capable of capturing them.

The country has since 1994 begun a process of transferring the police, hitherto controlled by the military, to civilian control. This process has generated a national debate because the armed forces continue pressing for military control of the civilian police authorities. In spite of the existence of a number of honest judges, much corruption exists in the judicial system, such as those in cases where military members are involved in the disappearances. Although allegedly involved in drugs-trafficking, theft of cars and the violation of human rights, these officials remain at large, without conviction.

An unholy alliance between certain members of the congress, the military and the private sector, representing powerful political and financial powers, has opposed the creation of a non-political and independent judicial system. The result is a weak judicial system which is unable to give individuals facing criminal charges a swift and fair trial. Apart from granting something close to general immunity to members of the military, political and social elite, the system has failed to the extent that 80 to 90 per cent of Honduras's prison population is incarcerated without having been convicted or having had their cases tried in court.

In 1996, detention of criminal suspects pending trial averaged eighteen months. Consequently, a large number or prisoners suffer from mental and physical problems. Furthermore the majority have been beaten and tortured by the military and the police during detention before going to prison. A constant lack of resources produces miserable conditions for the prisoners, such as severe overcrowding, undernourishment and horrible sanitary conditions. As a result, the last year has seen several riots and the burning down of prisons.

The health system is in a miserable state. A public health service exists which provides a majority of the population with poor quality care; there is a lack of medicines and resources. The service is expensive even for the middle class. There is a non-governmental sector consisting of a very expensive private service, and a small NGO sector that operates a free service. However, between 20 and 30 per cent of the population is deprived of health care; some 80 per cent of Hondurans suffer from poverty, and many poor patients cannot afford medical fees.

As things stand the government does not have sufficient command over resources to curb institutionalized violence, and to treat and rehabilitate survivors of torture.

Anti-torture work

Important steps have nevertheless been taken in the area of human rights in Honduras with the creation of the Prosecutors Office for Human Rights and the Commission for the Protection of Human Rights. The first national seminar on torture took place a couple of years ago with the participation of human rights and popular organizations, and in 1995 the Centre for the Prevention, Treatment and Rehabilitation of Victims of Torture and their Families 'Ole Vedel Rasmussen' (CPTRT) was founded (with technical, scientific, economic and moral support from PRODECA, RCT/IRCT).

The CPTRT strives for a better-functioning society in Honduras, with greater respect for human rights and democratic principles. Its work is organized in three primary programmes. The target group for the *rehabilitation* programme consists mainly of torture survivors, victims of organized violence, and the family members of both groups; family members of people who have 'disappeared' or been killed by death squads; prisoners and persons detained in prisons without sentence, suffering from inhumane conditions.

There is an extension of this programme which focuses primarily on *desalojados* (urban and rural population including indigenous groups, *campesinos*, who have been forcibly removed from their houses or land); refugees who have returned to Honduras; members of the legal system put under pressure by politicians and/or the military; and popular leaders and activists who receive death threats and/or psychological pressure. These activities are carried out not only in the CPTRT centre, but also in connection with rural health brigades and visits to the principal prisons of Honduras.

Complementing the rehabilitation activities is an intensive *prevention* programme, which includes training activities and workshops that seek to increase awareness and knowledge about ethics and human rights; this is directed at employees in the penal system, police authorities as well as professionals and students, primarily in the areas of medicine, nursing, law and psychology. The third primary programme is focused on the build-up of *local capacity*. It is carried out by a multidisciplinary team with training in medicine.

It is important to appreciate CPTRT's innovative approach in Central America. It seeks to accomplish its objective through a strategy which establishes a bridge between academic and alternative medicine. Besides the psychotherapy and general medicine, the patients benefit from homeopathy, massage, herbal medicine, Bach remedies, relaxation techniques, polarity and other alternative techniques. The combined alternative and academic therapies contribute to achieving greater credibility among patients of different cultural and religious beliefs.

The CPTRT is a non-governmental, non-profit organization and all its services are essentially free. During 1996, the CPTRT assisted a total of 1,269 persons. Of this number approximately 20 per cent were women. At least a hundred people with relevant academic backgrounds have been trained in the prevention of torture, ethics and human rights.

The staff is presently a multidisciplinary team of fourteen persons, which includes an executive medical director, an executive director, an assistant director, a general physician, a psychologist, an alternative therapist, a social worker, a nurse, an educator, and a documentalist.

An essential aspect of CPTRT's working method is to try to build linkages and cooperative relationships with other institutions and NGOs that seek to promote and protect human rights. Financial support and technical assistance is provided by PRODECA, DANIDA, RCT/IRCT from Denmark. CPTRT is also drawing on the RCT and IRCT international network for rehabilitation and prevention of torture. Among other international links, relations with the Inter American Institute for Human Rights in Costa Rica should be mentioned.

At the national level we are cooperating with the NGO environment, particularly human rights organizations, the National University and the Medical School, Honduras Health Exchange and The Public Defense. Furthermore, there are close relationships with the Honduran National Commissioner for Human Rights and the Special Human Rights Prosecutor. CPTRT attends to cases referred by the Honduras National Commissioner for Human Rights and by the Special Human Rights Prosecutor and notifies them about cases of human rights violation in prisons and police detention. CPTRT also participates in workshops and conferences organized by human rights governmental institutions.

National and international relationships are invaluable for our technical development. They are also a great moral support when our lives have been at risk. Threats against the families and leaders of human rights organizations, both governmental and non-governmental, are common. The National Commission for the Protection of Human Rights and the indigenous and popular organizations have called for general disarmament, as a result of which the personnel working at the CPTRT, as well as other members of human rights organizations, have suffered persecution, unauthorized phone-tapping and monitoring, and anonymous death threats.

The predicament

As indicated, the Honduran government has no official policies on the rehabilitation of torture survivors or institutional violence. There is a lack of knowledge and training among health and legal professionals and within the prison system, which leads to inadequate diagnosis and treatment of victims' sequelae. Nor does the government have the resources to undertake a satisfactory process of treatment.

Although the activities aimed at prevention take place in a complicated political environment, CPTRT seeks to increase understanding of human rights and to encourage the conditions necessary for systematic implementation of these values in the legal, judicial and penal systems of Honduras.

In order for CPTRT to become sustainable, a total change of power structures and attitudes, and subsequent fundamental structural change in society, will be necessary. Honduras functions as a pseudo-democracy. The country is ruled by militaries, landowners and multinationals. Therefore in the short term the project will be dependent on financial support from external donors.

To establish a treatment centre for survivors of torture in a country where government-sanctioned torture is still a practice requires the organization of a national group with the necessary resolution and audacity to work openly and with the courage to risk challenging the system. This role requires commitment, credibility and creativity on the part of the CPTRT group. Nevertheless, the work of CPTRT would not be possible without the international assistance it receives.

South Africa
Terence Dowdall

This section deals with the issues that faced the progressive health groupings and centres that offered treatment to survivors of torture and abuse at the hand of the South African security forces. We shall begin with a very brief introduction to the development of torture in South Africa, and will proceed to a discussion of the evolution of the progressive health groupings. We will look at the problems that they faced at each stage of their development, and the strategies that were used to try to cope with security force threats and pressures. Attention will also be given to the often complex problems that faced these new centres in the attempt to provide effective services in the context of civil conflict, in the very particular circumstances of the apartheid state.

Apartheid was a highly systematized strategy of social engineering intended to perpetuate white political and economic control in South Africa. It embodied vast numbers of controls and limitations on blacks and locked them into a state of subordination and oppression. Protest was met by state violence and increasing repression, and from the 1960s onwards the security police grew more and more powerful and less and less accountable to the law. Shielded by legal impunity, they increasingly resorted to violence and torture both to obtain information and to intimidate and undermine opposition by instilling fear in opponents of the National Party. In the 1980s increasing social unrest was met by increasing repression and torture – not only of political activists, but of anyone who took part in protest activities. Over the years in excess of seventy-five imprisoned activists died in detention and over 73,000 people, including children, were detained by the police and security forces. Very high proportions of detainees were tortured, and it was through this type of abuse that health professionals, both medical and psychological, became involved.

The problem of trust in politically dangerous situations

From the beginning of this work in the 1970s the health professionals involved operated in a political context. Torture as manifested in South Africa was a political act, one of a range of repressive strategies aimed at sustaining a particular political order. The people who were tortured were political opponents of that system, and that is why they were tortured. While in South Africa they could be re-detained at any time and subjected to further abuse or injury. Hence any treatment – and particularly psychological treatment – which they underwent needed to be undertaken by someone that they could reasonably trust, since the consequences could be dangerous and even fatal. In situations of civil conflict and repression, 'neutrality' is not valued or sought, since there are always suspicions about the real affiliations which neutrality may conceal. One has to bear in mind, too, that at certain times in the past decade, state hospital employees were being requested to inform the police of any people who came for treatment of injuries which may have been sustained during conflict associated with protest activity, and health professionals in general were regarded with some suspicion. This, then, was the first problem inherent in working with released detainees and people involved in the resistance movement.

It was dealt with initially on the level of personal connection: human rights lawyers made individual representations to psychologists or doctors whom they knew to be anti-apartheid in their sympathies, and asked them to give psychological or medical help to tortured ex-detainees. Therapists and doctors were 'vouched for' in this way. During the 1970s this was by and large workable because numbers were relatively low. However, in the early 1980s the wave of unrest which erupted in South Africa with successive States of Emergency led to massive rounds of detention and torture, and it became clear that a more coordinated response was needed. At this stage individual professionals began to come together in major urban centres like Johannesburg, Cape Town and Durban, to form organizations to address the problems which repression and apartheid posed for the health professions. One of the first problems which had surfaced was the covert politicization of the helping professions – law, medicine and psychology. Anti-apartheid professionals quickly realized that they could not expect moral or practical support from existing professional bodies, which while professing professional neutrality were in fact closely aligned to particular class, economic and political interests. Two of the major anti-apartheid health organizations which were formed in South Africa were the National Medical and Dental Associations (NAMDA) and the Organization for Appropriate Social Service in South Africa (OASSSA), and these combined with other progressive health organizations to set up a working interdisciplinary network of professionals who would specifically work with survivors of organized state violence and torture. This was known as Emergency Services Group (ESG) and from its beginnings in Johannesburg and Cape Town rapidly extended to many other urban centres. The issue of trust and political confidence was coped with through a loose political alliance which existed between the resistance movement and the progressive health organizations and the sense of basic working trust that members of the organizations vested in each other. As the health organizations expanded, membership was to some extent screened and no new members were accepted who could not be vouched for by at least two existing members, which seemed to be effective in blocking infiltration by the security police.

The problems of sustaining services and safeguarding dangerous information

The structure of the ESG services was carefully considered and a number of decisions were taken to see that it would have a good chance of surviving. It was decided early on that the primary function of the Emergency Services Groups was to provide medical and psychological assistance to anti-apartheid activists and their families and in order to be free to do this, the organization needed to keep a low public profile. In South Africa any organization which posed a visible threat was routinely 'banned', which meant that its operation became illegal and was greatly hampered. Actual centres – that is, premises with an infrastructure – were important for access and the effective delivery of services, and were usually leased in areas which were accessible to both health professionals and activists, without undue danger to either. International funding was raised for running expenses, a coordinator and a secretary/receptionist, but the therapeutic work was done entirely by volunteer health professionals, who worked at evenings and over weekends, and wherever they could find space during the day. Regular meetings were held for members so that ideas could be shared and common policy worked out. A number of practical problems faced these centres. One of the most important, of course, was the danger posed by the security police, who kept ESGs under a loose surveillance, and raided the offices from time to time. It was, of course, essential not to endanger inadvertently the people using the service, and a system of record-keeping was set up in which personal data like names and addresses were coded and kept in safe places, and where clinical records selectively omitted data which could be incriminating. Where individual activists were endangered or sought by the police, therapy sessions were not held at the centres but were conducted at changing, pre-arranged venues. Whilst this may have run contrary to conventional psychotherapeutic practice, it increased the confidence of the activists using the service, and very little damage was done to activists through their use of ESG health services. By and large the health professionals also kept clear of the security police. From time to time security police searched individual homes or attempted to harass or intimidate doctors or psychologists, and there were times when they were questioned or arrested for short periods, but the service was able to continue throughout the worst period of state repression. This did not, of course, mean that protest did not continue by the progressive health organizations against torture, but public statements inside South Africa were generally made by the parent bodies such as NAMDA or OASSSA. In international forums ESG spokespersons spoke out in detail against the repressive tactics and torture of the regime.

Problems of race, class and culture in civil conflict

In the South African context doctors and psychotherapists were mostly white and middle class. This applied also to most though not all of the progressive therapists working with torture survivors and their families, although these health workers were alienated from the South African professional bodies, which they believed acted in ways that perpetuated rather than challenged injustice. They were faced with a range of difficult and complex problems as they attempted to provide psychological assistance to security-force victims in the apartheid state. Membership of progressive health organizations affiliated to the mass democratic movement was sufficient to allay fears of betrayal. However, there remained deeper issues of trust across the racial gap in a nation divided along racial lines, where to be black was to have a history of being oppressed by the white establishment and often white individuals. A second major area of difficulty which was hard to acknowledge was the issue of competence. Whilst psychotherapists were formally trained in their disciplines, the therapeutic approaches were thoroughly rooted in Western middle-class culture, and the class and cultural gaps and the variance in expectations, assumptions and 'cosmologies' meant that therapist and survivor of torture 'missed' each other in important ways. The experience of the vast majority of white South Africans of black people had been in stereotyped 'service' roles, where very little real personal communication took place. In addition the strict residential and association limitations imposed by apartheid meant that white therapists seldom had much idea of the real day-to-day experiences of the survivors they were working with. The white suburbs were insulated from the sight of most of the violent repression that was happening. A further problem was that almost no psychotherapist could speak indigenous black languages. On top of all this was the limitation that professional training had been concerned much more with long-standing psychological problems rather than with acute stress and trauma, and this new area needed to be mastered effectively. Support and input from international organizations like the Danish Rehabilitation Centre for Victims of Torture (RCT) were of great value in the initial stages, but still needed to be adapted to local conditions.

It became clear that it was simply not possible to transplant the thera-peutic approach in an 'untransformed' way. An intensive learning process needed to take place for therapists to become as useful as possible to their clients. Most ESG groups set up therapist discussion and support groups to share ideas and brainstorm changes in approach.

One of the problems which therapists quickly realized they faced was how to treat activists in a situation where the trauma was far from over. The concept of Post-traumatic Stress Disorder tended to give way to a concept of Continuous Traumatic Stress Syndrome because of the on-going nature of acute stress that released activists experienced. They remained under surveillance, could be re-detained at any time and were frequently in hiding or 'on the run'. Assassinations were not uncommon. Their families were harassed and threatened. In these circumstances, a form of conventional and ongoing therapy, with regular appointments and the gradual removal of defences, was simply not a sensible option. Certainly, many activists were suffering very high levels of stress, but were not able to give themselves over to any form of treatment that would lower their vigilance or defences, since this would render them more vulnerable to capture and further harm. Accordingly, relatively brief methods of treatment needed to be developed which would shore up rather than break down defences in many of the people who were seen. Frequently a single extended session was all that was possible, in which limited catharsis, reframing and anxiety management training were the focus.

Apart from the brief interventions which were being developed for unpredictable circumstances, therapists increasingly moved towards a more 'community psychology' oriented approach. Many of the problems noted above were felt to be best addressed by forming working partnerships with people who could be described as being in the 'natural helping networks' of activists. Training and transfer of basic skills, and support of these 'natural helpers' – such as clergy, advice office workers, or people in resistance movements to whom members naturally turned for help – became a new focus. Direct therapeutic work of various kinds continued, but this second approach enabled the progressive health groups to extend support more widely to activists. The development of self-help strategies within this more community-based approach became more salient and necessary, given the irregular contacts which were often a hallmark of therapeutic contact with the progressive health organizations and clinics. Self-help manuals were drawn up for activists and their families as an additional back-up, often with the direct assistance of ex-detainees. This collaborative approach, between therapists and members of the organizations and communities within which they were working, to transform therapeutic and helping approaches increasingly became the strategy of choice as time went on.

In summary, then, our experience has been that therapeutic work with torture survivors within the country in which repression is taking place has actively challenged our thinking about psychotherapy and about the role of the medical and helping professions in fractured societies. We have had to face our own limitations, stereotypes, class interests and unproductive myths, and in some ways 're-create' our disciplines to make them more accessible. In the period of social reconstruction after the end of the civil conflict in South Africa the lessons learned in the period of state repression and torture have paradoxically been invaluable to help consolidate the peace.

Turkey
Ümit Erkol and Selim Ölçer

In Turkey, to call public attention to the problem of torture no longer shocks the person in the street. Many consider the infliction of torture on detainees an everyday occurrence, and do not react against it. When the course of history that led to today's Turkey is brought under scrutiny, it can be seen that the problem of torture predates the foundation of the republic. During the period of the Ottoman Empire, the practice of torture was mostly carried out in local police stations and following the arrest of dissidents. From then until now torture has been a permanent feature in the country.

The present Turkish Republic was founded on the ashes of the Ottoman Empire in 1923, constituting a mosaic of peoples and religions. A multi-party system was established in 1950, although there have been a number of military coups during the intervening period – in 1960, 1971 and again in 1980. The crippled democracy in today's Turkey carries the traces of that history.

At the end of the 1970s, interrogation under torture became fairly widespread as a result, first, of the impositions of martial law and then of the ensuing military coup, the prisons turned into dungeons where torture in detention became commonplace. During this period, the legal grounds were created for inflicting torture at every stage of investigation and prosecution, and the permitted detention period was increased to ninety days. According to Ministry of Justice data, some 215,000 people were put on trial at courts martial within a period of seven or eight years. Considering that one in every three detainees has been put on trial, according to the assessments of the Human Rights Association (IHD), some 650,000 people have either undergone interrogation under torture or have been put under the threat of torture for certain periods in locations where interrogation under torture is systematic.

The widespread practice of torture during the periods following martial law have been referred to by the Human Rights Foundation of Turkey (HRFT) and the IHD, and in the reports of the European Committee on Prevention of Torture published following the Committee's visits to Turkey in 1991 and 1992. It has been stated that people detained for both non-political and political crimes have been extensively subjected to torture. It is established that during the fifteen-year period following the coup, 460 people lost their lives due to torture in places of detention or in prison, or during hunger strike in prisons or because of health problems arising from torture.

A great deal of evidence can be presented regarding the prevalence of torture in Turkey. However, the figures given by President Kenan Evren in a press conference during his visit to the USA in 1988 are sufficient to reveal the facts. According to Evren's statement, 5,602 people were tried for inflicting torture. In these trials a total of 9,337 officers were arraigned, and 2,394 of them were sentenced. In the light of this data, it is quite easy to grasp the dimension of the social damage caused by torture in Turkey.[3]

Although torture and ill-treatment are banned under the constitution and in domestic law, the nature of political power and the judicial institutions in Turkey do not function to deter the perpetrators.[4] Those in power now argue that claims of torture are merely isolated instances, which represents a slight shift from the previous argument that it does not exist at all; this adjustment in the official position followed the rash of torture claims that have recently been certified by medical reports and detected by watch teams. However, the government can no longer maintain that there is no need for rehabilitation and treatment centres offering medical treatment to torture survivors.

Treatment of torture victims

The Human Rights Foundation of Turkey is an NGO set up in 1990. Its statutes declare: '(The Foundation) ... establishes, operates and helps others operate all manner of research, education and health institutions in relation with all human rights, as they are defined in international human rights documents and domestic laws.'[5]

The HRFT's work is organized around two projects, which have been in existence since the beginning: the Documentation Centre Project, and the Treatment and Rehabilitation Centres Project. Within the framework of the first project, human rights violations in Turkey are documented. The Documentation Centre issues reports in Turkish and English every weekday, and prepares an annual report on the basis of the daily reports. In addition to the daily and annual human rights reports, the Documentation Centre produces monographs in the field of human rights.

The Treatment and Rehabilitation Project aims to provide those whose health has deteriorated due to the torture inflicted on them with physical, psychological and social examination, and subsequently treatment and rehabilitation. The HRFT has established a treatment and rehabilitation centre in four provinces: Adana, Ankara, Istanbul and Izmir. All applicants to the centres claim to have been tortured, and apply on their own initiative following referral by a non-governmental institution, in particular by the medical Chambers, Human Rights Association, Bars and Contemporary Lawyers Association.

Staff members of the four centres include eight practitioners, four psychiatrists, three social workers and two medical secretaries. Each centre has an executive board composed of the staff working at the centre and volunteer medical professionals living in the provinces, headed by a volunteer physician. The number of volunteer physicians amounts to about 300. By the end of 1996 the four centres had treated and rehabilitated 2,767 torture survivors. The treatment and rehabilitation work of the HRFT is not limited to organizing the services it provides; it also involves scientific research and education programmes, with regularly published results.

The Foundations's position is strengthened by the contributions of the many professional and democratic mass organizations against torture that exist in the country – particularly the Human Rights Association (IHD) and Turkish Medical Chamber (TTB) – and by international support. The HRFT's work has been supported and financed since 1991 by the UN Voluntary Fund for Victims of Torture, the European Union, Amnesty International and the Swedish Red Cross.

The HRFT nurtures contacts with diplomatic missions to inform them about its activities and maintains relations with certain organizations that function in the supranational area, such as the aforementioned UN body, the Human Rights Section of the European Union. Moreover, it has ample contacts with NGOs and individuals from many countries, particularly in Europe.

The network of cooperating NGOs comprises organizations of various kinds: human rights organizations (e.g. Amnesty International, FIDH, APT); medical associations (e.g. British Medical Association, World Medical Association, Swedish Medical Association, Danish Medical Association); rehabilitation centres for torture survivors (e.g. IRCT, ICT, Berlin Centre for Victims of Torture, Medical Foundation, AVRE, Primo Levi); the Red Cross; humanitarian organizations (e.g. Caritas, Miserior) and charity organizations (e.g. Demokratische Turkei Forum); jurist organizations; journalist organizations; trade unions (e.g. ABF, Arbeitskreis Asyl Rhein-Neckar) and political parties sensitive to human rights.

The above-mentioned organizations and their representatives follow up human rights violations in Turkey, particularly torture. The reports prepared by the HRFT have a special place among their sources of information. The relations between the HRFT and all of these organizations are direct. HRFT makes an effort to keep them informed, on the grounds that human rights violations do not just constitute an internal problem of the country where they occur. Announcing and discussing the violations, and hence creating an atmosphere of international solidarity, is important.

Obstacles

There now exists a strong movement for the defence of human rights throughout the country. However, it is not possible to talk about a regular, functional relationship between the state and these organizations. HRFT has encountered persistent hostility since its inauguration. First, objections were raised against the founding of the HRFT in connection with a statement in its statutes. The HRFT gained legal status only after some revisions, as indicated above.

The Turkish authorities have instigated several legal moves against the publications and medical services of the Foundation, and the organization is kept under pressure on the pretext of official inspection of applicants. The purpose is to gain access to secret documents, and to reduce the trustworthiness of the HRFT by compromising its ability to keep confidential information about torture survivors, which in fact constitutes a legal and medical requirement for any establishment dealing with psychological and physical illness. Needless to say, such practices by the political powers are a great problem for the HRFT.

Pressures and restrictions against the HRFT increased in 1996. As a party to the general and regional human rights conventions and declarations, the Turkish government expected positive comments to be included in the US government's Human Rights Report on Turkey. However, while the report was at the drafting stage the Turkish authorities learned that it contained statements about systematic torture in Turkey, which were based on HRFT documents. Thereupon, the Ministry of Foreign Affairs attempted to prove the unreliability of the HRFT documents on which the US report was based.

The ministry put into action a plan to deal with the HRFT Treatment and Rehabilitation Centres, in operation since 1990, as if they did not exist or were carrying out illegal activities. It demanded an inspection of the Ankara, Istanbul, Izmir and Adana centres, whereupon, the general directorate of health services of the Health Ministry demanded that an inspection be carried out by the relevant Provincial Health Directorate. While the general directorate of foundations would carry out the audit, the Ministry of Health would determine that 'the centres did not exist or were in operation without permission'. The role of the Ministry of Justice in this campaign was to bring HFTR representatives and physicians to trial.[6]

A trial was begun of the representative of the Adana Office of the HRFT, who is also the physician of the Adana Treatment and Rehabilitation Centre. However, the political authority realized the groundlessness of its claims. While the proceedings were continuing in Adana, no charges were brought against the physicians of the Istanbul Representation, who have worked for a longer period of time and diagnosed and planned the treatment processes of a greater number of torture survivors. Statements by Ministry of Foreign Affairs officials confirm that they did not want to interfere in the relationship between patients and physicians since they had faced an international reaction to the Adana trial, which was precisely an attempt to intervene in this relationship. Debate over the fate of the physician will of course continue.

The negative attitude on the part of the authorities has important consequences. Scientific circles are reluctant to support the treatment and rehabilitation services of the HRFT because of pressures and biased propaganda. Human rights defenders are portrayed as an extension of political groups, which are called terrorist organizations on the grounds that most of the applicants who receive medical treatment at the rehabilitation and treatment centres were tortured for their political views. This makes the job more difficult for the HRFT, when, for instance, it has to apply for the use of facilities at state hospitals in cases that require technologically advanced medical examination, in-patient treatment or a surgical operation.

An additional difficulty is that torture survivors abstain from appealing to any human rights organizations, for fear of pressures, threats and subjection once more to torture, because they are only too aware of living in a country where torture is systematically inflicted. Nevertheless, confidence in the HFTR remains very high because it insists that the names and records of applicants should remain secret, and that applicants are able to depend on this secrecy.

Notes

1. Through voluntary contributions, the UN Fund subsidizes humanitarian organizations and projects that provide some kind of assistance to victims of torture. In 1996, a total amount of $2,434,000 was distributed to ninety-six projects or subprojects for torture victims around the world.

2. *Torture: Quarterly Journal on Rehabilitation of Torture Victims and Prevention of Torture*, vol. 7, no. 2, 1997.

3. Ü. Erkol and Y. Islegen, *Torture in Turkey and Proposals on Prevention of Torture*, HRFT Treatment and Rehabilitation Centers Report 1995, Ankara, 1996.

4. Ibid.

5. This statement of purpose was accepted by the authorities which nevertheless rejected the following draft: '[The Foundation] ... establishes, operates, and helps others operate rehabilitation centres for the medical treatment of those whose health has physically and psychologically deteriorated as a result of torture, inhuman or degrading treatment and punishment they had encountered in prison or custody without any discrimination between race, colour, sex, language, religion, political view and belief. It provides medical treatment, medicine and rehabilitation instruments to torture survivors.'

6. M. Çinkiliç, *The Story of the Adana Trial*, HRFT Treatment and Rehabilitation Centres Report 1996, Ankara, 1997, p. 48.

8

Torture and Asylum

Bent Sørensen

Why Leave Your Country?

To *go abroad*, away from your own country, can be a pleasure. To *flee* your country is quite another thing. It is often impossible to take more than the absolutely necessary things along, maybe not even those; the individual often has to flee with great haste – always out of fear.

Massive refugee streams are seen in war conditions, where people flee to escape the consequences of war; in fact they do so in order to avoid violations of human rights, first of all the right to life, but also the other civil rights like the right not to be tortured and the basic socio-economic rights – the right to food, heat and shelter. Refugee streams in hundreds of thousands are not uncommon.

In peacetime, people most often flee to avoid violations of their civil rights: they want to be able to express themselves freely, to be free to form unions and to organize, to practise whatever religion they wish, and to avoid being subjected to torture – even if they are fighting for human rights.

Torture

Research carried out during the past twenty-three years at the Rehabilitation and Research Center for Torture Victims (RCT) in Copenhagen has revealed how large a role torture plays in this context. The research has demonstrated that states in peacetime use torture deliberately as a *means of power*.[1] Furthermore, as can be seen from the chapter by Lone Jacobsen and Edith Montgomery (Chapter 6), torture leads to very *severe after-effects* – so severe that the person has difficulty in, or is not capable of, performing normal work. The government exploits this fact: the persons who fight for human rights are exactly those who form the target group of government-sanctioned torture. They are being tortured so that they cannot function properly and are subsequently sent back to their own community. They are then no longer able to continue the fight for human rights, and they end up as deterrent examples to their relatives, friends, the whole community. The citizens of the state are held in a grip of terror which to a very large extent is based on the use of torture. Torture has become a common health-care problem.

Torture may be considered as the most flagrant violation of human rights, and in living persons torture is the intervention which leads to the severest after-effects. For many people flight out of the country is the only means to escape.

How Many People Flee Because of Torture?

There are few investigations that help to clarify the question of how many flee from torture *eo ipso*; such investigations are difficult to undertake (see the section below on torture victims' problems during the asylum-seeking phase).

At the RCT, a Ph.D. monograph has been written on the problem.[2] The study was based on the total number of asylum-seeking children arriving from the Middle East in the period from 1 February 1992 to 30 April 1993. The parents of these children were all investigated to reveal whether they had been tortured (the definition of torture used was that of the Tokyo Declaration).[3] The investigation was performed partly by means of a questionnaire, partly by means of an in-depth psychological interview. In the case of discrepancy between the two methods (which only occurred in three out of 123 cases), the decision whether torture had taken place or not was made, anonymously, by an expert (the author), based on the various papers in the particular case. The result showed that 55 per cent of the men and 12 per cent of the women who were parents of the arriving children had been exposed to torture. Some 51 per cent of all the children who had arrived in the time-period had one or both parents who had been subjected to torture, the severe after-effects of which on children are described by Jacobsen and Montgomery.

Dr Ron Baker,[4] who collected the literature until 1992, states that between 4 and 35 per cent of all refugees, worldwide, have been subjected to torture, and furthermore that the fear of being tortured is one of the main reasons for fleeing. Dr Douglas A. Johnson, in testimony on 8 May 1996 before the Committee on International Relations of the US House of Representatives, repeated the above-mentioned figures and stated that according to calculations there are now 400,000 tortured refugees living in the USA. The conclusion must be that a considerable number of refugees have been subjected to torture in the country they have fled, and that torture is one of the main reasons for fleeing.

The Handling of Asylum Applications

Applications for asylum are dealt with according to the domestic laws of the various countries. Initiatives are under way within the European Union (EU) to introduce a standardized asylum policy, with common rules and one common border for the fifteen EU countries, but the proposal has not yet been accepted (the Amsterdam Treaty). The legal rules, however, are satisfactory in most of the countries: the domestic law in practically all countries contains a passage saying that persons must not be sent back to a country where they risk being subjected to torture. Furthermore, there is nearly always the possibility of appealing against a decision before a higher court. What follows deals only with practical problems, and only in peacetime.

The first meeting

Having arrived in a country, the first person an asylum-seeker is confronted with is a passport control officer, then often officials of the immigration authority. Prior to arrival, the person has fled. He may have come out of prison or a police station by means of bribery, or been underground in his own country, before he was successful in getting out with his own passport – or more often a falsified passport; alternatively he has been smuggled out. The travel continues by air, often with some stops and changes of plane on the way. On arrival, the asylum-seeker not infrequently turns out to have destroyed his own passport, if he had one. He is confronted by a police officer wearing a uniform, not unlike the uniform his torturers were wearing. Generally there are language difficulties, and an interpreter is called in.

The scenario

It is important to realize that the police see themselves as kind, good-hearted persons who are there to assist and protect the citizens of the country – which luckily is correct, by and large. The asylum-seeker, however, sees uniformed police officers as similar to those who tortured him – as he knows nothing at all about the police in the foreign country. The asylum-seeker is now questioned about his identity – his passport perhaps having been destroyed – and the flight route, and about the reason for seeking asylum. Everything is written down carefully with a view to subsequent handling of the case by the asylum board. In dealing with torture survivors, confidentiality is of paramount importance (see the preceding chapter). What is more, it often takes years before a person will talk about torture – after what is the most horrible act a human being can perpetrate against a fellow human being. In this connection, it is hardly surprising that a woman who has been repeatedly raped for months in her own country, and who subsequently manages to escape, only to find herself sitting two days later in front of a police officer who is wearing a uniform much the same as her rapist's, does not at once inform about the rape.

The waiting time

If a person is immediately refused entry at the border, he will often have to spend a period of time at the airport, before he is sent back. The Council of Europe's Committee for the Prevention of Torture (CPT) has visited a number of such localities and found that they are rarely of an adequate standard. If the stay exceeds a few hours, the CPT demands that the person is given access to his luggage; that there is an acceptable place to stay with access to toilets and sleeping facilities; and, if the person must stay longer, there should be access to outdoor activities. Thus, even if the person has to leave the country, the authorities must ensure that in the meantime he can stay under decent conditions.

If a person is not rejected immediately, his asylum application will be handled according to the laws of the country. Thus, there will be a waiting time. This can in itself be a great strain; it often takes two to three years before a final decision is reached, and naturally it is of great importance where the asylum-seeker spends his waiting time.

It goes without saying that it is quite unacceptable to place the person in a police station except for a very short stay, a maximum of twenty-four hours. Here again one must be mindful of the after-effects that afflict a torture victim, and the fact that most torture takes place in a police station. Besides, police stations are not suited for long stays, even for the country's own citizens.

It is also unacceptable to place asylum-seekers in prisons, as they are not sentenced criminals, or suspected of having committed crimes. Rather, special camps for asylum-seekers have been established in most countries. Conditions in different countries vary considerably: from small, over-crowded cells to fairly good accommodation with free access to relaxation rooms, association and free areas, with the possibility of receiving visitors, and with good health conditions and access to medical care. One problem, however, is that persons are gathered together from many different countries, which often maintain hostile relations. There are language problems, cultural problems concerning for example food, and then the essential fact of having been deprived of liberty. A stay in such a place, together with uncertainty about the outcome of the asylum application and the uncertainty about the time horizon, places a great strain on those asylum-seekers who have not been exposed to torture. For persons who have been tortured, the strain is almost unbearable and leads to a deterioration of the person's mental condition during the stay, even though torture has stopped and the process of recovery is under way. In its 7th Annual Report,[6] the CPT articulated the problems and put forward suggestions for improvements in conditions.

The state's obligations

The state has an obligation as regards physical conditions for refugees, and also as regards the special demands made on personnel; finally it has a responsibility to effect as smooth and efficient a handling as possible of asylum applications.

The physical demands have been described above. The state must, of course, ensure adequate physical conditions. Great demands must be made of personnel. The first person the refugee sees may be decisive for his general well-being. The staff member must therefore possess a mature personality and a knowledge of human behavioural patterns, especially that of torture survivors. He/she should know the interpreter well, and be able to collaborate with him or her so that the asylum-seeker and the interpreter are able to understand one another completely. Patience is of course a valuable quality: calm and dignified behaviour is a necessity. Thus, staff members should be recruited on the basis of their meeting these criteria; they should also have undergone special postgraduate training. Moreover, this is in fact a *requirement* of all countries that have ratified the Convention Against Torture,[7] Article 10 of which reads as follows:

> Each State Party shall ensure that education and information regarding the prohibition against torture are fully included in the training of law enforcement personnel, civil or military, medical personnel, public officials and other persons who may be involved in the custody, interrogation or treatment of any individual subjected to any form of arrest, detention or imprisonment.

Personnel must of course also know the Refugee Act in detail, in particular that persons may not be sent back to a country where there are 'substantial grounds for believing that he would be in danger of being subjected to torture' (Article 3 of the Convention Against Torture).

The demands placed on personnel in refugee camps are thus great and difficult to meet. Nevertheless, certain general principles may be mentioned. The staff should be sufficient in number. They should be mature, have good interpersonal communication skills, be calm and able to handle difficult situations. They should be well-trained in international rules and the consequences for refugees of the adopted policy. Furthermore, it is desirable that they be knowledgeable about the prevalent cultures, including the specific behavioural norms, and respect them. For example, if there are Muslims staying in a camp, facilities for cooking after sunset during the Ramadan period should be provided, and they should not be offered pork; Hindus, for their part, should not be offered beef; and so on. Personnel should receive special training to help them understand the psyches and behavioural patterns of torture survivors. Monitoring is essential, and Article 11 of the Convention Against Torture bears directly on police, prison and refugee camp personnel (if the country in question has ratified the Convention):

> Each State Party shall keep under systematic review interrogation rules, instructions, methods and practices as well as arrangements for the custody and treatment of persons subjected to any form of arrest, detention or imprisonment in any territory under its jurisdiction, with a view to preventing any cases of torture.

Article 10 of the Convention, then, sets standards for training; Article 11 covers control by the police (interrogation methods, etc.) as well as by prison staff and staff in refugee camps (detention). This is only followed to a limited extent in practice, however. In Europe, the CPT functions as an international control body.

If immigration officials rule that a person be expelled immediately, this person should have access to assistance from the UNHCR and possibly also legal advice, which is mostly provided by NGOs. If the person wishes to contact his embassy (which rarely happens in practice, as he is fleeing his country), this request should of course be met.

The refugee boards

In practically all countries the composition of refugee boards is satisfactory, seen from a democratic point of view; the same goes for appeal courts. In addition, the domestic law in most countries contains a passage which prohibits the repatriation of persons to a country where they would be at risk of being tortured. Thus, on the face of it, everything seems to be in perfect order.

If a country has ratified the Convention Against Torture and declared in favour of Article 22, persons in the country (not only citizens of the country) can complain about breaches of the provisions of the Convention. This also goes for Article 3, the full text of which is as follows:

1. No State Party shall expel, return [*refouler*] or extradite a person to another State where there are substantial grounds for believing that he would be in danger of being subjected to torture.

2. For the purpose of determining whether there are such grounds, the competent authorities shall take into account all relevant considerations including, where applicable, the existence in the State concerned of a consistent pattern of gross, flagrant or mass violations of human rights.

The conditions required for the UN Committee Against Torture (which consists of ten persons) to consider a complaint are the following: (1) The complaint must not be handled by another international forum; and (2) all domestic remedies must have been exhausted.

In recent years, the CAT has received an increasing number of complaints relating to Article 3 – currently some thirty per year. In consequence, the Committee has gained a good deal of experience. Based on the decisions made (which are published in the Annual Reports of the Committee), an evaluation can be made of where the weak spots in the national handling of asylum applications seem to be.

First observation

Naturally enough in trials, national authorities concentrate on 'inconsistencies' in a communication: how can a person be trustworthy if he says one thing at the first interrogation, other things at the next, and then something different at subsequent interrogations? Why did the person not admit right away to having been exposed to torture? After all, this is essential information. The reason was indicated above: torture is so horrible that you definitely do not want to talk about it unless you absolutely have to. Furthermore, as stated, many torture victims suffer from severe after-effects. These after-effects may be identical to or resemble so-called post-traumatic stress disorder (PTSD): the person is unable to speak about it because he or she does not remember in the way we do. Moreover, they realize that they have a poor memory, which they try to cover up so as not to reveal that torture has taken place – they are ashamed. Thus, 'inconsistencies' and other apparent inaccuracies may be caused by the fact that the person suffers from the sequelae to torture.

Second observation

As mentioned, most countries have a rule that forbids repatriation of a person to a country where he is at risk of being tortured. When the CAT goes over cases where asylum has not been granted, this rule is rarely mentioned – even though decisions by the national boards are very detailed. The problem seems to be that the issue has not been discussed; at any rate it is not clear from the relevant papers whether it has been discussed or not.

Third observation

Many countries respect the rule of not granting asylum to 'a terrorist'. Many of those who have been tortured – who, indeed, fought for human rights in their home country – would be characterized as terrorists in that country. Some perhaps are, others not. This is, however, of little importance. If there are 'substantial grounds for believing that he would be in danger of being subjected to torture', the person must not be sent back. And this applies whether he is a mass murderer or a terrorist. If the country is unable to grant asylum to a person, his stay must be secured in another way.

The above-mentioned observations illustrate why the CAT, on the basis of documents, sometimes arrives at a conclusion contrary to that of the refugee board in a country, which after all has also had the possibility of interviewing the person and not just basing its conclusion on 'paperwork' (a situation, incidentally, which certain countries seem to have difficulty in accepting). In my view, this situation also suggests that certain facts are not always taken into consideration in the handling of asylum applications, such as the reason why torture is used, the identity of the persons who constitute the 'target groups' (leaders of ethnic minorities, trade union leaders, student leaders, journalists, politicians, etc.), and finally and most importantly, the nature of the most frequent sequels to torture. This latter factor accounts for the often deviant character of torture survivors and the problem of 'inconsistency'.

The remedy is obvious: improved training and information, and perhaps also a change of attitude. The legal background for implementing such training is to hand, if the country has ratified the UN Convention Against Torture: Article 10.

The General Public

In many countries there is strong public opinion against receiving refugees. It is not only the refugee boards but also the 'people' who therefore should be informed of the real facts, as described above. This could help contribute to a change in public attitude, to the benefit of both asylum-seekers and society. In my view, refugees – especially perhaps those strong persons who have been tortured because they fought for human rights in their homeland – are not a burden on the host country. Rather, they are a gift for the country. As always, gifts should be received with humility and gratitude; otherwise there is no joy either for the donor or the receiver.

Notes

1.   I. Genefke, 'Achievement after More than 20 Years of Health Professionals' Work against Government Sanctioned Torture', *Journal of the Indian Medical Association*, no. 7, 1996, pp. 94, 262–5.

2.   E. Montgomery, 'Refugee Children from the Middle East', *Scandinavian Journal of Social Medicine*, Supplementum no. 54, forthcoming.

3.   See Kellberg, Chapter 1 of this book.

4.   R. Baker, 'Psychological Consequences for Tortured Refugees Seeking Asylum and Refugee Status in Europe', in M. Basoglu, ed., *Torture and its Consequences: Current Treatment Approaches*, Cambridge University Press, Cambridge, 1992, pp. 83–106.

5.   D.A. Johnson, *Testimony: Hearing before the Subcommittee on International Operations and Human Rights of the Committee on International Relations, House of Representatives*, US Government Printing Office, Washington, 1996, pp. 89–100.

6.   *7th General Report on the CPT's Activities Covering the Period 1 January to 31 December 1996*, European Committee for the Prevention of Torture and Inhuman or Degrading Treatment or Punishment (CPT), Council of Europe, Strasbourg, 1997.

7.   'United Nations Convention Against Torture and Other Cruel, Inhuman or Degrading Treatment or Punishment' reprinted in *The Committee Against Torture*, Human Rights Fact Sheet No. 17, United Nations, Geneva.

Part IV

The Struggle against Torture

9

Foreign Policy and Torture

Katarina Tomaševski

There is a yawning gap in the enforcement of international human rights law: whereas freedom from torture should be a universally guaranteed human right, governmental obligations are territorially delimited. Few exceptions exist: international treaties relating to torture require governments to extradite or prosecute suspected torturers, while international treaty bodies interpret the absolute prohibition of torture to inhibit expulsion or deportation to countries where there is a risk of torture. Governmental behaviour beyond national borders remains, however, beyond international human rights litigation.

International mobilization around freedom from torture exposed this gap. The Convention Against Torture is silent on the issue, as are its regional sister-treaties. In the absence of law, attention switched to foreign policy as a means of constraining governmental behaviour beyond national borders. This chapter examines the place of freedom from torture in foreign policy. It highlights how governments alternate between facilitation of torture abroad and condemnation of governments on whose territory torture takes place. External governmental support is poorly documented because foreign assistance intended to facilitate torture is cloaked behind foreign policy priorities such as 'national security' or 'combating international terrorism', which precludes access to information, limits public scrutiny, and inhibits the application of human rights safeguards. Condemnation of other governments for torture is better documented because governmental conduct is to a large extent publicly recorded. These two options – facilitation and condemnation – are sometimes exercised by the same government at the same time, in relation to the same country, as aptly noted by Human Rights Watch:

Some of the Governments that are denouncing torture before [the United
Nations Commission on Human Rights], including the United States, are at the
same time providing extensive international assistance to the authorities which
consistently engage in this practice.[1]

Such conventional state-centred analysis exposes conflicts within
foreign policies. Israel, Turkey and Central America are used below as
mini case studies. Conflicts within foreign policy have intensified in the
1990s. The notion of national security has been broadened to include
terrorism, drug trafficking and organized crime. Military and police
functions have become blurred, as have human rights and humanitarian
law. The term 'human rights violation' no longer applies to governmental
conduct alone; annual resolutions of the Commission on Human Rights
voice concern 'at the gross violations of human rights perpetrated by
terrorist groups.'[2] Domestic concerns, especially protection against the
import of violence and terrorism, increasingly guide foreign policies and
justify assistance for combating such problems abroad. Foreign involvement in policing inevitably follows, and exposes how ill-equipped international human rights law has been – and remains – in effectively responding to changing foreign policy.

Gaps in the Law

Human rights obligations address vertical relations of unequal power
between the government (endowed with monopoly over the use of force
and violence) and the individual (whose resort to violence is generally
outlawed). Governmental self-restraint is embodied in human rights safeguards. Exceptions are few and these are stringently regulated. Freedom
from torture is not among those exceptions because it enjoys the highest
possible degree of protection in international human rights and humanitarian law. International human rights bodies have decided cases where a
violation of the right to life was justified (in combating terrorism, for
example), but no exception or justification has ever limited the universal
validity of freedom from torture. The Vienna Conference on Human
Rights confirmed that 'freedom from torture is a right which must be
protected under all circumstances, including in times of internal or international disturbance or armed conflicts.'[3]

That special status of freedom from torture has not been accompanied
by a corollary extension of governmental obligations beyond their national
borders. Exceptions have been recognized in the principle *aut dedere aut
judicare* for persons suspected of having committed torture and the prohibition on exposing any person to torture by expulsion or deportation.

The initial cases before the Committee Against Torture (CAT) dealt with the interpretation of that obligation, and the CAT found that applicants from countries such as Switzerland and Canada should not be returned to Zaire and Pakistan.[4]

International jurisprudence concerning governmental conduct abroad provides a much narrower interpretation of governmental obligations. The Strasbourg jurisprudence affirmed governmental responsibility only when 'actual governmental authority' is exercised abroad, such as through military occupation.[5] The International Court of Justice failed to extend governmental reponsibility beyond national borders unless evidence could be furnished that another government exercised effective control of operations which included absolutely prohibited conduct, such as torture.[6]

That legal gap comes to light when foreign policy tolerates or endorses torture abroad in pursuance of some important foreign policy objective. Pacification of an armed population may entail torture. Quite a few cases of torture carried out by Blue Helmets during the US/UN military/humanitarian intervention in Somalia were reported in international media, when Blue Helmets were brought before military courts and commissions of inquiry in the USA, Canada, Belgium and Italy in response to evidence that they tortured Somali detainees.[7] The accompanying publicity demonstrates that exposing torture does not necessarily lead to effectively opposing it. The absence of human rights safeguards for governmental behaviour abroad is an obstacle.

The assumption that a government will take another to court because of human rights violations on its territory is embodied in international human rights law, but that body of law lies dormant. (The exception relating to Turkey is mentioned below.) In the case of Somalia, there was (still is) no government to protect its population against abuses committed by the domestic, foreign or international military or police. In other cases there may be a government theoretically willing to take another to court because of a breach of prohibition of torture, but practically incapable of doing so because the price of embarassing another government may be too high. As a consequence, no government has ever been held responsible for torture abroad.

Authoritative findings that torture is prevalent in specific countries should be – but are not – translated into foreign policy towards such countries. Frequent recommendations to governments to refrain from facilitating torture abroad testify to the gap between 'should' and 'is'. The Parliamentary Assembly of the Council of Europe expressed in 1989, just as the cold war was ending, a typical attitude whereby the responsibility of countries exporting torture equipment stops at the borders of the importing countries:

Many arms exports may be used for the violation of human rights over which the exporting country has no control, except to refuse to export arms which could be used for domestic repression.[8]

The European Parliament called for inclusion of repressive technologies in controls of arms exports so as to diminish the risk of facilitating torture abroad. The Parliament had to acknowledge, however, in the same resolution 'the hypocrisy of governments who breach their own export controls'.[9]

Some countries have partially closed that gap by adopting legal prohibitions on the export of torture equipment and technology. Among the options is to develop lists of countries to which military and/or security exports are prohibited, as was done in Canada's legislation of 1986 on control of the export of military goods and technology. It included among the criteria 'countries whose governments have a persistent record of serious violations of the human rights of their citizens, unless it can be demonstrated that there is no reasonable risk that the goods might be used against the civilian population'.[10] Similarly, the European Union's initial attempts to develop criteria for arms export control within its emerging common foreign and security policy included 'the respect of human rights in the country of final destination.'[11]

That approach follows from the inclusion of human rights in foreign policy in the West/North, which often aims to foreclose co-operation with human rights violators. By the criterion of documented torture, such a list would encompass more than half the countries in the world. The 1997 report of the UN Special Rapporteur on torture names more than seventy countries, including *inter alia* Austria, Canada, France, Germany, Italy, Spain, Sweden and the United Kingdom.[12] If information available from *all* international human rights bodies was combined, a list of torture-free countries would be very short. Nevertheless, even if the world as a whole seems to be moving away from broadening the scope of freedom from torture, there is a substantive difference between incidence of torture and evidence of institutionalized and/or legalized torture.

The UN's Exposure of Torture and the Foreign Policy Response

Governments acting collectively possess the authority to find a government responsible for human rights violations, and such indictments are tabled at the annual meetings of the UN Commission on Human Rights. Peer pressure ensures human rights obligations are observed; its absence enables governments to ignore them. The number of countries indicted for human rights violations since the UN started investigative and condemnatory action in the 1970s encompasses almost half of the UN membership. That portrays both the strength of the system and its weakness: quite a few governmental delegations who take part in discussing human rights violations have the unpleasant task of responding to allegations of violations against the states they represent. The main purpose of human rights – to prevent the abuse of power – requires those who wield power to police themselves. Identification of violators reveals the inherent conflict between the two roles of the government – as violator and protector of human rights. The strength of the system is that governments *do* police each other; its weakness is that they do so reluctantly and the results of their deliberations are political decisions. A country for which there is evidence of prevalent torture will not necessarily be found on the UN list of human rights violators.

The UN human rights system was not designed to police governments, but only to assist them in policing themselves. It cannot deter or punish gross and systematic violations. Its achievement has been to define violations and make them visible – exposure is the sanction. A further step to oppose the continuation of violations happens rarely and is, again, a political decision. Political decision-making was in the 1980s supplemented by thematic procedures which broadened the reach of the UN's investigative powers worldwide. Those procedures were initially established for disappearances, torture and summary executions, the three phenomena most closely related to the governmental monopoly over the use of force and violence.

Table 9.1 summarizes recent results of the first thematic procedures of UN human rights bodies which deal with abuses of physical power by governments. Those procedures were designed to enable the United Nations to achieve two aims: first, to concentrate on those abuses that were accepted by states as apparent human rights violations; and second, to overcome the political obstacles to exposure of such apparent violations in countries for which a political decision could not be reached.

Only those countries in which all three phenomena were documented through the respective procedures are included in Table 9.1. That list only partially overlaps those countries whose governments have been condemned for human rights violations by the UN Commission on Human Rights, and illustrates the political obstacles. Countries torn by armed conflict – for example, Angola, Burundi, El Salvador, Haiti, Lebanon, Rwanda, Sudan, Yugoslavia, Zaïre – are routinely condemned for human rights violations, as are two long-term foci of condemnatory UN action, Iran and Iraq. There is, however, a long list of countries included in Table 9.1 but not in the condemnatory resolutions of the Commission

Table 9.1 Countries listed in special procedures on torture, disappearances and summary executions, 1993–96

1993–94	1994–95	1995–96
—	Algeria	Algeria
Angola	Angola	—
—	Argentina	Argentina
—	Bolivia	Bolivia
Brazil	Brazil	Brazil
Burundi	Burundi	Burundi
Cameroon	Cameroon	—
Chad	—	—
Chile	Chile	Chile
China	China	China
Colombia	Colombia	Colombia
Ecuador	Ecuador	Ecuador
Egypt	Egypt	Egypt
—	El Salvador	—
Equatorial Guinea	—	Equatorial Guinea
Ethiopia	Ethiopia	Ethiopia
Guatemala	Guatemala	—
Haiti	Haiti	—
India	India	India
Indonesia	Indonesia	Indonesia
Iran	Iran	Iran
Iraq	Iraq	Iraq
Israel	Israel	Israel
—	Lebanon	—
—	—	Libya
Mauritania	—	Mauritania
Mexico	Mexico	Mexico
Morocco	—	Morocco
Nepal	Nepal	Nepal
Nigeria	—	—
Pakistan	Pakistan	Pakistan
Peru	Peru	Peru
—	Philippines	Philippines
Rwanda	—	—
Saudi Arabia	Saudi Arabia	Saudi Arabia
South Africa	South Africa	South Africa
Sri Lanka	Sri Lanka	Sri Lanka
Sudan	Sudan	Sudan
Syria	Syria	Syria
Tajikistan	—	—
—	Togo	Togo
Turkey	Turkey	Turkey
—	Uzbekistan	Uzbekistan
—	Venezuela	Venezuela
—	Yemen	Yemen
Yugoslavia	Yugoslavia	Yugoslavia
Zaïre	—	Zaïre

on Human Rights: Brazil, China, Egypt, India, Mexico, Pakistan, Saudi Arabia, Syria and Turkey.

Two countries from the list in Table 9.1, Israel and Turkey, are discussed below to illustrate the ambivalence of the West/North regarding torture. Israel has achieved the unglamorous status of the longest-lasting inclusion on the list of violators – it has been condemned by the Commission on Human Rights since 1968; Turkey has not achieved this status. The choice has been purposeful because both Israel and Turkey continue to be on the list of largest recipients of aid, including military aid, while ongoing torture has been documented for both countries by authoritative international human rights bodies, including the Committee Against Torture.

Israel

There have been few instances where the international community has responded to human rights violations with one voice, and where condemnation for gross and systematic human rights violations was accompanied by sanctions. Rhodesia and South Africa were early precedents. Israel was – and remains – a different precedent: condemnations for human rights violations have been repeated by various UN bodies since 1968 and Israel continues to be the longest-standing item on the UN list of violators (1968–98), and yet it continues to be one of the largest aid recipients. Although much of that focus on Israel is attributable to international politics, the Committee Against Torture found Israel in breach of the Convention in 1997.

Political and financial support from the USA makes Israel immune to sanctions. Israel has been routinely condemned for human rights violations, but the US veto in the Security Council protects it from sanctions: the USA used its veto more than sixty times between 1970 and 1993, with half of those vetoes expended to block proposals to sanction Israel.[13] Although Israel's GDP per capita of more than $16,000 is well above the upper limit of eligibility for aid, Israel remains among the largest recipients of US aid, occasionally changing places with Egypt. The Middle East accounts for 40 per cent of US aid, and those allocations are not affected by human rights or development criteria.

Source: United Nations Commission on Human Rights – Torture and other cruel, inhuman or degrading treatment or punishment, Report of the Special Rapporteur, Mr. Nigel S. Rodley, U.N. Doc. E/CN:4/1994/31 of 6 January 1994, E/CN.4/1995/34 of 12 January 1995, and E/CN.4/1996/35 of 9 January 1996; Report of the Working Group on Enforced or Involuntary Disappearances, U.N. Doc. E/CN.4/1994/26 of 22 December 1993, E/CN.4/1995/36 of 30 December 1994, and E/CN.4/1996/38 of 15 January 1996; Extrajudicial, summary or arbitrary executions, Report by the Special Rapporteur, Mr. Bacre Waly Ndiaye, U.N. Doc. E/CN.4/1994/7 of 7 December 1993, E/CN.4/1995/61 of 14 December 1994, and E/CN.4/1996/4 of 25 January 1996.

The European Union (EU; formerly the European Community, EC) suspended aid to Israel on a number of occasions, and individual governments have imposed arms embargoes. In 1987–88 the European Parliament refused to give assent to an agreement with Israel because of human rights violations.[14] Although Israel has had a trade agreement with the EC since 1975, her attempts to strengthen ties were routinely linked to progress in the peace process.[15] Israel's suppression of *intifada* triggered sanctions. *Intifada*, the Palestinian unarmed uprising against Israeli occupation in the West Bank and Gaza Strip, prompted the European Parliament to veto a trade agreement with Israel; that agreement was subsequently made conditional upon 'progress towards an Arab–Israeli peace agreement.'[16] Cooperation with Israel was suspended again in 1990. In July 1995, the EU signed two agreements with Israel, one on trade and another on research and development, thus 'rewarding Israel for its efforts in the Middle East Peace process'.[17]

The Committee Against Torture (CAT) requested a special report from Israel following widespread publicity for the legalization of physical pressure against detainees by Israel's judiciary, and found such interrogation practices in breach of the Convention.[18] The Committee had already found Israel in breach of the Convention in 1994, when it examined her initial report, because torture was not outlawed; subsequent judicial decisions legalized the use of physical pressure in interrogation,[19] and a great deal of publicity followed. The CAT requested a special report from Israel, in which interrogation practices were cursorily described (the official justification was that interrogations would become ineffective if suspects knew in advance what could and could not be done to them), and the much-criticized court judgement was attached. That judgement confirmed that 'physical pressure is permitted in a situation where conditions for the defence of necessity exist.'[20] As Israel's delegation stated before the UN Commission on Human Rights in March 1996, 'the State of Israel was at war against terror and was exercising its right to self-defence.'[21] Such necessity existed when interrogation could prevent a terrorist bomb from being exploded, and the representatives of Israel clarified that investigators were required to balance 'anticipated danger to the population, the urgency of obtaining information, and alternative ways of averting the danger'.[22]

Turkey

A wide range of human rights issues have been raised in the relations of the West/North with Turkey: the lack of protection for detainees against torture and ill-treatment; the broad definition of 'terrorism', which includes publication of texts critical of the government's human rights policy and practice; protracted armed conflict in the southeastern part of the country; the military occupation of northern Cyprus (with the Turkish Republic of Northern Cyprus recognized by Turkey alone). None of these criticisms has had much impact, however. The main reason is Turkey's strategic importance. It is defined as the cusp between West and East, Europe and the Middle East. Turkey's strategic importance increased in the Gulf War and during its aftermath. The USA has supported Turkish military and civilian governments by providing military and economic aid as well as occasionally reporting enthusiastically on the improvement of the human rights situation. The *1983 State Department Country Report on Human Rights Practices* noted the 'declining numbers of complaints of torture by prisoners, and increasing numbers of convictions of police personnel for torture'.[23]

Just prior to publication of that report, Germany suspended approval of a loan to Turkey in response to the military coup of September 1980. The European Union has had an association agreement with Turkey since 1963, and the European Parliament's initiative in linking human rights to the EC's cooperation first focused on Turkey in 1983; Turkey has remained an almost permanent item on the European Parliament's agenda. In 1987, Parliament refused to give its assent to agreements with Turkey and Israel, in both cases because of human rights violations, although that was not the sole reason.[24] The European Parliament made human rights in Turkey a widely publicized issue in 1994–96 concerning the approval of the customs union with the EU. Both constitution and anti-terrorism legislation were amended so as to obtain approval of the EU–Turkey customs union treaty, and some political prisoners were released.[25] At exactly that time, ten contributors to a book published by the Human Rights Foundation of Turkey under the title *We Protect Human Rights with Imperfect Constitution and Laws* were indicted for the criminal offence of insulting the 'laws of the Republic of Turkey'.[26] The European Parliament again suspended aid to Turkey in September 1996 because of 'Turkey's poor human rights record.'[27]

Turkey's military raids to root out the PKK (Kurdistan Workers' Party) led to concerns among its main donors. In July 1994, Turkey reportedly rejected $364 million military aid from the USA because Congress was debating prohibition of misdirection of US aid for internal security. The USA relented because 'America depends on military bases in Turkey'.[28] Germany and Denmark stopped military sales to Turkey during its 1995 military operation in northern Iraq and Turkey retaliated by banning arms purchases from Denmark.[29] Human Rights Watch reported that, besides Denmark and Germany, the Netherlands, Norway and South Africa suspended military sales to Turkey because weapons has been used in counter-insurgency and/or anti-terrorism operations.[30] Military exports to Turkey subsequently resumed, as did controversy.[31]

While donors' concerns were directed at the use of their financial and military aid, none has been voiced thus far about Turkey's refusal to implement its human rights obligations relating to the prohibition of torture. Turkey rejected cooperation with the European Committee for Prevention of Torture (CPT), and then with the Committee Against Torture (CAT). It thereby created a test case for the enforcement of international human rights obligations by other parties to the two treaties.

Whilst governments are generally reluctant to take other governments to court over human rights violations, an exception was the case against Turkey brought by Denmark, France, the Netherlands, Norway and Sweden under the European Convention on Human Rights. The case ended in 1985 with a friendly settlement, which included a commitment by Turkey to report on measures it adopted against torture. Turkey may or may have not prepared such reports (three were to be made): no public information has ever been made available.[32] Torture reappeared as an issue of controversy in 1992, with the CPT's public statement on Turkey. The reason was that torture was continuing, particularly in police cells. In defiance of the European Convention for the Prevention of Torture, which obligates parties to allow the CPT access to all places where people are held in detention, to liaise with the CPT, and to follow up on its recommendations, Turkey refused to cooperate. The CPT is a unique international body with a preventive rather than condemnatory role. It issues confidential reports based on visits to prisons, addressed to the respective government and suggesting measures to improve protection against ill-treatment of detainees. Despite the harsh criticism to which the Committee subjects all governments, ranging from Denmark to Spain, and from the United Kingdom to Hungary, all cooperate with the Committee. The CPT's public statement on Turkey was motivated by findings from its two visits and the failure of the government to implement the Committee's key recommendations to strengthen safeguards against torture and constrain the powers of anti-terrorism units.[33] A similar path was followed by the Committee Against Torture (CAT) within the United Nations. The CAT initiated in 1990 a confidential examination of information indicating that torture continued in Turkey; it found that torture was systematic, and made its conclusions public.[34]

Conflicts within US Foreign Policy

Israel and Turkey are far from being isolated cases that can be cited as evidence of conflict within foreign policies, where human rights lose out to other foreign policy objectives, while denials of human rights are justified by the threat of terrorism. The USA is taken below as an example of conflicts between different objectives of foreign policy and the effects of their translation into aid. A brief summary of US aid to Central America over past decades highlights the effects of a change of governance on retroactive questions of US complicity during decades of institutionalized repression. During the Cold War, *the* foreign policy priority was containment of communism; this overshadowed human rights considerations that were intended to constrain US complicity in abuses abroad. The end of the Cold War did not elevate human rights as a foreign policy concern; on the contrary. Torture is implicitly justified in policies designed to suppress terrorism or drug trafficking abroad, while there is no ready-made human rights response to challenge them.

Central America

Self-granted impunity has often accompanied changes of governance in South America, and has raised many unanswered questions about foreign – especially US – support for previous regimes. In El Salvador, US economic aid in the period 1980–91 exceeded $3 billion and military aid $1 billion – averaging an annual $100 per inhabitant.[35] US support was suspended on few occasions, despite the presence of human rights criteria in US foreign policy. In December 1983 an announcement was made that aid would stop unless killing by death squads diminished, and indeed they did.[36] In 1985, US legislation (which had prohibited assistance to foreign police) was modified so as to exempt El Salvador; such assistance was conditioned by requiring the US president to notify Congress that El Salvador was making significant progress in eliminating human rights violations.[37] President Reagan thus certified that El Salvador was making progress in human rights, while the US State Department reported serious violations, including torture.[38]

The previous role of the USA came to light when transition in El Salvador began. In September 1991 nine members of the armed forces were tried for the murder in November 1990 of six Jesuit priests, professors at the Central American University. Their housekeeper and her daughter were also killed because the officers had been instructed not to leave witnesses. Two officers were condemned to thirty years' imprisonment, but seven soldiers were acquitted because they had followed orders. That trial, which the UN Special Rapporteur called a 'landmark in the recent history of criminal justice',[39] was one of the first steps in the process of peace-making. The trial revealed the dark side of US assistance because 'all of the soldiers who stood trial were products of the US military training.'[40]

The USA had also been the major source of military aid and training for Guatemala's armed forces, all the way from the US-supported military coup of 1954 to the prohibition by Congress of further military aid to Guatemala in 1978 because of widely reported military atrocities. The legislative prohibition of military aid to Guatemala lasted till 1983, but it did not prevent the continuation of US military support, which was merely re-labelled.[41] The underlying reasoning for linking US aid to human rights in the early 1970s, namely to halt complicity in human rights violations, came to light again in the 1990s. The US intervention of 1954 had set up 'an institutional structure of domination built to violate human rights',[42] and the open acknowledgement of support to military regimes increased, not only in the case of Guatemala but also Honduras. Because the USA could not have been brought before the Inter-American Court of Human Rights in the precedent Velasquez case, its complicity was discussed in the media: 'The Hondurans got millions of dollars of aid (much of which went straight to the army), and America's blessing on the human-rights record of the police and the army.'[43] Domestic legal remedies were used in the USA for Guatemala. General Hector Gramajo, a former defence minister of Guatemala, was found responsible for violations in nine cases of torture and summary executions, and victims' families were granted $47.5 million punitive damages by US courts.[44]

The inclusion of human rights in foreign policy may, with the benefit of hindsight, have opened the way to holding governments accountable for supporting and/or tolerating institutionalized human rights violations abroad. Such accountability has thus far been retroactive and limited to exposure. Making it proactive rather than retroactive would necessitate profound changes in foreign policy.

Terrorism and drug trafficking

During previous decades, human rights activism focused on prominent political dissidents in various countries and regions. Public support was easily mobilized for victims of political killings and harassment; it would have been much more difficult to mobilize public support for the protection of drug traffickers or terrorists. Because human rights activism is often associated with *Amnesty International*, victims of human rights violations are seen as people who were tortured or killed because of their ideas or ideals.

Problems of anti-government violence imposed themselves upon human rights activists, academics and governments. They began with controversies related to the legitimacy of armed struggle for national liberation, and broadened in the 1990s to all types of violence. Governments reacted rapidly in self-defence. Peru and Colombia tabled an initiative before the United Nations Commission on Human Rights to place terrorism on the human rights agenda,[45] and the issue attained prominence at the 1993 Conference on Human Rights, which found that terrorism aimed at destruction of human rights should be combated.[46] Terrorism was added to the draft document for the 1993 World Conference on Human Rights, and the representative of Turkey asked

> what in the West made some, perhaps most, human rights circles sympathize with terrorist movements. It would seem that they thought that the deep frustration caused by 'repression' created terrorists, who originally were delicate souls ready to sacrifice themselves for others.... These circles generally supported terrorism warfare as an unfortunate but necessary path to a more humane order.[47]

The failure of the final document of the Vienna Conference to stress the necessity of responding to terrorism with human rights safeguards was rectified by the General Assembly in December 1993, which called upon governments to combat terrorism 'in accordance with international standards of human rights'.[48]

International human rights bodies faced the situation whereby terrorism served as the main justification for government policies that denied individual rights and freedoms, often including freedom from torture. The Inter-American Commission on Human Rights avoided including terrorism into its mandate by pointing out, first, the heritage of justifications of systematic human rights violations by the threat of terrorism, and, second, the absence of a definition of terrorism, which enables governments to use the label of terrorism as justification for the denial of human rights.[49] The Human Rights Committee expressed its concern at terrorist violence in Peru in the 1990s, but censured the 'excessive force and violence used by the military'; it concluded that 'combating terrorism with arbitrary and excessive State violence cannot be justified under any circumstances.'[50]

Peru had in 1987–90 the largest number of documented disappearances in the world. Inter-governmental human rights bodies condemned 'the persistence of recourse to terror and indiscriminate violence as instruments for the settlement of social and political conflicts'.[51] The USA, however, endorsed Peru's claim that 'the chief source of human rights violations remained *Sendero Luminoso*'.[52] Peru had been ruled mostly by the military this century. At the time of the 1980 elections, which aimed to return the country to civilian rule, Sendero Luminoso (Shining Path) started military operations (or terrorist actions, in the government's preferred language) to disrupt elections. During the 1980s, with changing civilian governments, Peru suffered numerous casualties in the terrorism versus anti-terrorism battle. Alberto Fujimori was elected in 1990, promised victory in the battle against terrorism, and in 1992 suspended parliament and the judiciary in order to achieve it. A new constitution was adopted in May 1993, and Fujimori was re-elected in 1995, having defeated Sendero Luminoso. The US government defined the 1992 *autogolpe* as a constitutional crisis rather than an interruption of democracy, while the US media defined it as 'Fujimori's military-backed clampdown on dissent and democracy'.[53] Advocates of continued US support to Fujimori's Peru were many. They included William Odom, the director of the National Security Agency 1985–88, who urged the West to differentiate amongst dictators and assist those committed to privatization and free-marketization.[54] The Inter-American (OAS) political bodies 'deplored' but did not condemn Fujimori's *autogolpe*; nor did they call for sanctions. The USA suspended military aid, but not for law enforcement.[55] The priority attached to combating terrorism and drug trafficking in US foreign policy justified such continued support.

The 1996 compromise on Colombia within the UN Commission on Human Rights illustrates a similar conflict between human rights and foreign policy priorities. Neither investigative nor condemnatory UN action could be agreed upon for Colombia, despite extensive documentation of ongoing abuses. The compromise was to set up an office of the High Commissioner on Human Rights in Colombia, with the task of monitoring 'violations committed by agents of the state as well as paramilitary groups, guerilla groups and, possibly, persons involved in drug trafficking and the cartels'.[56] The chairman's statement embodied that agreement, and noted that arbitrary killings, disappearances and torture take place in Colombia but cannot be combated because the military exercises jurisdiction, but does not prosecute agents of the state. The future office of the High Commissioner was mandated to 'assist the Colombian authorities in developing policies and programmes for the promotion and protection of human rights and to observe violations of human rights in the country, making analytical reports to the High Commissioner.'[57] Because human rights assistance was previously provided to Colombia, little enthusiasm accompanied that compromise. While the UN's assistance was plagued with controversies, the USA was providing assistance to Colombia for the suppression of drug trafficking: 'The bulk of military items donated or sold to Colombia since 1989 have been provided under the guise of war on drugs.'[58]

The Reagan administration declared in 1986 that drug trafficking constituted a national security threat to the USA. The US International Narcotics Control Act of 1989 provided grounds for assistance to Bolivia,

Colombia and Peru.[59] Bolivia and Colombia were exempt from human rights criteria otherwise included in US foreign policy because priority was attached to suppression of drug production and trafficking. The USA demanded the resignations of the minister of the interior and the head of national police in Bolivia in 1991 because of their suspected involvement in drug trafficking, and they resigned so that $100 million in aid could be disbursed.[60] In 1992 Colombia received $143 million from the United States and 'President George Bush warned the U.S. Congress that he would veto attempts to attach conditions to aid.'[61] UN human rights bodies looked into disappearances and summary executions in Colombia in 1988 and 1989, but, despite ample documentation and NGO lobbying, Colombia was investigated and provided with advisory services. That programme consisted, as it usually does, of support for legal reform and national institutions. Its evaluation in 1993 broadened the scope of inquiry to include 'paramilitary groups, terrorism, drug trafficking, widespread armed violence, impunity and corruption'.[62]

Obstacles to Opposing Torture beyond National Borders

The two pillars of international human rights activism are exposing and opposing human rights violations. For countries such as Israel and Turkey, the work of international human rights bodies made exposure authoritative, but opposing the continuation of torture is beyond their powers. For countries such as El Salvador and Guatemala, a change of regime opened the way towards retroactive accountability domestically, but foreign involvement remains beyond the powers of those domestic institutions. For foreign policy priorities such as combating terrorism and drug trafficking, systematic exposure of abuses will only happen if obstacles to access to information can be overcome. Opposing torture beyond national borders requires, however, a profound change in foreign policy.

When human rights conditionality became a prominent topic of international human rights politics, the focus was on the human rights performance of aid-receiving rather than aid-giving countries. Nevertheless, the complicity of the latter inevitably entered the debate. One important reason was that human rights was added to foreign policy because previous complicity was exposed and opposed. The responsibility of aid-giving countries for such misbehaviour has rarely been tackled, however. One reason is the already mentioned limitation of governmental responsibility for human rights violations to the territory and people under its jurisdiction. Another reason is the orientation of debates about human rights in foreign policy towards development rather than military and/or security aid. Such an orientation is largely the result of obstacles to the access of information about all relevant facets of military and/or security aid, especially when such aid is used for internal repression. The inclusion of human rights in foreign policy – paradoxically – reduced access to information and further confused issues by relabelling. Foreign assistance does not have to mention an objectionable term such as 'internal repression' and can be earmarked instead as support for combating terrorism and drug trafficking. Human rights safeguards are at their weakest when governments pursue such apparently legitimate and publicly supported objectives; when that pursuance takes place beyond national borders, potential – if weak – safeguards often evaporate.

Human rights have become a part of foreign policy of most countries in the West/North, and are mainly used as eliminatory or punitive criteria. Human rights as eliminatory criteria make a recipient country ineligible for aid, while aid will be suspended if a recipient's human rights record is negatively evaluated by the donor. One aim of foreign policies which interpret human rights as eliminatory and/or punitive criteria is to dissociate the donor from violative practices by the recipient.[63] That should – but sometimes does not – preclude supplying torture equipment and training foreign military and/or security personnel in its use. The former UN Special Rapporteur on Torture noted in his 1986 report that US export regulations encompassed the licensing of 'specially designed implements of torture',[64] a decade after human rights had become part of US foreign policy and supporting legislation. Public calls demanding the accountability of the US government for torture abroad accompanied profound changes of governance in Latin and Central America during the last decade. Layers of conflict within US foreign policy came to light: while US foreign policy professed commitment to human rights, US assistance for combating terrorism implicitly justified the absence of human rights safeguards, while the combating of drugs trafficking effectively excluded such safeguards. Torture can be used to curtail dissent or to curb criminality, but the official justification is routinely the latter. The international outcry is proverbially strong when political prisoners are victims, while the fate of people who are referred to as 'common criminals' does not prompt international publicity. When the allegation is that victims of abuse were terrorists or drug traffickers, few voices are raised demanding governmental accountability.

The basic premise of international human rights is national protection. Each government, representing the state, is obliged to secure human rights protection within the borders of that state. Complaints of human rights violations cannot target another government even if factual evidence could be gathered to demonstrate that a foreign rather than national government had institutionalized torture. That legal gap cannot be closed by reliance on foreign policy. Richard Bilder pointed out a long time ago that the basic problem of human rights in foreign policy was 'finding selfish national interest reasons why governments should be concerned with denials of human rights in other countries.'[65] Such selfish national interests guide foreign policy, in which people in other countries have no say because democracy ends at national borders. Securing freedom from torture abroad is therefore impeded by double jeopardy: both democratic and legal safeguards end at national borders.

The absolute prohibition of torture implies that there can be no legitimate security purpose for its use, external or internal. Previous decades focused on external security, responding to the prevalence of international conflicts. The international arms control regime which evolved over past decades prioritized international security, and was oriented against nuclear proliferation and weapons of mass destruction. The heritage of the Cold War counterpoised the national security of exporting countries by restricting the export of military and strategic goods and technologies to Cold War enemies. Efforts to constrain outside involvement in armed conflicts failed more often than not, and counter-insurgency strategies legitimized outside involvement so as to prevent changes in the geopolitical division of the world at the time – a strategy embodied in the containment of communism.

In the 1990s the pattern of conflicts was transformed by the prominence of internal security. This is reflected in arms exports. The export of police and riot-control equipment from the USA in the 1980s averaged $10 million and increased fivefold in the early 1990s.[66] The lack of a post-Cold War international control regime and the absence of knowledge of governmental practices to inform such a regime make safeguards against facilitating torture beyond national borders a formidable task. Free trade in goods and services (that is, trade in torture equipment and training in its use) is a profitable business, in which the West/North seems to be leading. Although torture can be effective without imported modern equipment, it is undoubtedly facilitated through continuing free trade in such goods and services.

Notes

1. *Commission on Human Rights: Military Aid to Governments Practising Torture: Written Statement Submitted by Human Rights Watch*, U.N. Doc. E/CN.4/1995/NGO/ 6 of 31 January 1995, para. 1.

2. *Commission on Human Rights: Human Rights and Terrorism*, resolution 1996/47 of 19 April 1996, preamble.

3. *United Nations: World Conference on Human Rights, Vienna: Vienna Declaration and Programme of Action*, 14–25 June 1993, U.N. Doc. A/CONF.157/23 of 12 July

1993, part II, para. 56.

4. Communications No. 13/1993 (Mutombo *v.* Switzerland) and No. 15/1994 (Khan *v.* Canada).

5. 'European Commission of Human Rights: Cyprus versus Turkey', *Yearbook of the European Convention of Human Rights*, vol. 18, 1975, p. 118.

6. *International Court of Justice: Military and Paramilitary Activities against Nicaragua: Nicaragua versus USA*, Judgement of 27 June 1986, para. 115.

7. J. Hoagland, 'Missteps in Somalia, but Overall the Operation is Encouraging', *International Herald Tribune*, 15 April 1993; H. Clarke and R. Rollnick, 'Belgian "Racist" Troops Row', *The European*, 15–18 July 1993; R. Graham, 'Italy to Probe Torture Claims', *Financial Times*, 14–15 June 1997; S. Bates, 'Peacekeeping "Torturers" Go on Trial', *Guardian Weekly*, 29 June 1997.

8. *Parliamentary Assembly of the Council of Europe: Resolution 928 (1989) on arms sales and human rights of 27 September 1989*, reproduced in U.N. Doc. E/CN.4/1990/65, para. 5, 17.

9. 'European Parliament: Export of Repressive Technologies, Resolution of 19 January 1995', reproduced in *Human Rights Law Journal*, vol. 16, no. 1–3, 1995, para. 3, 74.

10. E. Regehr, 'Military Sales', in R.O. Matthews and C. Pratt, eds, *Human Rights in Canadian Foreign Policy*, McGill–Queen's University Press, Kingston and Montreal, 1988, p. 215.

11. P. Eavis and A. Shannon, 'Arms and Dual-use Export Controls: Priorities for the European Union', *Saferworld Briefing*, Bristol, June 1994, p. 9.

12. *Commission on Human Rights: Report of the Special Rapporteur, Mr. Nigel S. Rodley: Torture and other cruel, inhuman or degrading treatment or punishment*, U.N. Doc. E/CN.4/1997/7 of 10 January 1997.

13. S.D. Bailey, *The UN Security Council and Human Rights*, St. Martin's Press, New York, 1994, pp. 127–8.

14. M. Zwamborn, 'Human Rights Promotion and Protection through the External Relations of the European Community and the Twelve', *Netherlands Quarterly of Human Rights*, vol. 1, no. 1, 1989, p. 18.

15. H. Carnegy, 'EC Links Trade Deal to Israeli Peace Progress', *Financial Times*, 11 July 1991.

16. Ibid.

17. L. Barber, 'Haggling Ends with EU–Israel Trade Accord', *Financial Times*, 19 July 1995.

18. 'A UN Finding of Torture: Panel Says Israel is Violating Convention', *International Herald Tribune*, 10–11 May 1997.

19. 'Legitimizing Torture: The Israeli High Court of Justice Rulings in the Bilbeisi, Hamdan and Mubarak Cases', Israeli Information Centre for Human Rights in the Occupied Territories, B'Tselem, Jerusalem, January 1977.

20. *Committee Against Torture: Special report by Israel submitted in accordance with a request made by the CAT on 22 November 1996*, U.N. Doc. CAT/C/33/Add.2 of 6 January 1997, para. 4, 7.

21. *Commission on Human Rights: Statement of Mr Landman (Observer for Israel): Summary record of the 3rd meeting, 19 March 1996*, U.N. Doc. E/CN.4/1996/SR.3 of 30 April 1996, para. 24.

22. *Committee Against Torture: Statement of Mr Nitzan (Israel): Summary record of the 296th meeting of the CAT on 7 May 1997*, U.N. Doc. CAT/C/SR.296 of 15 May 1997, para. 31.

23. 'Country Reports on Human Rights Practices for 1983', Department of State, Washington DC, February 1984, p. 1108.

24. Zwamborn, 'Human Rights Promotion and Protection', p. 18.

25. H. Pope, 'Kurdish MPs Freed for "Europe's Sake"', *Independent*, 27 October 1995.

26. 'International Helsinki Federation for Human Rights: Once again, Turkey prosecutes human rights defenders. Their "crime": criticising Turkey's laws', press release of 15 December 1995.

27. P. Buonadonna, 'Union Struggles with Human Rights', *The European*, 26 September–2 October 1996; 'Turkey: Two-faced', *The Economist*, 26 October 1996, p. 45.

28. 'Turkey: Hold the Funds', *Newsweek*, 4 July 1994; 'Arms Aid to Turkey?', *International Herald Tribune*, 18 October 1995.

29. 'Turkey Bans Arms from Denmark', *International Herald Tribune*, 1 June 1995.

30. 'Weapons Transfers and Violations of the Laws of War in Turkey', Human Rights Watch, New York, 1995.

31. 'The United States and Europe Plan Further Weapons Sales to Turkey Despite Continuing Violation of Human Rights', Human Rights Watch, Brussels, 17 January 1997.

32. M.T. Kamminga, 'Is the European Convention on Human Rights Sufficiently Equipped to Cope with Gross and Systematic Violations?', *Netherlands Quarterly of Human Rights*, vol. 12, no. 2, 1994, pp. 153–64.

33. *European Committee for the Prevention of Torture and Inhuman or Degrading Treatment or Punishment: Public Statement on Turkey of 15 December 1992*, Doc. CPT/Inf (93)1, para. 2.

34. *Committee Against Torture: Summary account of the results of the proceedings under article 20 of the United Nations Treaty against Torture concerning Turkey of 9 November 1993*, U.N. Doc. A/48/44/Add.1, para. 5.

35. 'El Salvador's Decade of Terror', Americas Watch, New York, 1991, Appendix A, p. 141.

36. 'From the Ashes. A Report on Justice in El Salvador', Lawyers Committee for Human Rights, New York, 1987, pp. 3–4.

37. Congressional record H. 6718 of 29 July 1985.

38. D.C. Kramer, 'International Human Rights', in T.E. Yarborough, ed., *The Reagan Administration and Human Rights*, Praeger, New York, 1985, pp. 234–6.

39. *Commission on Human Rights: Final report to the Commission on Human Rights on the situation of human rights in El Salvador by Mr. José Antonio Pastor Ridruejo*, U.N. Doc. E/CN.4/32 of 16 January 1992, para. 88.

40. C.J. Arnson, 'Bizarre Justice in El Salvador', *International Herald Tribune*, 4 October 1991.

41. K. Sikkink, 'The Effectiveness of US Foreign Policy, 1973–1980', in L. Whitehead, ed., *The International Dimensions of Democratization. Europe and the Americas*, Oxford University Press, Oxford, 1996, p. 98.

42. E.S. Herman, 'The United States versus Human Rights in the Third World', *Harvard Human Rights Journal*, vol. 4, 1991, p. 91.

43. 'Honduras: Breeze of Change', *The Economist*, 3 April 1993, pp. 49–50.

44. C.B. Daly and P. Thomas, '$47.5m Blow for Guatemalan General', *Guardian Weekly*, 23 April 1995.

45. Resolution 1990/75 of 7 March 1990, United Nations.

46. *United Nations: World Conference on Human Rights, Vienna: Vienna Declaration*

and Programme of Action, 14–25 June 1993, U.N. Doc. A/CONF.157/23 of 12 July 1993, para. 17.

47. *Commission on Human Rights: forty-ninth session, summary record of the 46th meeting, 1 March 1993*, U.N. Doc. E/CN.4/1993/SR.46 of 8 March 1993, para. 11.

48. *United Nations: General Assembly resolution 48/122 of 20 December 1993: Human Rights and Terrorism*, para. 2.

49. 'Groups of Armed Irregulars and Human Rights', *Annual Report of the Inter-American Commission on Human Rights 1990–1991*, Doc. OEA/Ser.L/V/II.79.rev.1, Doc. 12, Washington DC, 22 February 1991, p. 513.

50. *Human Rights Committee: Comments of the Committee relating to the consideration of the second periodic report of Peru*, U.N. Doc. CCPR/C/79/Add.8 of 25 September 1992, para. 8.

51. 'The Inter-American Commission on Human Rights: Press Release No. 9/89', Lima, 12 May 1989, p. 2.

52. *U.S. Department of State: Country Reports on Human Rights Practices for 1993*, Washington DC, February 1994, p. 530.

53. 'Peru's President Tightens his Grip', *International Herald Tribune*, 8 April 1992.

54. W.E. Odom, 'Durable Democracy Requires a State that Works', *International Herald Tribune*, 14 April 1992.

55. *Human Rights in Peru One Year after Fujimori's Coup*, Americas Watch, Washington DC, April 1993, p. 45.

56. J. Bauer, 'Highlights of the 1996 Commission on Human Rights', *Human Rights Tribune*, August–September 1996, p. 40.

57. *Commission on Human Rights: Chairman's statement on the situation of human rights in Colombia of 23 April 1996, Report on the Fifty-Second Session*, U.N. Doc. E/CN.4/1996/177, p. 299.

58. State *of War: Political Violence and Counterinsurgency in Colombia*, Human Rights Watch/Americas, New York, December 1993, p. 130.

59. A. Laars and K. O'Flaherty, 'Colombia: Human Rights Implications of United States Drug Control Policy', *Harvard Human Rights Journal*, vol. 3, 1990, pp. 186–94.

60. 'Bolivia: It's All Money', *The Economist*, 23 March 1991, p. 48.

61. N. Maharaj, 'In Colombia, US is Not Practising what it Preaches', *Terra Viva*, 23 June 1993, p. 8.

62. *United Nations: Report of the evaluation mission on the support project for the Office of the Presidential Adviser for the Promotion and Protection of Human Rights in Colombia*, U.N. Doc. E/CN.4/1993/61/Add.3 of 6 September 1993, para. 128.

63. K. Tomaševski, *Between Sanctions and Elections: Human Rights Performance of Donor Governments*, Pinter Publishers/Cassell, London, 1997.

64. *Commission on Human Rights: Report by the Special Rapporteur, Mr. P. Kooijmans: Torture and other cruel, inhuman or degrading treatment or punishment*, U.N. Doc. E/CN.4/1986/15 of 19 Feburary 1986, para. 120.

65. R. Bilder, 'Human Rights and U.S. Foreign Policy: Short-term Prospects', *Virginia Journal of International Law*, vol. 14, 1974, p. 615.

66. M.T. Klare, 'The Arms Trade in the 1990s: Changing Patterns, Rising Dangers', *Third World Quarterly*, vol. 17, no. 5, 1996, p. 870.

10

The Contribution of Truth Commissions
Priscilla B. Hayner

At the point of transition following a brutal and repressive regime, a state and its people are left with a legacy of violence, bitterness and pain – and often many hundreds or thousands of perpetrators who deserve prosecution and punishment for their crimes. Yet the experience of successful prosecutions after a period of massive atrocities has been limited, as under-resourced and sometimes politically compromised judicial systems struggle to confront such widespread and politically contentious crimes. Struggling with the limited options for confronting past atrocities, and with an eye towards the challenge of building a human rights culture for the future, many new governments have turned to mechanisms outside the judicial system to both confront and learn from the horrific crimes of the past. There has been increasing interest, especially, in mechanisms of official truth-seeking, through the creation of temporary commissions to dig up, investigate and analyse the pattern of politically motivated rights crimes of the past.

Such transitional truth-seeking bodies have become much more common in the 1990s, and have taken on the generic name of 'truth commissions'. Officially sanctioned by the government (and sometimes with the agreement of the former armed opposition), these bodies focus on documenting and investigating a pattern of abuses in the past, and set down recommendations of how to prevent the recurrence of such practices in the future. Each of these truth-seeking bodies to date has been unique, different in form, structure and mandate from those that have gone before. Not all, in fact, are formally called truth commissions: in Guatemala, for example, there was a 'Historical Clarification Commission' created out of the United Nations-negotiated peace accords; in Argentina, a 'Commission on the Disappearance of Persons', and in some countries they are simply called commissions of inquiry. Nevertheless, these bodies all share certain common elements and are created for similar purposes. By 'truth commission', a fairly specific kind of investigatory commission is implied. I point to four identifying characteristics: first, a truth commission is focused on the past. Second, it investigates not a singular event, but the record of abuses over a period of time (often highlighting a few cases to demonstrate and describe patterns or large numbers of abuses). Third, a truth commission is a temporary body, generally concluding with the submission of a report. And finally, a truth commission is somehow officially sanctioned by the government (and/or by the opposition, where relevant) to investigate the past. This official sanction allows the commission more power, access to information and protection to undertake investigations, and a greater likelihood that its conclusions and recommendations will be given serious consideration.

We should expect differences between commissions, as each country must shape a process from its own historical, political and cultural context. Unlike courts, which generally stand as permanent bodies, and about which there are many international norms regarding their appropriate structure, components, powers, and the minimal standards under which their proceedings should be undertaken, there are many aspects of truth commissions which will differ from country to country. Some are given subpoena powers, or even strong search-and-seizure powers, and hold public hearings in front of television cameras. Others hold all investigations and interviews of victims and witnesses behind closed doors, may not have the power to compel witnesses to testify, and release information to the public only through a final report. Also, commissions' mandates will differ on the types of abuses to be investigated, perhaps including acts by the armed opposition as well as government forces, for example, or perhaps limited to certain specific practices such as disappearances. Such variations are a natural reflection of the differences in countries' politics, political culture, history and needs.

Truth commissions can play a critical role in a country struggling to come to terms with a history of massive human rights crimes. A number of past commissions have been notable successes: their investigations welcomed by survivors of the violence and by human rights advocates alike, their reports widely read, their summary of facts considered conclusive and fair. Such commissions are often referred to as having a 'cathartic' effect in society, as fulfilling the important step of formally acknowledging a long-silenced past. But not all truth commissions have been so successful. Some have been significantly limited from a full and fair accounting of the past – limited by mandate, by political constraints or restricted access to information, or by a basic lack of resources, for example – and have reported only a narrow slice of the 'truth'. Some commission reports have been kept confidential after being submitted to the government.

A truth commission should be distinguished from a government human rights office set up to watch over current human rights abuses, and also from nongovernmental projects documenting past abuses. There are also important distinctions between these truth commissions and criminal prosecutions, with important strengths and weaknesses in either approach. A truth commission is not a court of law; it does not determine individual criminal liability or order criminal sanctions. On the other hand, a truth commission can do many things that courts can't or generally don't do. Trials focus on the actions of specific individuals; truth commissions focus on the large pattern of overall events. It is true that some trials help shed light on overall patterns of rights violations, but this is generally not their focus or intent.[1] Also, courts do not typically investigate the various social or political factors which led to the violence, or the internal structure of abusive forces, such as death squads or the intelligence branch of the armed forces, all of which might be the focus of a truth commission. Courts do not submit policy recommendations or suggestions for political, military or judicial reforms. And finally, while court records may be public, court opinions are generally not widely distributed and widely read, as is typical of truth commission reports. In brief, a truth commission's strengths are in those very areas which fall outside the parameters or capabilities of a court.

Similarly, these truth-seeking bodies should be distinguished from international tribunals, such as the International Criminal Tribunal for the Former Yugoslavia and the International Criminal Tribunal for Rwanda, both created by the United Nations, or the permanent International Criminal Court which was agreed to in July 1998, and will soon be established. These international tribunals have been established in response to massive state violence, but they function with the purpose and powers of a court, very different from a commission of investigation, which typically has fewer powers but a much broader scope of inquiry.

The Increasing Use of Truth-Seeking as a Transitional Tool

Truth commissions have been multiplying rapidly around the world and gaining increasing attention in recent years.[2] Although there have been some twenty such bodies in the past 23-odd years, many have received very little international attention – such as those in Chad, Sri Lanka, Uganda and the Philippines – despite considerable attention from the press and public at the national level. Others, such as the Truth and

Reconciliation Commission in South Africa, which is to publish in 1998; the United Nations sponsored Commission on the Truth in El Salvador, which finished in 1993; the Chilean National Commission on Truth and Reconciliation, completed in 1991; or the Commission on the Disappeared in Argentina, which published its report in 1984, have received much international attention and have helped to define the field and shape the new models that are being created elsewhere.

Because a truth commission is by definition a government-sanctioned body, it can play a particularly strong role in a transition. If it is done well, such a commission can be used to begin a process of serious reform, offer reparation to victims, and strengthen other forms of accountability. Compared to nongovernmental projects, a truth commission's official status may give it greater access to government information and documentation, greater security or protection in its investigations, more attention from the press and the international community, and wider distribution of its report. Of course, there should always be concern that a government truth-seeking body will be created with no coinciding commitment to institute real reform. A commission itself does not have the power to institute reforms or make policy changes, and thus must depend on the political will and interest of the government for its recommendations to be given force.

Latin America has had some of the better known truth commissions to date. The 'National Commission on the Disappeared' in Argentina was the first truth commission to attract significant international attention. It was set up by Argentine President Raúl Alfonsín in 1983 as one of the first acts of the post-military government. In nine months, the commission compiled information documenting nearly nine thousand cases of disappearance that took place under military rule from 1976 to 1983. The commission's report, *Nunca Más*, quickly became a bestseller in Argentina: over 150,000 copies were sold in the first two months after its release, and about 5,000 copies continue to sell each year, now over thirteen years after its release. It is now one of the most-sold books ever in Argentina.[3]

The Chilean truth body, the 'National Commission on Truth and Reconciliation' was also started almost immediately after that country's return to civilian rule, in 1990. Unlike most truth commissions, it was able to investigate all cases reported to it that fit within its mandate (disappearances, political killings, politically motivated kidnappings, and deaths due to torture). It concluded its report in nine months, and President Patricio Aylwin released it to the public with an emotional appeal, broadcast on national television, begging pardon and forgiveness from the families of the victims.[4] Unfortunately, a few high-profile political killings in the weeks and months following the release of the report derailed a planned process of national discussion and public recognition of the commission's findings.[5]

The 'Commission on the Truth for El Salvador' was created through a United Nations negotiated peace accord between the government and the armed opposition, the Farabundo Martí National Liberation Front (FMLN), in 1991. Initially given six months, the commission worked for nearly nine months, including preparation time and a two-month extension, and covered a much broader set of human rights violations than the commissions of the southern cone. Directed to investigate 'serious acts of violence ... [whose] impact on society urgently demands that the public should know the truth', the commission took testimony about torture, disappearances, political killings, massacres, and politically motivated rape during twelve years of civil war, 1980–91. The report also outlined the blatant obstruction of justice by members of the judiciary and the military during this period. In contrast to the presidentially appointed and government-funded commissions in Argentina and Chile, the commission in El Salvador was sponsored by the United Nations, funded by voluntary contributions from UN member states, and staffed only by non-Salvadorans, led by three high-level, internationally respected commissioners from Colombia, Venezuela and the United States. It released its report to the public in March 1993, which included the names of over forty people responsible for abuses or for covering up evidence and blocking investigations, including senior members of the armed forces and FMLN and the president of the supreme court.[6]

The Truth and Reconciliation Commission in South Africa has brought a whole new level of interest to the subject of healing through confronting past pain, reconciling through admitting wrongs, and washing even the worst of past crimes in the public view of television cameras and public audience. The commission was established in 1995 through national legislation after over a year and a half of public debate, and strong input from all political parties and many sectors of civil society. It was given two and a half years to collect information about gross human rights violations by state bodies or by the armed opposition between 1960 and 1994, to hold public hearings, and to publish a report with recommendations for reparations and reform. Over twenty thousand victims came forward to provide testimony. In addition, the commission held a number of thematically focused hearings to examine the role of the churches, the medical establishment, the legal sector, the business community, and other institutions in passively or actively contributing to the rights violations of the past. With the use of a strong subpoena power, the ability to grant amnesty to perpetrators who confessed to politically motivated crimes, and with the many high-level political leaders that appeared before it, the commission was in the centre of the news for the full period of its work.

In addition to official truth commissions, which are sponsored or authorized by the national government (sometimes in agreement with the armed opposition), there are many examples of nongovernmental projects which have documented the patterns and practices of abuses of a prior regime. Most commonly, these are sponsored by national human rights organizations: *Uruguay: Nunca Más*, for example, was produced out of the offices of a national human rights organization, SERPAJ (Servicio Paz y Justicia, or Peace and Justice Service).[7] In Russia, the nongovernmental organization Memorial was set up in 1987 around the question of account-ability and fact finding over past events. Its staff has collected extensive archives on abuses back to 1917, and has published several books with lists of victims' names and analyses of state policies of repression.[8] There are also examples of church backing for such projects: in Paraguay the *Nunca Más* series was sponsored by the Committee of Churches;[9] in Brazil the Archbishop of São Paulo, in conjunction with the World Council of Churches, supported the efforts towards *Brasil: Nunca Mais*.[10] Because the Brazil project was carried out secretly, Church backing not only provided financial support, but also lent legitimacy to the published report. The military, having just turned over power to elected leaders, was not in a position to attack the Church (as the only identified author) when the report was published.[11]

Despite the limitations to their work, usually including restricted access to information, these unofficial projects have sometimes produced remarkable results. For the project in Brazil, for example, a team of investigators was able secretly to photocopy all of the official court papers which documented prisoners' complaints of abuse. The *Brasil: Nunca Mais* report is thus an analysis of the military regime's torture practices over fifteen years, based on these official records. When the report was released, it quickly climbed to number one on the country's bestseller list.[12]

Understanding and Preventing Torture: What Contribution from Truth Commissions?

Although the specific mandate and form may differ between commis-sions, all aim to contribute to learning about the past, offer official acknowledgement to victims, suggest political, military, police or judicial reforms necessary to keep such abuses from being repeated, and often to recommend reparations for victims. Understanding and preventing torture is a prominent aspect of this work.

A window into the practice of torture

The first task is to establish exactly what did happen, remove the silence shrouding often still painful and controversial events, and make the information publicly accessible so that it cannot be further denied. Towards this end, many commission reports have included horrifying accounts of torture, sometimes presented in the victims' own powerful voices.

The Argentine commission report is perhaps the strongest in this respect. Although its mandate was to focus on those disappeared under the seven-year military dictatorship in Argentina, the commission relied on survivors of the military detention centres to understand the practices of disappearance, which often included months of torture before being killed. Many of the 450 pages of the commission's report include passages like this one, excerpted from the testimony of Dr Norberto Liwsky – which the commission calls 'typical' of all the cases it heard. Liwsky testifies:

> One day they put me face-down on the torture table, tied me up (as always), and calmly began to strip the skin from the soles of my feet. I imagine, though I didn't see because I was blindfolded, that they were doing it with a razor blade or a scalpel. I could feel them pulling as if they were trying to separate the skin at the edge of the wound with a pair of pincers. I passed out. From then on, strangely enough, I was able to faint very easily....
>
> In between torture sessions they left me hanging by my arms from hooks fixed in the wall of the cell where they had thrown me.... Sometimes they put me on to the torture table and stretched me out, tying my hands and feet to a machine that I can't describe since I never saw it, but which gave me the feeling that they were going to tear part of my body off....
>
> The most vivid and terrifying memory I have of all that time was of always living with death. I felt it was impossible to think. I desperately tried to summon up a thought in order to convince myself I wasn't dead. That I wasn't mad. At the same time, I wished with all my heart that they would kill me as soon as possible.[13]

Or this passage of Teresa Celia Meschiati, who testified, after describing intense torture with electric prods,

> I tried to kill myself by drinking foul water in the tub which was meant for another kind of torture called *submarino*, but I did not succeed.
>
> The gradually increasing intensity of the electric prod was matched by the sadism of my torturers. There were five of them, whose names were: Guillermo Barreiro, Luis Manzanelli, José López, Jorge Romero, and Fermín de los Santos.[14]

When the commission excerpted testimony which happened to include the names of accused perpetrators, they chose to reprint the names as cited. The commission made no conclusions about culpability, however, and did not publish a final and complete list of those found to be responsible for abuses.[15]

In addition to testimony of survivors, the Argentine commission was able to reconstruct the location and even the floor plans of over three hundred secret detention centres, visiting each one, with survivors, to confirm them. This list is included in the commission report. It is not known how many people survived these detention centres, as the commission only kept track of the disappeared, those who were abducted and never seen again. The annex to the commission report lists by name each of the close to nine thousand disappeared that it was able to document.

In El Salvador, the UN Commission on the Truth took direct testimony from over 2,000 people, accounting for 7,000 victims. Of these, 20 per cent reported acts of torture (another 15 per cent concerned enforced disappearances, many of whom were likely also tortured). A statistical analysis of the testimony collected by the commission (as well as testimony handed into the commission from the files of non-governmental organizations, United Nations bodies and the government) is included in the appendix to the report, an extremely useful window into understanding the pattern of abusive practices over time and across the different regions of the country, how it affected different population groups, and what groups the accused perpetrators were from – including the military, police, death squads and the armed opposition. The text of the report itself, however, includes little detail on the practice of torture, as the approximately thirty cases chosen for in-depth investigation are all disappearances, extrajudicial executions, assassinations by death squads, or large-scale massacres. Thus a first-hand narrative, such as in the Argentine report, or even a descriptive overview of common practices, summarizing testimony received, is not included.

Not many truth commissions have held public hearings, due to serious concerns for security and fear of witnesses. In Latin America, public hearings were considered virtually unthinkable, for just these reasons (some survivors were even too fearful to appear for a private, confidential hearing). In Africa, however, a number of commissions have held public hearings, allowing victims a public stage to receive recognition for the pains suffered, and allowing the process of the truth commission to be shared nationally. The Truth and Reconciliation Commission in South Africa, tasked to uncover 'as complete a picture as possible' about 'killings, abduction, torture, and severe ill-treatment', has gone the furthest in this regard. In addition to receiving testimony in camera, the commission held public hearings all around the country, in poor black townships and in major cities, in large churches and dusty town halls, where over two thousand victims, survivors or witnesses were heard. Each of these hearings was videotaped by a special camera crew from the South African Broadcasting Corporation, and clips of the hearings were shown on the nightly news. Five hours or more of live coverage of the hearings were broadcast on the radio each day. Torture survivors described details of their torture; mothers described how sons were killed; fathers recounted land mines that had killed infant children. Over a period of more than a year, the country was washed over with story upon story of abuse and killings, to the point where it was no longer possible for anyone reasonably to deny the extent of abuse that had taken place. It was widely understood, however, that even the approximately twenty thousand victims documented by the commission were but a small portion of the true total.

In addition to hearing from victims, the South African commission also received public testimony directly from perpetrators, who admitted to the gruesome details of their own past crimes. In the first example ever of public admission from so many perpetrators (and occasionally what seemed to be genuine apology), hearing upon hearing presented torturers and killers sitting on stage, under oath, answering days of questions from lawyers, commissioners, and even directly from their former victims. These amazing scenes were possible only because the commission offered something in return: amnesty for those who disclosed the full truth and proved their crimes to be politically motivated and proportional to the political end pursued. Over 7,000 perpetrators applied for amnesty, some 1,600 of them for gross violations of human rights (other applications were for politically motivated property crimes, illegally transporting weapons, or similar acts which did not constitute a gross violation of human rights).

In many circumstances it is impossible to count the total number of victims of a previous regime. Often, where there have been years of abusive practices, it is simply impossible for a commission to document every case – for lack of time and resources, and in the interest of focusing the commission's energies on investigation as well as collecting information. In addition, some of those who lost a loved one or witnessed disappearances or massacres may not want to give testimony: some are still traumatized, or fearful of the consequences of speaking out; others, such as some former anti-apartheid activists in South Africa, simply don't consider themselves to be victims. 'I knew the consequences, the sacrifices, of fighting against the government', they say, and they don't want to ask for sympathy now. While it is thus difficult for a commission to tabulate an accurate number of torture survivors, even preliminary numbers can help to signal what the total might be. This can be important not only for historical purposes but also can assist in designing support services that would be appropriate for the needs of this population.

But some truth commissions have explicitly excluded torture survivors in their count of victims, such as the commissions in Chile, Argentina and Uruguay. The focus of a truth commission's investigations is determined by the terms of reference handed to it upon creation, which in the case of Chile and Argentina was through a presidential decree, and in Uruguay from parliament. The mandates of these commissions were focused on the investigation of the disappeared (and, in the case of Chile, also killings), and they therefore did not even try to keep track of or calculate the number of people who suffered from torture and survived.

The Uruguayan commission[16] missed the majority of the human rights violations that had taken place during the military regime because of this limited mandate: illegal detention and torture, which affected a huge proportion of the population, were ignored. As the Chilean rights advocate José Zalaquett noted, 'A systematic practice of "disappearances" as in Argentina, or, on a lesser scale, as in Chile, was not part of the Uruguayan military's repressive methodology.'[17] Writing in 1989, Zalaquett continued,

> Although it is public knowledge in Uruguay and abroad that torture was systematically practiced during the military rule, there is no officially sanctioned record documenting this practice. The military does not publicly admit to it. In private it attempts to justify torture as a last resort and a lesser evil.[18]

The Argentine commission was also tasked to investigate only disappearances, and the Chilean commission was given the slightly broader (but still limited) mandate to cover disappearances, executions, kidnappings, attempts on life by private citizens for political purposes, and torture that resulted in death.[19] In both countries, the commissions took testimony from surviving victims of torture better to understand the experience of those killed or disappeared, but the survivors themselves were not counted in the total calculation of victims, nor were their names printed in the commissions' published list of victims.

In stark contrast to the Argentine commission report, the Chilean report includes almost no direct testimony or first-person accounts of torture or other abuse. Instead, it describes, in relatively few pages and in general terms, the kinds of torture used and the effect that it had on prisoners. Yet it is clear from these descriptions how uncompromisingly brutal the torture was, such as this description of the period between September and December 1973 (the most violent period of the Chilean dictatorship, immediately following the coup):

> During these months mistreatment and torture were an almost universal feature of detention.... Torture methods were extremely varied. An almost universal technique was violent and continued beating until blood flowed and bones were broken. Another form was to make detention conditions so harsh that

they themselves constituted torture.... It was also common to hang prisoners up by their arms with their feet off the ground for very long periods of time. They might be held under water, foul smelling substances, or excrement to the brink of suffocation. There are many accusations of sexual degradation and rape. A common practice was simulated firing squad.[20]

In a number of cases, the report describes prisoners being 'tortured to the point of madness'.[21] And it makes clear how widespread torture was:

It would be impossible to present a comprehensive list of all the torture sites – there were so many – in our country during the period we are considering. During these months torture was not practiced in every single detention site, but certainly in most of them.[22]

Yet, despite these horrifying descriptions, the Chilean report defines those who survived such treatment not to be victims – only those who died from torture. '[T]he Commission has defined as victims of human rights violations those who were subjected to: ... torture resulting in death', the report makes clear.[23] Ironically, the reason for this narrow definition was because the universe of torture survivors was so large. Gisela von Muhlenbrock, as assistant to the president of Chile who helped to draft the executive decree which established the commission, says that they limited the universe of victims according to how much they would be able to afford to pay in reparations. When I asked her why torture victims were not counted as victims, she said, 'We asked ourselves, "How much can we afford?" We couldn't afford to extend compensation to everyone; so we limited the universe in terms of things we could finance.' A number of commissioners and the executive secretary of the follow-up reparations body described this limited definition as both logical and necessary. 'It would have been impossible to cover torture; there were far too many cases to investigate them all', they said.[24]

This narrow definition of 'victim' by this well-known commission in Chile contributed to a skewing of the popular understanding of who counts as a victim of the military regime: just as the commission defined it, the popular understanding is that those who survived the torture camps are not 'victims', only those who died. In an interview in Chile in 1996, for example, one journalist, who herself was twice arrested and tortured under the military regime, told me, 'Those who survived torture are not victims in Chile. They are not considered victims. When we say "victim", we mean only those who were killed or disappeared.'[25] Many others told me the same.

This narrow definition of victim has had a number of significant consequences. First, because the focus was on those who died, no one has a clear sense of how many people survived detention and torture in

Chile. Human rights activists and other close observers of the human rights situation in Chile cite numbers ranging from 10,000 to 200,000. Some human rights professionals, when asked how many torture survivors there were, wouldn't even hazard a guess.[26] The correct figure is probably somewhere between 50,000 and 100,000.

The second important consequence of this narrow definition of victim is in restricting who has access to reparations: virtually all reparations in Chile are targeted to the families of those who died or disappeared. There is an extensive reparations programme for these families, including monthly cash payments, educational and medical benefits, and exemption from military service. Victims of torture, however, receive neither official recognition nor reparation (with the exception of access to a special mental health programme, although this programme is not well known and very few have taken advantage of it). The executive secretary of the Corporation for Reparation and Reconciliation, the follow-up body to the Chilean truth commission, told me how he sometimes saw first hand the lack of fairness in this policy: 'One woman came into my office and sat down to say, "The tragedy of my family is that they didn't kill my father. He's destroyed, but they allowed him to live. It would have been better if they had killed him." Her family gets no reparations, but her father is completely destroyed as a person.'[27]

Reparations to victims

Many truth commissions have recommended that financial or other reparations be awarded to surviving victims or to families of those killed or disappeared. In Chile and Argentina, individual reparations programmes were targeted to the families of those victims listed in the commissions' reports (and also those who later reported a case that should have been included). A similar programme is expected in South Africa, where a central aspect of the commission's mandate is to study and propose a reparations policy. Commissions elsewhere have also recommended financial reparations programmes, such as in El Salvador, Haiti and Uganda, but these recommendations have not been implemented, largely due to limited resources and competing financial priorities.

The Haitian commission, for example, recommended that a special reparations commission be created as a follow-up body, to determine the 'legal, moral, and material obligations' due to victims of violence.[28] Listed first in its long chapter on recommendations, the commission outlines this proposal in some detail, suggesting that funds should come from the state, from national and international private donations, and from voluntary contributions via the United Nations.

The El Salvador report called for a special fund, 'an autonomous body with the necessary legal and administrative powers to award appropriate material compensation to the victims of violence in the shortest time possible'. It further recommended that not less than 1 per cent of all international assistance that reaches El Salvador be set aside for this fund.[29] But neither the Salvadoran government nor the international community was enthusiastic about this proposal, and the recommended fund was never established.

The likelihood that a reparations programme will be implemented in any country will be determined by the level of political interest and political will, the resources available to the state, and the number of victims that require compensation. Where resources are very limited, symbolic, community or development-oriented reparations might be considered, such as memorials, days of remembrance, or schools or community centres built in the name of victims. Many commissions have left detailed recommendations in support of such initiatives.

Preventing abuses in the future

Ultimately, a commission of inquiry into past abuses aims not only to describe what happened, but to put forward measures that will prevent such abuses from happening again. Although these commissions themselves do not have the power to implement policies or reform, they are often asked to make substantial recommendations for changes necessary in political, military, police or judicial structures, in the legal framework to protect rights, or in the social or educational sphere to promote a wider understanding of basic human rights.

The commissions in El Salvador and Chile put forward the most significant and detailed recommendations, and both of these reports were given considerable attention over the ensuing years as policy-makers used these recommendations as a guide in designing reform packages.[30] But the reforms suggested were not always easily or quickly implemented. In El Salvador, for example, there was considerable resistance in parliament to the proposal that extrajudicial confessions be prohibited from being submitted as evidence in court, which would remove a primary motivation for torturing suspects, as well as to the recommendation that the right to an attorney be guaranteed from the moment of arrest, and other recommendations to protect the rights of detainees. As common crime rose and popular demands for hard-line measures against criminals increased, politicians balked at such restrictions on what they considered to be tools in their crime-fighting strategy. But the recommendations from the Salvadoran truth commission were considered to be obligatory, by prior agreement between the parties to the peace accords, and the United Nations therefore continued to push for their implementation. After considerable delay, it was only with the intervention of a senior United Nations envoy from New York, Alvaro de Soto, that some of these reforms were passed, although some in slightly compromised form.[31]

Yet the challenge of halting years or decades of abusive practices goes far beyond writing new laws and passing new regulations. Many states which have all the right laws in place, as well as other layers of safeguards or protections, still continue to battle ongoing abuses by security forces (the New York City police force, for example, received much attention in 1997 for serious abuses against detainees). Therefore, while truth commissions have certainly contributed to necessary reforms, they have not necessarily put a stop to torture.

For example, fourteen years after the end of military rule in Argentina (and thirteen years after its truth commission report was released), torture by the police and prison guards continued. In late 1997, a UN Human Rights committee criticized Argentina for 'tolerating the continued practice of torture', despite the fact that the country is a signatory to the International Convention Against Torture. 'Many Argentines die after being tortured by the police, and the Argentine authorities have done little to stop the practice', the *New York Times* reported, citing comments of Gonzales Poblete, vice president of the UN Committee.[32] These practices of torture do not appear to be politically motivated, but are certainly reminiscent of the common practices under military rule.

Serious problems also continue in Brazil. Jim Cavallaro, Human Rights Watch representative in Brazil, told me in late 1996 that 'Torture in Brazil neither began nor ended with the military dictatorship.' They have been torturing people for years, with clear evidence of death squads back into the 1950s, he said.

> The end of the military dictatorship was by no means an end to the practice of torture, although it did end the legitimacy of torturing people from an upper middle-class background. But torture against poor, darker-skinned people is routinely practised in Brazil.[33]

Cavallaro continued

> Some say there is more torture now than during the military dictatorship. Or that it's easier to torture people now than during the military dictatorship. Before, it was possible to torture the wrong person – the cousin of a general, for example – but no one living in a *favela* [a city slum], selling drugs, with a second grade education, is the cousin of a general.

No one is keeping track of the how much torture goes on, he says; no one reports it.[34]

Even as the South African Truth and Reconciliation Commission was under way, with daily hearings airing accounts of torture and killings, there were new charges that torture was still practised by the police. It is estimated by human rights observers, such as Peter Jordi of the Witswatersrand University Law Clinic, that 1 to 2 per cent of all detainees suffered some form of torture in 1997; the primary methods employed were suffocation and electrocution.[35] In one three-month period in 1997, the Independent Complaints Directorate of South Africa, the police oversight body, reported that 255 people died in police custody or due to police action, many from shootings.[36] These charges of ongoing abuses received far less attention than the truth commission hearings about the past, although there were some serious proposals on the table to address the problem, as well as attention from the truth commission regarding what policy reforms or police-training initiatives should be recommended in their report.

Special Considerations

Women's experiences underreported

In many cultures, rape carries great social stigma, embarrassment and shame for the victim. Many women are thus understandably uncomfortable providing testimony about sexual abuse in public hearings, or even in private hearings if their testimony would then be published in a public report – with their name, and perhaps the name of the accused, printed for all to see. As a result, the full truth about women's experiences in periods of widespread conflict and repression has not been effectively recorded or reported by most truth commissions.

A number of truth commissions have been aware of the underreporting of the experiences of women victims, especially in the area of sexual crimes. In South Africa, for example, the commission found that although women made up about half of the deponents giving testimony, much of their testimony reported violence against men – their husbands, brothers or sons, for example. Women's own experiences seemed to be overshadowed or silenced. This underreporting was especially severe on the subject of sexual violence, where an extremely small number of cases were reported compared to the known widespread occurrence of rape by the police and in the inter-communal violence of the KwaZulu–Natal region.[37]

Clearly, without special attention to facilitate or encourage the reporting of women's experiences, the true picture of these violations will remain largely shrouded in silence and hidden from the history books. There are a few examples of special attention towards this issue, although none entirely successful. In South Africa, the commission held three special women's hearings, with female commissioners on the panel and, in one case, allowing women to give testimony about sexual abuse from behind a screen, out of the view of the public and television cameras. Only in Haiti, however, has a truth commission been specifically directed in its founding mandate to pay special attention to sexual abuses against women. This resulted in considerable attention being given to the issue in the commission's investigations, and a whole chapter of its report dedicated to the subject.

The Challenge of Healing and Reconciliation

> If someone had asked me when I was set free: did they torture you a lot? I would have replied: Yes, for the whole of the three months... If I were asked that same question today, I would say that I've now lived through seven years of torture.
>
> Miguel D'Agostino, file No. 3901, Argentine National
> Commission on the Disappeared[38]

Healing from torture is a painful and long-term process, as the expanding literature on this subject makes clear. Many survivors of torture must struggle daily to live with their memories. As should be expected, the idea of forgiving one's torturer and reconciling with one's former opponents or repressors is an idea that not all are willing to embrace. These two tasks – healing and reconciliation – together form the backbone of perhaps the most difficult side of any transition out of a repressive past. While negotiated transitions or constitutional agreements can settle the political differences between former opponents and lead to formal peace, many victims and former fighters of the resolved conflict may be left both traumatized and unwilling to forgive their former opponents. When victims and perpetrators run into the many tens of thousands, or when the country is deeply polarized down ideological, race, class or geographic lines, some sort of national process may be necessary to confront and try to counter these differences. It is partly out of this felt need to give greater attention and support to victims, as well as consciously to promote national reconciliation, that truth commissions have become such an attractive transitional mechanism.

Truth commissions claim many purposes and goals, and promoting healing for victims and reconciliation for the nation are prominent among them. The names of some commissions make their aim clear: the National Commission on Truth and Reconciliation in Chile and the Truth and Reconciliation Commission in South Africa, for example, set the tone for these commissions and the debate and discussion around them. Posters around South Africa, and large banners hung behind the stage of every public hearing, announced the truth commission with the bold motto 'Truth. The Road to Reconciliation.'

Yet it should not be assumed that truth always leads to healing and reconciliation, or at least not for every person. For some, it helps enormously to have the opportunity to tell one's story to an official state body. But for others, healing will require access to longer-term structures for psychological and emotional support. Likewise, it has yet to be proven that reconciliation will always be advanced from confronting the pains of past conflict. Healing and reconciliation are both long-term processes that go far beyond the capacity of any one short-term commission. Yet, given the scarcity of transitional mechanisms and the limited resources to pour into peacemaking projects, many national leaders pin high hopes on the ability of truth commissions to carry a country down the path of reconciliation, healing and peace, and many couch their support for such a commission in those terms.

Clearly, some scepticism about the inherent healing qualities of truth commissions is deserved. Many questions remain that demand greater study and exploration. But this scepticism should be tempered by indications of quite positive contributions from national truth-seeking in some circumstances. For example, I have spoken with many victims who say that only by learning the full truth about their past horror can they ever begin to heal. Only by remembering, telling their story, and learning the full details about what happened and who was responsible are they able to put the past behind them. Similarly, in South Africa, many survivors told me that they could only forgive their perpetrators if they were told the full truth; almost incomprehensibly, hearing even the most gruesome details of the torture and murder of a loved one somehow brought them some peace.

In South Africa, as elsewhere, the future will be shaped by the past. And a past that carries silenced pain, resentment and unaddressed latent conflict will not be soon forgotten nor easily shaped into a peaceful future. A truth commission can help to unsilence this past, pay respect to victims, and outline needed reforms. Yet it cannot work alone. Real change in the future will depend on the political will of national and local leaders, a commitment to institute far-reaching reforms, and a long-term view towards developing a culture of respect for basic human rights.

Notes

The research for this chapter was made possible by research and writing grants from the John D. and Catherine T. MacArthur Foundation and from the United States Institute of Peace. The opinions, findings, and conclusions or recommendations expressed in this chapter are those of the author and do not necessarily reflect the views of the MacArthur Foundation or the Institute of Peace.

1. The Nuremberg trials are often noted for the great amount of information they publicly exposed on the extent of the Nazi crimes. The international tribunals on the former Yugoslavia and on Rwanda may also serve this function. These tribunals, created under the auspices of the United Nations, are exceptional cases that were set up in part to establish a public record of events.

2. For a more detailed description of truth commissions since 1974, see Priscilla B. Hayner, 'Fifteen Truth Commissions', *Human Rights Quarterly* 16, 1994; or Priscilla B. Hayner, 'Commissioning the Truth: Further Research Questions', *Third World Quarterly* 17, 1996.

3. *Nunca Más: Informe de la Comisión Nacional Sobre la Desaparición de Personas*, National Commission on the Disappeared, Editorial Universitaria de Buenos Aires, Buenos Aires, 1984; or, in English, *Nunca Más: The Report of the Argentine National Commission on the Disappeared*, Farrar Straus Giroux, New York, 1986. Sales figures from Editorial Universitaria de Buenos Aires.

4. 'Discurso de S.E. el Presidente de la República, Don Patricio Aylwin Azocar, al dar a Conocer a la Ciudadania el Informe de la Verdad y Reconciliación', 4 March 1991, p. 11.

5. Phillip Berryman (translator), *Report of the Chilean National Commission on Truth and Reconciliation*, University of Notre Dame Press, Notre Dame, 1993.

6. *Report of the Commission on the Truth for El Salvador, From Madness to Hope: The 12-Year War in El Salvador*, U.N. Doc. S/25500, Annexes, 1993, English version.

7. *Uruguay Nunca Más: Informe Sobre la Violación a los Derechos Humanos (1972–1985)*, Servicio Paz y Justicia Uruguay, Uruguay, 1989.

8. See, for example, *Links: Historical Almanac, Volume I*, Progress Phoenix, Moscow, 1991, a collection of historical essays, and *List of Executed People: Volume I: Donskoi Cemetery 1934–1943*, Memorial, Moscow, 1993. All Memorial publications are in Russian (unofficial translation of titles). For an excellent description of Memorial's activities, see 'Making Rights Real: Two Human Rights Groups Assist Russian Reforms', *Ford Foundation Report*, Summer 1993, pp. 10–15, or Nanci Adler, *Victims of Soviet Terror: The Story of the Memorial Movement*, Praeger, New York, 1993.

9. Jose Luis Simon G., *La Dictadura de Stroessner y los Derechos Humanos*, Serie Nunca Más, vol. 1, and Guido Rodriguez Alcala, *Testimonios de la Represión Política en Paraguay 1975–1989*, Serie Nunca Más, vol. 3, Comite de Iglesias, Asunción, Paraguay, 1990.

10. *Brasil: Nunca Mais*, Arquidiocese de São Paulo, Editora Vozes, Rio de Janeiro, 1985.

11. For an excellent description of the Brazilian project, see Lawrence Weschler, *A Miracle, A Universe: Settling Accounts with Torturers*, Penguin Books, New York, 1990.

12. Ibid.

13. *Nunca Más: The Report of the Argentine National Commission on the Disappeared*, Farrar Straus Giroux, New York, 1986, pp. 22–3.

14. Ibid., p. 39.

15. For further discussion on the controversy around naming names of perpetrators in truth commission reports, see the book on truth commissions by Priscilla B. Hayner, forthcoming.

16. The parliament of Uruguay set up the 'Investigative Commission on the Situation of "Disappeared" People and Its Causes' in April 1985. After seven months, the commission reported on 164 disappearances during the years of military rule, providing evidence of involvement of the Uruguayan security force, which

they forwarded to the Supreme Court. For further information, see Priscilla B. Hayner, 'Fifteen Truth Commissions', *Human Rights Quarterly* 16, 1994, pp. 116–17.

17. José Zalaquett, 'Confronting Human Rights Violations Committed by Former Governments: Principles Applicable and Political Constraints', in *State Crimes: Punishment or Pardon*, The Justice and Society Program of The Aspen Institute, Washington DC, 1989, p. 59.

18. Ibid., p. 61.

19. See Executive Branch Supreme Decree No. 355, reprinted in *Report of the Chilean National Commission on Truth and Reconciliation*, p. 6.

20. *Report of the Chilean National Commission on Truth and Reconciliation*, p. 134.

21. Ibid., p. 136.

22. Ibid., p. 134.

23. Ibid., p. 39.

24. Interviews by author, November and December 1996.

25. Interview by author with Monica Gonzalez, Chile, 27 November 1996.

26. Interviews by author in Chile in November and December 1996.

27. Interview by author with Andres Dominguez, executive secretary of the Corporation for Reparation and Reconciliation, 27 November 1996.

28. *Si M Pa Rele* ('*If I Don't Cry Out*'), National Commission for Truth and Justice, Haiti, 1996, ch. 8.

29. Report of the Commission on the Truth for El Salvador, From Madness to Hope: The 12–Year War in El Salvador, U.N. Doc. S/25500, Annexes, 1993, English version, p. 186.

30. The South African commission is also expected to propose significant and detailed recommendations; that report was not yet published at the time of writing. Some of the other reports, such as in Argentina, have left only general recommendations not specific to any one branch or policy.

31. See Jack Spence, David R. Dye, Mike Lanchin and Geoff Thale, 'Chapúltepec: Five Years Later: El Salvador's Political Reality and Uncertain Future', Hemisphere Initiatives, Cambridge, Mass., 16 January 1997, p. 20.

32. Calvin Sims, 'Buenos Aires Journal: Argentina's Bereft Mothers: And Now, a New Wave', *New York Times*, 18 November 1997, p. A4.

33. Interview by author with Jim Cavallaro, Rio de Janeiro, Brazil, 18 December 1996.

34. Ibid.

35. As cited in Ros Atkins, 'Lukewarm About Torture', *Frontiers of Freedom*, South African Institute of Race Relations, no. 4, 1997, p. 27.

36. Brandon Hamber and Sharon Lewis, 'An Overview of the Consequences of Violence and Trauma in South Africa: Occasional Paper of the Centre for the Study of Violence and Reconciliation', Johannesburg, South Africa, 18 August 1997, p. 16.

37. Interviews by author with Janis Grobbelaar, information manager, and Venessa Barolsky, researcher, Truth and Reconciliation Commission of South Africa, Johannesburg, and with Beth Goldblatt, Researcher, Gender Research Projects, Centre for Applied Legal Studies, University of the Witwatersrand, Johannesburg, South Africa. For an excellent analysis of women and the South African commission, see Beth Goldblatt, 'Violence, Gender and Human Rights: An Examination of South Africa's Truth and Reconciliation Commission', presented at the Law and Society Association Annual Meeting, St Louis, Missouri, 29 May–1 June 1997.

38. *Nunca Más: The Report of the Argentine National Commission on the Disappeared*, p. 20.

11

The Role of Non-governmental Organizations

Rita Maran

The Growth of Non-governmental Organizations

Thousands of non-governmental organizations (NGOs) now operate within the orbit of the United Nations. Their fields of activities are those of the United Nations, and their numerical growth over the past two decades is unprecedented. Significance of the work of NGOs has for the past dozen or more years received increasingly respectful recognition on the world scene, from heads of state to Secretaries-General of the United Nations. In his early days as United Nations Secretary-General, Kofi Annan greeted representatives of hundreds of NGOs from all regions of the world who gathered as they do every September for the opening session of the UN General Assembly. The Secretary-General took the opportunity to set the scene for the UN/NGO partnership that would ensue during his tenure when he described the relationship as 'not an option, but a necessity'.[1]

Non-governmental organizations are broadly defined here as non-profit citizens' voluntary entities organized locally, nationally or internationally, with activities determined by the collective will of members. NGOs are an embodiment of civil society; they serve to fill in societal gaps and failures with respect to disparate issues ranging from the environment and sustainable development, to women's human rights, health and nutrition, and civil and political rights, among many others. NGO mandates cover an equally broad spectrum, and usually include outreach activities to educate local, national or international governments and institutions. As their workforce is often composed of volunteers, NGOs educate members as well as stimulate public consciousness about the concern central to their formation.

For this chapter, the term 'NGO' refers to: (1) NGOs accredited with consultative status to the UN Economic and Social Council (ECOSOC); and (2) grassroots organizations whose work tends to be localized, and who may be unconcerned about the possibility and potential of – or indeed the existence of – official UN accreditation. In the first instance, NGOs with formal accreditation to ECOSOC now number over 1,611. Of that number, this chapter will survey approximately thirty whose core mandates are representative of the larger number of NGOs concerned in various ways with torture. As for category (2), the numbers defy speculation, since grassroots organizations exist in every corner of the globe, and every passing day sees new organizations come into existence and old ones fade. Once an organization has put down roots and established a stable and permanent presence, it may come to recognize good reasons for gaining consultative status. Accredited NGOs can make oral and written interventions in sessions on human rights, receive UN human rights documents, lobby and exchange information with delegates and each other at UN sessions and conferences, and so on. It is also the case that in less hospitable countries, being formally recognized by the UN may afford a measure of protection from physical or legal harassment. That said, it should also be noted that accredited NGOs offer helping hands to unaccredited NGOs, to help newcomers become familiar with the system, and the lack of accreditation does not constitute a stumbling-block over the first years of a new organization's life.

In 1996, a much-discussed reconsideration of the role and functions of NGOs took place within the UN. The General Assembly called in November 1996 for discussions 'on the methodology as well as on the substantive issue of facilitating the participation of non-governmental organizations in all areas of the work of the United Nations'. Following that call, the Ambassador of Pakistan undertook to arrange for 'informal soundings', with meetings to commence in December 1996.[2] Informal soundings, as they were called, and formal restructuring meetings were held. The objectives in both circumstances were similar: first, to examine the methodological and procedural aspects of the process by which the General Assembly examines participation of NGOs, and second, to consider the desirability of increased interaction between the UN on the one hand and NGOs and civil society on the other.[3]

Two of the decisions reached were: agreement on maintenance of the existing system of categories for NGOs; and a new procedure for participation of national NGOs, rather than international NGOs only, as before. It was further specified that human rights NGOs would not face any additional conditions in their work with the UN. As the subject was

'New Arrangements for Consultation with Non-governmental Organizations Adopted by Economic and Social Council', specific substantive issues were intentionally not on the agenda at those meetings.[4]

This chapter looks at the development of human rights NGOs, particularly but not exclusively those that fall within the orbit of the system established for the UN–NGO relationship. The chapter goes on to discuss the anti-torture work of a set of the major NGOs, with mandates that include actively working against torture, providing service to survivors, or both. The chapter identifies key issues that those NGOs have selected to address, and offers comments on characteristics of individual organizations, the identified populations they serve, linkages with other service organizations, audiences they aim to inform, and sources of funding.

Human Rights NGOs

In countries in transition and in countries under repressive systems of governance, numerous obstacles have impeded the development and performance of NGOs. In lower-income countries, the community's lack of history or experience of grassroots public sector activities – the sort of experience far more integral to Western industrialized countries – has constituted a serious obstacle to the development of NGOs. Lacking precedents or models, start-up NGOs had to cut new ground. In addition, many countries' restrictive or ambiguous legal requirements by governments concerning the establishment and structure of grassroots organizations also impeded their formation and development.

In what is now acknowledged as a strongly linked UN–NGO complementary relationship, human rights NGOs undertake research on issues under consideration by UN bodies, particularly the Commission on Human Rights (the Commission) and its Sub-Commission on Prevention of Discrimination and Protection of Minorities (the Sub-Commission). NGOs assist in the drafting of proposed Commission and Sub-Commission decisions and resolutions; supply research and up-to-date, verified data for inclusion in the Commission and Sub-Commission's deliberations; and act as intermediaries and interpreters of human rights issues between governments, the larger NGO community, and the public at large. To be sure, NGOs are imperfect organizations and, as such, are subject to flaws, inconsistencies and inadequacies; notwithstanding this, their efforts are credited with broadening and deepening the understanding of rights issues by their constituencies, by national and international legislators, diplomats and officials, and by the public at large.

NGOs that Combat Torture: The Frame of Reference

Out of the necessity generated by the widespread institutionalized practice of torture by governments around the world in the period between the 1960s and the 1980s, the need became clear for organizations that were not connected to governments and that would actively and authoritatively combat torture. People were being tortured by governments not here and there, randomly, but intentionally in great numbers in many countries. There was an imperative that torture be stopped – in Greece, in Argentina, in Chile, in Paraguay, in Brazil, in Turkey, and so on. The practice had to be publicly exposed and condemned. Prevention, punishment and eradication of the practice were essential. And most immediately, people who were emerging from torture – respectfully termed victims some of the time, equally respectfully termed survivors at other times – needed to be helped, in both the short and the long term.

By 1975, the UN General Assembly had adopted the Declaration on the Protection of All Persons From Torture and Other Cruel, Inhuman or Degrading Treatment or Punishment, a critical step along the way to promulgating a binding treaty. In 1987, the Convention Against Torture and Other Cruel, Inhuman or Degrading Treatment or Punishment (the Convention) came into force. The Convention carries legal weight, and, once ratifed by a State Party, the Convention's legally binding nature can be invoked. The Convention requires under Article 14 that

> 1. Each State Party shall ensure in its legal system that the victim of an act of torture obtains redress and has an enforceable right to fair and adequate compensation, including the means for as full rehabilitation as possible.

Over the last thirty or forty years since start-up efforts by groups not connected to governments (at that early stage, they would not have thought of themselves as 'NGOs' in upper case), several dozen now formally constituted NGOs around the world have made substantive contributions in the anti-torture movement. Some NGOs focus their work on the victims; some, on actions to abolish the practice; some, on both.

Those that work to uncover the facts surrounding torture, identify the torture agents, and bring the facts into the public arena have moved governments of disparate political structures in the direction of correction, remedy, and reform. In countries where the right to be secure from torture is grievously lacking, NGOs – often at risk to themselves – act as megaphones, broadcasting factual information about what is happening. Anti-torture NGOs may find themselves confronting the state, as their activities to prevent further acts of torture throw an unwanted spotlight in that direction. Peter Burns, one of the longest-sitting members of the

UN Committee Against Torture, said: 'The Committee could not function properly without input from NGOs. We rely heavily on NGOs to provide us with commentaries on the States Parties' reports – to point out areas that the States have overlooked and any misrepresentation (even if inadvertent) that may have occurred.' No small tribute to their work.[5]

Efforts are best judged by accomplishments:

- turn-around calls for urgent action on behalf of people undergoing or at immediate risk of torture;
- development of culturally sensitive methodologies for treatment of survivors;
- formulation of legal, legislative and administrative initiatives that narrow the possibilities for torture by governmental agents;
- creation and education of a broadly based public movement for the prevention and punishment of torture;
- alerting of professional organizations, especially medical and legal, to enable focused anti-torture activities within professions across borders;
- setting up technologically dedicated global networks for dissemination and sharing of information.

Anti-torture NGOs, the UN, and the Regional Systems

Most organizations do their work in the context of international human rights principles established through the UN. The International Bill of Human Rights[6] constitutes the basic legal foundation, along with the Convention Against Torture and Other Cruel, Inhuman and Degrading Treatment or Punishment. Regional human rights systems in Africa, the Americas and Europe add legal weight to the global legal instruments that prohibit torture. Anti-torture NGOs thus not only reinforce established juridical principles of human rights, but also give life to the pragmatic, clinical application of those principles.

Numbers of human rights organizations, Amnesty International for one, have relatively broad mandates in which torture is earmarked among other civil and political rights violations. Other human rights organizations – the Geneva-based World Organization Against Torture, and the Center for Victims of Torture in Minneapolis are examples – set up tighter single-issue mandates that focus more exclusively on torture.

Groupings of NGOs not infrequently join forces for action under their accreditations as NGOs within the UN system. In 1996, for example, the Association for the Prevention of Torture (APT) exercised its right of intervention at the Commission on Human Rights on behalf of itself and other NGOs concerning the draft Optional Protocol to the Convention Against Torture. The NGOs stated that the purpose of the Optional Protocol – namely, visits by authorized missions to places where torture was alleged to be taking place – would be undermined if prior consent by the government were to be required.[7]

Most recently, human rights NGOs have supported the development of norms by UN human rights bodies concerning reparation, rehabilitation and compensation for torture victims. Defined norms concerning reparations, once made known to individuals in treatment, are considered to have a positive impact on the healing and recovery process. The victims themselves and health-care professionals attending them have attested that the salutary effect of reparations goes beyond the financial compensation involved. Further, the 'Basic Principles and Guidelines on the right to reparation for victims of gross violations of human rights and humanitarian law' include rehabilitation as a form of reparation.[8]

According to the Rules of Procedure of the treaty-based Committee Against Torture (the Committee), established under the Convention Against Torture and Other Cruel, Inhuman or Degrading Treatment or Punishment, the Committee may invite NGOs in consultative status with ECOSOC to submit information, documentation and written statements that are relevant to the Committee's activities.[9] Information supplied by anti-torture NGOs in the eighteenth session of the Committee for the discussion on methods of interrogation in Israel led to the Committee's assessment that breaches of the Torture Convention were evident, despite Israel's assertion to the contrary.[10]

How Many Torture Victims Are There?

When a problem of global proportions such as torture emerges and help is needed, public acknowledgement that the problem does in fact exist produces the baseline question: 'how many people are we talking about?' The number of self-identified torture survivors seeking and finding assistance appears relatively low, by routine statistical standards. In regularly functioning treatment centres, the number of people being received may vary from very few in a given week, to an annual total of no more than several hundred. The universe of individuals who have suffered torture can only be approximated. In the United States, for example, estimates are that as many as a third of those who seek political asylum have survived torture. To hazard a guess based on US organizations' estimates, some 200,000 to 400,000 victims of torture are living in the United States. In an effort to learn more precisely what the actual number of torture survivors may be, a bill has been proposed in the US Congress that would have the Centers for Disease Control and Prevention conduct an epidemiological study for that purpose.[11] In the absence of statistics, an even heavier burden of proof is imposed on the torture survivor.

In US treatment centres, unlike centres in countries where torture is committed, a large percentage of staff activities is devoted to writing evaluations for torture survivors seeking asylum. To be granted asylum, refugees must present acceptable documentation. Centres are often dependent on *pro bono* volunteer medical care-givers and a part-time administrative staff of one or two professionals. Treatment centres that function in 'safe' countries to provide assistance to survivors arriving from torturing countries naturally face fewer problems, and in some instances are recipients of funds from home governments. In torturing countries, human rights NGOs whose educational and lobbying functions deal with torture in that country may face dangerous adversarial situations with the government.

Further to the question of numbers, a conference on 'Human Rights and Mental Health' in Sarajevo in July 1997 brought together mental health specialists and lawyers from Spain and their counterparts from Bosnia. An estimated one million people, out of the total population of four million Bosnians, including Bosniacs (Muslims), Serbs and Croats, underwent torture and other maltreatment during the recent three-and-a-half-year war. Conferees discussed the psychosocial needs of those who survived unspeakable horrors and who are now without therapeutic resources to address the sequelae. Speakers presented the pros and cons of establishing an institute to carry out assessments and identification of the survivors of torture and other wartime trauma, and to serve as a research and resource centre in Bosnia. The institute would set up new agencies offering practical means of assistance, with formal support from government and professional associations.[12]

On a smaller but statistically precise scale, an epidemiological study carried out in the Zagreb area of Croatia in 1995 found that of 1,926 Bosnian war refugees, 24 per cent had been tortured and were in need of treatment for the aftermath.[13]

Practical Issues of NGO Service Providers

Torture is a unique phenomenon; the centres dealing with its consequences are, however, widely divergent. NGOs were formed out of the necessity to effect some kind of remedial action. Principal consideration was given to the needs of torture 'victims' and 'survivors' (the use of both words here reflects the usage of both words by the organizations working in the field). Some NGOs became highly centralized, focusing uniquely on the individual who experienced torture. Others are organized in a relatively decentralized mode, with more sweeping approaches that regularly handle related problems of refugees, asylum seekers, and victims of politically driven violence.[14]

In cases involving asylum-seekers, the organization must make difficult decisions about the relationship it should seek to maintain with the particular governmental authorities in whose offices they are required to file asylum requests. What may be a relatively normal bureaucratic procedure in a non-torturing country can be a virtual landmine in a torturing country, in which an equally normal bureaucratic procedure becomes disastrous.

Many NGOs maintain programmes of medical, physical and/or psychosocial therapy, and rehabilitation of torture survivors. Other activities include work on development of methodology, documentation, research, education and training of personnel, and public information activities. NGOs limit their mandates for such practical reasons as financing; professional expertise available; and ability to keep an office open in the country of location. Widely differing mandates reflect diverse areas of concentration; geographical scope, number and cultural characteristics of people being treated; activities that are politically or technically possible in the country where the NGO is based; legal requirements for such organizations; institutional operating methods. In some organizations, workers take decisions on practical and operational matters and decide priorities: in what order to seek to prevent, stop, monitor, intervene, advocate, deliver services, and finance the organization? How to maximize reliability of information and consequent credibility? With respect to others in the same field, how best to collaborate and coordinate? How best to deal with competing demands for funding from the same sources? How firm and reliable, and of what duration, are financial resources?

The number of NGO service centres for torture victims has grown steadily since the early 1970s. Amnesty International's survey in 1993, for example, listed some seventy service providers in twenty-three countries, and one year later noted a steady increase in the number. In the 1970s and 1980s, some NGOs (by no means all, since the UN human rights–NGO system was not that well known at that time) hoped that by establishing a linkage with UN human rights bodies, that protective institutional umbrella might afford them some measure of security.

Practical, ethical, safety and financial questions that NGOs must consider take on different priorities within the context of changing political, social and economic circumstances. Early anti-torture NGOs faced decisions with respect to the direction and scope of their work; priorities in the work they were beginning to undertake; considerations of safety for their clients and indeed for their own staffs; sources of funding for an untried field of work; ways to ensure fiscal sobriety so as to attract ongoing funding sources.

Newly established anti-torture NGOs in diverse countries usually lack predecessors from whose files experiential wisdom, methodological approaches and illustrative case studies could be drawn. The new NGOs had no choice but to develop innovative structures. They proceeded out of an informed determination to devise ways to help victims of state-inflicted violence who need mental and physical rehabilitation. In some instances, service providers then and now risk a fate similar to that of victims, when by their work they declare to the world the reality of torture by the government in their country.

NGO rehabilitation services address themselves to primary and/or to secondary victims of torture, secondary victims being the immediate relatives of primary victims. Rehabilitation services in general address refugees from countries with repressive regimes and/or a traditional practice of torture; people living in countries with previous or current repressive regimes and/or a traditional practice of torture; either or both of the above, during times of international or internal armed conflict.

Organizations are attentive to the guidelines established by the Chilean Medical Association, which are consistent with the recommendations of the British Medical Association and the Amnesty International twelve-point programme for the practical control and eradication of torture. The guidelines call upon physicans not to care for patients under the following circumstances: the physician has been ordered not to identify her/himself, or to conceal her/his identity; the physician encounters a blindfolded, hooded, or otherwise vision-impeded patient; the patient is being held in a secret detention centre; contact between the patient and the physician can be carried out only in the presence of a third party.

With financial resources a continuing concern, anti-torture NGOs have on appropriate occasions joined ranks to maximize information and resources. The World Organization Against Torture (OMCT), for example, worked with Defense of Children International and Physicians for Human Rights in gathering information presented to the Committee Against Torture and the Committee on the Rights of the Child. OMCT is, as well, working with more than sixty civil and human rights organizations in preparing a report on the status of the US government's report to the Committee on Torture.[15]

To date, so far as is known, none of the centres has accepted as a patient someone who has committed torture. As one psychologist said, 'It would be like running a treatment centre for survivors of the Holocaust – and at the same time treating Nazis.' Torturers are turned away in order to ensure the peace of mind of other patients, and to obviate anxiety or concern on the part of patients who must feel sure they are in a safe and secure environment. The current experience in South Africa, in which some officers who personally committed torture have come forward to confess in the hope of being amnestied, may produce changes in the overall picture of treatment available to torturers.[16]

Overview

By way of surveying a field that has multiplied in recent years, this chapter now turns to an overview of NGOs that work to combat torture. The following NGOs include those that do treatment and those that do not. The title of the organization usually (but not always) indicates whether it is offering therapeutic service. In describing organizations' goals and methods, in so far as practicable I have gone directly to their own literature – brochures and newsletters – as well as scholarly writings. The listings are alphabetical by country, then by city, using English-language names for countries and for NGOs.

The Centre for Torture Victims, Sarajevo

The Centre, which opened its doors in April 1997, is an independent, humanitarian, non-partisan organization. It actively cooperates with the Bosnian Health Care System, and welcomes Bosniacs, Bosnian Croats and Bosnian Serbs. It has a staff of psychiatrists, psychologists, a researcher, general practitioners, a medical technician, a physiotherapist, and an office supervisor. Before opening the Sarajevo office, the Centre had been based in Zagreb, Croatia.

People who come to the Centre have in some cases been subjected to torture in their own homes, sometimes by people known to them who may now be among those indicted by the International Criminal Tribunal for the former Yugoslavia in The Hague. Some clients come to Sarajevo from nearby towns to which they have been involuntarily relocated. In the first few months of operations, the Centre identified a few hundred torture victims, and performed psychological, medical and physiotherapy rehabilitation treatment.

The Centre seeks to carry out education and training of health-care professionals on the medical, social, legal and ethical aspects of torture. It works with the World Health Organization on continuing the development of post-trauma therapy. The Centre also educates and raises public awareness of torture, and organizes and participates in conferences and seminars. It draws financial support from the Council of Europe, the Danish government, and the RCT/IRCT in Copenhagen, of which it is a network member.

*The Rehabilitation and Research Centre for Torture Victims (RCT),
Copenhagen*

Established in 1982, RCT started its activities by undertaking rehabilitation
of victims of torture who were arriving in Denmark from countries on
other continents. Intense work with torture victims in the hospital clinic
highlighted the need for ongoing services ranging from psychological
therapy to mental health care. With support from the Danish government
and the University Hospital, a building on the grounds of the hospital
was turned over for use as a clinic by the RCT. The University Hospital
supplied up to four beds at any given moment. RCT carried out research
on torture, the nature of sequelae, consequences of torture, and methods
for development of rehabilitation models.

From the outset, in addition to clinical work with torture victims,
RCT, which enjoyed the cooperation of the Danish government, published documented research (some of it emanating from Amnesty International) on government-sanctioned torture, and on preventing torture.
The care of victims of torture, research and dissemination of information
on torture, and the abolition of torture have remained the organizations's
goals.

*International Rehabilitation Council for Torture Victims (IRCT),
Denmark*

The RCT was joined in 1987 by the IRCT, which was supported by the
Danish Ministry of Foreign Affairs, the European Community, and the
UN Voluntary Fund for Victims of Torture. IRCT is a private, humanitarian, non-political organization whose essential function is advocacy for
provision of resources for torture victims and for prevention of torture.

The genesis of this two-pronged organization, RCT/IRCT, can be
traced to the exodus of Greek victims of torture under the junta starting
in 1967, and of Chileans after the coup that overthrew the Allende government in 1973. A sizeable cohort from those two countries made their
way to Denmark, and were received by the Danish government with
medical and social services. An Amnesty International group of medical
professionals in Copenhagen set up an independent organization to offer
medical assistance to refugee survivors of torture in their countries of
origin. Given that medical and social services are outside the AI mandate, the medical group in time splintered off to form the RCT.

The joint RCT/IRCT took as its goals not only the direct hands-on
work with torture survivors living in Denmark, but also vigorous initiatives in countries on other continents where there was clear need for a

separate Centre for Torture Victims. The RCT/IRCT has proved an important forerunner in the spread of similar organizations to other countries, some that were, like Denmark, receiving torture survivors from other countries, and others receiving torture survivors from within their own society.

The joint organization has enjoyed stable funding, and has become the hub of much of the international work to treat survivors of torture. RCT/IRCT is now linked with over 123 rehabilitation programmes in 58 countries, and with another 21 initiatives in 18 countries. They range from Albania, Bangladesh, Bosnia–Herzegovina, Cameroon and Nepal, to Zimbabwe. Since 1991, RCT has published a quarterly journal, *Torture*, on rehabilitation of torture victims and prevention of torture. In 1996, IRCT was accredited as an NGO in consultative status with ECOSOC.

Some telling statistics: over five thousand health professionals received training from RCT/IRCT in 1996, one-third abroad and two-thirds in Denmark. Among many topics the RCT/IRCT concern themselves with today are problems associated with the use of interpreters in psychotherapy for torture victims, and country-specific problems such as genocide in Rwanda and torture in the Spanish Basque region.

In its early days, the RCT/IRCT was just one fledgling organization in a small but growing field of NGOs. The RCT/IRCT mandate was healthcare-based; over time it became well acquainted with the UN system and the body of international law on torture. As time passes, anti-torture NGOs network with other similarly focused organizations. Most have become familiar with international human rights law, and many are actively engaged in formulating new standards for survivors and survivors' families' rights, including means of redress of the harm done, reparations, compensation and rehabilitation.

The RCT/IRCT has a US affiliate: the Rehabilitation Fund for Torture Victims, Inc. Based in New York since 1986, the Fund raises and distributes funds in support of a wide range of activities which will contribute to the rehabilitation of torture victims, the fight against torture, and the prevention of torture. Some centres in different parts of the world have been established as a result of the Fund's support, and the Fund offers direct help to individual torture victims in rehabilitation centres around the world. The Fund supports education of health professionals about the prohibition against torture and about rehabilitation, including the curriculum of professional schools and training centres for healthcare personnel. The Fund carries out research activities including epidemiological as well as clinical studies of torture victims and related studies of remedial initiatives.

Amnesty International, London

The development of international norms and laws concerning torture that have come about since 1961 must acknowledge first the work of Amnesty International (AI). Although AI does not operate a treatment centre, it maintains close links with treatment centres around the world. Further, AI has established institutional policy, and is central to work against torture in many parts of the world.

AI's initiatives with respect to torture can be seen in a historical and chronological perspective. The organization had been in existence only six years when it drew attention to particular cases of torture as an administrative practice. At that same time, the UN and NGOs were drafting norms and operating procedures by which to fight systematically against institutionalized torture. The international legal regime establishing the absolute non-derogable nature of the right to be secure from torture was in early stages of development. Since that time, authoritative language is in place citing the non-derogable nature of the right of everyone to be secure from torture. AI sought to mobilize political will among governments to invoke and apply norms against torture.

In the world of the 1970s, when torture was universally deplored but widely prevalent, AI and the International Commission of Jurists, a long-standing Geneva-based NGO devoted to the rule of law, gathered verified information from reliable sources. The two organizations analysed the existing and the needed but not yet existing legal instruments by which torturing governments could be deterred. It was, seen broadly, the opening of the much-needed worldwide movement to prohibit, criminalize, prevent and punish governmental torture.

From the time of the first AI Campaign for the Abolition of Torture in 1972–73, AI set standards that were applicable not only to its own work but, as time passed, equally to the work of other human rights NGOs in the field. In 1972, the public campaign used a three-part strategy: publicity, international legal efforts, and new action techniques. The Campaign – the first of its kind – helped mobilize interest about institutionalized torture among government officials and politicians, as well as at the UN and among NGOs. AI helped establish high standards for gathering and disseminating information; those standards in turn made possible collaborative efforts with governments, the UN, and grassroots organizations. Again, by 1975, the UN General Assembly had adopted the Declaration Against Torture, and in 1987, the Convention Against Torture and Other Cruel, Inhuman or Degrading Treatment or Punishment came into force.

From the beginning, the AI Medical Programme incorporated research on torture, medical ethics with respect to torture, and work for individual prisoners and torture victims.[17] The current UN Special Rapporteur on Torture was for the first twenty years of AI's life the Legal Director. The Special Rapporteur reports regularly to the Commission on Human Rights concerning specific cases he is monitoring in different countries and the standards he is using.

In 1984, AI had issued guidelines clarifying its position with respect to rehabilitation centres. The guidelines remain valid at this time:

1. AI supports the principle of rehabilitation of victims of torture.

2. AI does not fund rehabilitation centres. Medical groups and individual doctors who may also be AI members do medical work against torture outside the AI system.

3. AI makes no commitment to comment or pass judgement on any particular treatment protocol.

4. AI is committed itself to maintaining good working relationships with centres doing medical treatment work with torture victims.[18]

Redress, London

Redress is an NGO working since 1992 to promote effective mechanisms for reparation for torture, and to assist survivors of torture to obtain redress. The Convention Against Torture and Other Cruel, Inhuman or Degrading Treatment or Punishment requires that States Parties ensure that victims of torture or maltreatment obtain redress, with an enforceable right to fair and adequate compensation including rehabilitation. This NGO states that successful attempts at redress play an important role in the healing and empowerment of survivors of torture.

Redress is concerned with the lack of effective remedies available to survivors of torture, and with the right to reparation, which includes compensation, rehabilitation, restitution, acknowledgement of wrongdoing, and guarantees of non repetition. Principles and guidelines on this topic are being drafted for the current agenda of the UN Commission on Human Rights.[19]

Redress is working towards a mechanism that will be feasible at national and international levels. Such a mechanism would take into consideration the factors of cost, political visibility, and acceptance by successor states of legal obligation for harms done by previous states. As the Statute for the proposed International Criminal Court proceeds in the UN system, containing as it does an emphasis on the notion of retributive justice, Redress, along with other NGOs including AI, seeks to promote the notion of restorative justice.

Redress receives its major grants from the European Community and the UN Voluntary Fund for Victims of Torture, with additional donations from numerous foundations and trusts.

Action of Christians for the Abolition of Torture (ACAT), Paris

L'Action Chrétien pour l'Abolition de la Torture, founded in 1974, is Paris-based with national sections in other countries. ACAT has a well-developed support system within Church-based communities in France and other European countries. ACAT has built a stable organization with staying power over the past two decades, perhaps attributable to a common religious base. Guided by a French jurist who is also a scholar and activist on international human rights law, ACAT publishes books on subjects surrounding torture.[20]

ACAT has helped develop coalitions of organizations that are linked through their work against torture. They are able to share substantive accredited information and, thanks to a committed membership, to make information available to governmental and UN authorities responsible for preparing normative and legal documents.

The International Federation of Action of Christians for the Abolition of Torture (IFACAT), to which all national sections belong, makes interventions on related issues to the Commission on Human Rights. One intervention, for example, supported the long-proposed International Criminal Court, and encouraged the UN to hold a diplomatic meeting in 1998 to adopt a draft for the International Criminal Court, a proposal that has been under discussion for many years within the UN system.[21]

The Association of Israeli-Palestinian Physicians for Human Rights (PHR–Israel), Tel-Aviv

PHR–Israel is a non-partisan non-profit organization founded in March 1988 that brings together health professionals from Israel, the West Bank and Gaza Strip who work against abuses of human and medical rights in those locations. With a broad medical rights mandate, its work against torture is done largely through research, publishing and public campaigns, often jointly with other Israeli human rights organizations. A point of reference is the World Medical Association 'Declaration of Tokyo, 1975', by which doctors reject participation in torture regardless of circumstances. PHR–Israel has an extended network of volunteer health professionals, whose mainly *pro bono* services cover prisons, detention centres, and rural villages.

PHR–Israel works also for positive change in government policies and legislation through the utilization of policy papers and High Court appeals. An example is the issue of prolonged solitary confinement in Israeli prisons; PHR–Israel was instrumental in the adoption of new recommendations for improvements, albeit limited, by the Ministry of Internal Security.

On the issue of torture, PHR–Israel, as one member of a local human rights coalition, took issue with two legislative initiatives drafted by the Ministry of Justice that continued previous lacunae in legislation concerning the use of physical force during interrogation. Conferences are held jointly. 'Dilemmas in Professional Ethics Resulting from Medical Doctors and Psychologists Involved in Torture' was held in 1993.

PHR–Israel publishes papers, newsletters and books, often jointly with other related NGOs. *Torture: Human Rights, Medical Ethics and the Case of Israel* (published jointly with Zed Books, London, 1995), came out of the 1993 conference 'The International Struggle Against Torture and the Case of Israel', organized jointly with the Public Committee Against Torture in Israel. The book launched a year-long campaign to combat public apathy in Israel concerning the use of torture by Israeli interrogators. PHR–Israel funding derives from memberships within the Israeli medical community, NGOs, medical centres, and foundations.

World Organization Against Torture/SOS–Torture, Geneva

The World Organization Against Torture (OMCT) is the world's largest network of human rights organizations, set up to fight all forms of torture and other cruel, inhuman or degrading treatment, summary execution, and other more subtle forms of violent repression such as disappearance and psychiatric internment for political reasons. Since its inauguration in 1986, OMCT has come to the aid of people undergoing or at immediate risk of torture. The network operates very much like Amnesty International's Urgent Action Network with respect to sending out alerts, and filing reports on particular countries and issues involving torture-related problems. OMCT circulates information on individuals being tortured or under immediate risk of torture.

The SOS–Torture network comprises over two hundred affiliated organizations, most with headquarters in Third World countries or in Eastern Europe. Each case submitted to OMCT must be sponsored by a member of the network who agrees to take responsibility for the information and the account given by the victim. OMCT in addition offers advice to organizations in the field of international human rights; encourages the promotion and implementation of international instruments against torture; and provides emergency aid to victims and to those attempting to help them in the field.

In 1996, OMCT took action on behalf of '6394 persons in 61 countries whose rights had been or were in danger of being severely violated'.[22] In some cases, individuals who had within the past few days been arrested and were at risk of torture were released following interventions by the SOS network. In other cases, victims were given assistance funding.

OMCT has consultative status with the UN, the International Labour Organization, and the African Commission on Human and Peoples' Rights. OMCT ties its work closely to the various UN mechanisms and procedures concerning torture; these include the Special Rapporteur on Torture, the Commission on Human Rights Working Group on Arbitrary Detention; the individual experts reporting to the Commission on the situation concerning specific countries (Peru, East Timor, Guatemala, Colombia, Mexico and Bahrain, among others); the Special Rapporteur on Summary Execution; the Special Rapporteur on Violence against Women; the High Commissioner for Human Rights; and the Voluntary Fund for Victims of Torture. OMCT intervenes with respect to items on the agendas of the UN Commission on Human Rights (the Commission), and the Sub-Commission on Prevention of Discrimination and Protection of Minorities (the Sub-Commission).[23]

OMCT addresses specific forms of violence against women in interventions before the Commission: war-related sexual violence, as in 'ethnic cleansing' in the former Yugoslavia; violence permitted by law 'as a form of punishment for women who do not follow certain social or customary rules'; and violence related to birth-control policies (in Tibet, by Chinese authorities). OMCT points out that those three types of violence are prohibited under the terms of Article 1(1) of the Convention Against Torture, and urges the need for more specific attention to violations of women's rights throughout UN mechanisms and procedures.

A programme on behalf of children was begun by the OMCT in 1992. Since then, the figures of children who are tortured have increased manyfold, leading to the conclusion that torture of children is extremely frequent and global. Documentation concerns Pakistan, Bahrain, Guatemala, Israel and Honduras, among others.

OMCT adds substantively to the more generalized human rights movement discussions about such issues as democracy, rule of law, the interplay between civil/political rights and economic/social/cultural rights, and the relationship between NGOs and the regimes in their home countries. OMCT has sponsored conferences on these topics over recent years, and addresses those fundamental questions in editorials in their quarterly publication, *Bulletin OMCT*.[24]

The World Organization Against Torture USA, Washington DC

This is the US affiliate of the SOS–Torture Network, which is administered by the international secretariat of the World Organization Against Torture in Geneva. The US affiliate concentrates on US compliance issues, with a particular focus on the death penalty, the juvenile death penalty, refugee policies involving *refoulement* (especially under the new expedited processing and removal provisions of US immigration law), and abuse of prisoners in custody, with a special emphasis on sexual abuse of women in prisons. The US affiliate chairs a coalition of sixty or more mostly domestic US groups dealing with those issues, in order to compile NGO reports under the Convention Against Torture and the International Convention on the Elimination of All Forms of Racial Discrimination that are filed in conjunction with the US government's official submissions to the respective committees under those treaties.

The US affiliate also assists affiliated groups worldwide. Currently it administers a project funded by the National Endowment for Democracy to provide computer equipment and training to human rights groups in Africa. The US affiliate brought together more than forty human rights groups in Africa in July 1997, to begin the process of evaluating their computer and electronic communications needs, providing them with equipment and training, and setting up an African electronic communications information clearing house and training centre.

The Center for Victims of Torture, Minneapolis

The Center, a private, non-profit organization founded in 1985, and located in Minnesota in the heartland of the USA, is the largest programme of its kind in the United States. The Center offers a comprehensive assessment and treatment programme of direct care and rehabilitation to torture survivors. It informs and educates a general public and members of Congress about the need for governmental assistance across a wide range of needs. Its newsletter, *The Storycloth*, is substantive in informing about UN and US legislative developments, about NGOs in the field, about international developments relating to torture survivors, and about the Center's own projects.

Approximately ten to twelve thousand torture survivors currently reside in the state of Minnesota. Of that number, the Center has provided assistance to roughly four hundred survivors from over forty countries. Two-thirds of the Center's clients are people seeking political asylum. For people who have undergone torture and other related trauma, the procedures required in order to qualify for asylum may be impossible to comply with. For some, it means the horror of retelling and therefore reliving the event. It means, for others, reconnecting those parts of themselves from which they intentionally tried to dissociate while undergoing torture. Many find it extremely difficult to speak articulately, if at all, about what they have lived through, and some asylum-seekers narrate the horrifying story in a dispassionate and unemotional way. It is precisely that testimony that is necessary to validate the credibility of their fear of persecution in their home country.

With the Center's help, the Comprehensive Torture Victims Relief Act (see above) has been reintroduced in the present Senate. The legislation has a twofold objective: to earmark additional funds for rehabilitation programmes, and to help in the training of immigration and asylum officers. Training of government asylum officers would put the officers in a better position to understand the ways in which torture has affected the survivor's ability to respond well to questioning.

At a relatively early stage of the war in the Balkans, the Center sent a physician, a psychologist and a nurse to the former Yugoslavia to provide emergency training for care providers in the region. At that same time, they assessed what future role the Center might play in the healing process, and whether activities should take place in the Balkans or in Minneapolis. In return, that year, the Center hosted a month-long training of fourteen health professionals from Bosnia–Herzegovina, and from Croatia, funded by the US Agency for International Development.

Another key activity assisted by the Center was the first US goverment-sponsored conference, 'Survivors of Torture: Improving our Understanding', held in Washington DC in April 1997.[25] The Center made a key presentation about the psychological, physical and socio-political impact of torture, and presented the important findings of a new multi-disciplinary care programme that involved 220 torture survivors in care at the Center from 1991 through 1995.

The Center maintains a special representative in Washington DC, who regularly meets with legislators and government bureaucrats to whom he furnishes information and documentation, and with whom he lobbies for legislation to assist torture survivors.

The Center receives gifts and matching grants from private foundations, the UN Voluntary Fund for Victims of Torture, and from individual donors. Up to the present, the Center has allocated roughly 50 per cent of its budget for client care, and 50 per cent goes to public policy work, with a small percentage allocated for training. In the future, client care may be allocated somewhat less than half, training slightly more, with public policy receiving the rest.

Human Rights Watch (HRW), New York

Human Rights Watch was established in 1978. It monitors and promotes the observance of internationally recognized human rights in Africa, the Americas, Asia, the Middle East, and among the signatories of the Helsinki Accords. HRW investigates and works to stop human rights abuses, including torture, summary execution and arbitrary detention, among others, in over seventy countries worldwide. It provides timely, reliable information on human rights, based on standards of universal civil and political rights as embodied in international laws and treaties. It seeks to enlist the influence of the US government, the UN, the European Union and the World Bank in its goal of holding governments publicly accountable for transgressions of the rights of their people. It makes a priority of protecting human rights monitors who are tortured in many countries. HRW special projects are arms, children's rights and women's rights.

HRW publishes an annual *World Report* that covers human rights abuses in the specified countries. Its publications on individual countries contain, as relevant, complete reports on the practice of torture and its victims. HRW is supported by contributions from private individuals and foundations worldwide.

Survivors International (SI), San Francisco

Founded in 1988 by a clinical psychologist,[26] Survivors International began by offering *pro bono* help to immigrants in the San Francisco Bay area who had undergone torture and other forms of severe trauma. After several years, Survivors International was able to expand its list of volunteer health-care professionals and its client rolls. SI's network of professionals includes the fields of psychology, medicine, social work, public health and the law. SI provides medical and psychological assistance to survivors from thirty-nine countries around the world, whose backgrounds range from landowner to peasant, professional to blue-collar worker, political activist to politically unaffiliated, and who are members of minority as well as majority ethnic groups. Currently, between thirty and thirty-five survivors are assisted each week. SI receives grants from the UN Voluntary Fund for Victims of Torture, the San Francisco Foundation, and foundation and private donors.

Conclusion

This chapter has discussed two types of organizations working against torture: those that offer direct hands-on service to survivors, and those that do not. The latter organizations have broader mandates that includes torture among other violations of mainly civil and political rights that they address. Most but not all organizations are formally accredited to the United Nations. There is a correlation between NGOs that have been active in the human rights over many years and accreditation with consultative status.

The number of centres assisting torture victims is anticipated to grow considerably, surpassing two hundred in 1999.[27] Centres need to be able to count on stable and reliable financial support, in order to do efficient long-term planning. If estimates of increasing number are correct, funding will be needed in proportion to the increasing number of victims seeking help from an ever-growing number of centres throughout the world.

It is appropriate to conclude with a few words about collaboration and resources with respect to the UN, whose full potential for progress in this field has yet to be tapped. The UN Voluntary Fund for Victims of Torture works to provide medical, psychological, social, legal and economic aid to torture victims and their families. The Fund received requests for funds in 1996 amounting to more than $5 million, for ninety-six projects in fifty-four countries. The amount available was $2,535,500, making it necessary for the Fund to limit its grants to between 30 per cent and 48 per cent of the total request of approved projects. The same has been true in previous years; because of a shortage of contributed funds, the Fund has found it necessary to award no more than a third to a half of the sums that were requested and duly approved on the basis of merit. Since it is fair to assume that the requests will increase each year, in order to meet its obligations the Fund will need to take in double the current contributions. Between $5 and $6 million contributions to the Fund per year will be requisite, if the Fund is to fulfil its mandate responsibly.[28]

The office of the the UN High Commissioner for Refugees is another of the UN-affiliated agencies that collaborate on this issue, from its mandate covering millions of refugees in every part of the world. The newly named Office of the High Commissioner for Human Rights, redesignated from its former title of Centre for Human Rights, symbolizes hope that the High Commissioner will breathe new life into that critical link in the human rights chain. In a joint human rights venture, the World Health Organization, the UN High Commissioner for Refugees, the European Community Task Force in Zagreb, the World Federation for Mental Health, and others collaborated in a project of the Netherlands-based Pharos Foundation to develop 'Guidelines for Evaluation and Care of Victims of Trauma and Violence'.[29] Greater intercommunication among UN agencies and between them and NGOs have begun, to what we hope will be good effect.

Notes

1. The S-G so spoke to the 637 NGOs from 61 countries assembled at UN Headquarters in New York in September 1997, Press release SG/SM/6320 PI/ 1027 of 10 September 1997.

2. H.E. Mr Ahmad Kamal was then the Ambassador of Pakistan. *Journal of the United Nations*, 27 November 1996, no. 1996/231.

3. U.N. Doc. A/50/24 1996, para. 13.

4. See U.N. Doc. General Assembly A/50/24 and A/50/227; ECOSOC/ 5684 of 25 July 1996; ECOSOC resolution 1296 (XLIV) of 23 May 1968 (the original authority for NGO arrangements with ECOSOC).

5. Interview with Laurie Wiseberg in *Human Rights Tribune*, vol. 4, no. 4, September 1997.

6. The Universal Declaration of Human Rights and the two International Covenants, one on Civil and Political Rights and the other on Economic, Social and Cultural Rights.

7. The NGOs were: Amnesty International, Human Rights Watch, International Commission of Jurists, International Federation of ACAT, International Federation of Human Rights Leagues, International Service for Human Rights, and the Women's International League for Peace and Freedom. *Commission on Human Rights*, E/CN.4/1997/33 of 23 December 1996.

8. Theo van Boven, 'Draft basic principles and guidelines on the right to reparation for victims of gross violations of human rights and humanitarian law', per Commission on Human Rights Resolution 1996/35 of 19 April 1996 and E/ CN.4/1997/29 of 23 January 1997, and Sub-Commission resolution E/CN.4/ Sub.2/1996/17 of 24 May 1996.

9. *Committee Against Torture: Rules of Procedure, Rule 62*, CAT/C/3/Rev.2 of 31 January 1997.

10. CAT/C/XVIII/CRP.1/Add.4 of 11 April 1997.

11. The Comprehensive Torture Victims Relief Act, first introduced in the US Senate in August 1994, has been reintroduced in the present Senate by a bipartisan team.

12. The three-day 'International Symposium: Human Rights and Mental Health', took place at Kosevo Hospital in Sarajevo, 11–13 July 1997. It was co-sponsored by Médicos del Mundo and the Madrid Bar Association, along with mental health specialists and other medical staff of Kosevo Hospital, the Human Rights Centre of the Faculty of Law of the University of Sarajevo, the Psychiatric Association of Bosnia–Herzegovina, and specialists from the European medical community.

13. Study done for the RCT/IRCT journal *Torture*.

14. For a discussion of the early groups helping torture victims, see the chapter by James Welsh, 'Violations of Human Rights: Traumatic Stress and the Role of NGOs', in Yael Danieli, Nigel S. Rodley and Lars Weisaeth, eds, *International Responses to Traumatic Stress*, published for and on behalf of the United Nations by Baywood Publishing, Amityville, NY, 1996.

15. The US report has been overdue since the scheduled delivery date in November 1995. *Committee Against Torture: Provisional Agenda and Annotations*, CAT/ C/40 of 31 January 1997.

16. Suzanne Daley, 'South Africa Commission Itemizes Brutality of Past', *New York Times*, 9 November 1997, p. 1. The article notes that one of the torturers received help from a private therapist.

17.   An AI Medical Seminar was held in 1978 in Greece, at which several national medical groups – Denmark, The Netherlands, the USA, Sweden, Greece, and France – reconsidered the medical profession's responsibilities and activities in their future work. *Violations of Human Rights: Torture and the Medical Profession*, Index: CAT 02/03/78, August 1978.

18.   Author's communication with James Welsh, AI IS, October 1997. See also *Role of Health Professionals in the Exposure of Torture and Ill-Treatment*, AI Index: ORG 44/01/84, AI International Secretariat, London. Also *BIBLIOGRAPHY – Publications on health and human rights themes: 1982–1997*, AI Index: ACT 75/03/97, Amnesty International, September 1997.

19.   *Report of the Secretary-General to the Commission on Human Rights: Question of the Human Rights of All Persons Subjected to Any Form of Detention or Imprisonment: Right to restitution, compensation and rehabilitation for victims of grave violations of human rights and fundamental freedoms*, U.N. Doc. E/CN.4/1997/29 of 23 January 1997, in which states provide information about legislation adopted or that will be adopted on this issue.

20.   Guy Aurenche, French lawyer and member of ACAT and the International Federation of ACAT, is the author of *Bonne Nouvelle à un monde torture*, Centurion, Paris, 1986; *Guerre, genocide, torture: La réconciliation, à quel prix?*, Desclée de Brouwer, Paris, 1997; and other works on torture.

21.   *Commission on Human Rights: Follow-up to the World Conference on Human Rights*, UN Doc. E/CN.4/1997/NGO/52 of 14 March 1997. Another intervention urged the Commission's attention to protecting the defenders of human rights; E/CN.4/1997/NGO/13 of 10 March 1997.

22.   *OMCT – Operating the SOS–Torture Network*, no. 58, November–December 1996.

23.   One of the OMCT publications, *In the Eye of the Storm: Report on Gross Violations Against Human Rights Defenders* (1997), for example, is an outgrowth of the study by the Commission Working Group concerning 'The Rights and Responsibility of Individuals, Groups and Organs of Society to Promote and Protect Universally Recognized Human Rights and Fundamental Freedoms'. The Report presents an annotated listing of cases in which OMCT has intervened involving human rights defenders under attack by governments in fifty-two countries.

24.   *OMCT Bulletin*, no. 59, January 1997.

25.   The conference was co-sponsored by the National Institute of Mental Health, Office of Refugee Resettlement, and the Center for Mental Health Services.

26.   Gerry Gray founded Survivors International.

27.   *Torture*, vol. 7, no. 2, 1997.

28.   The number of states that have contributed to the Fund has risen from five in 1982 to twenty-six in 1996. The Fund reports its finances annually to the General Assembly and to the Commission on Human Rights. *Report of the Secretary-General to the Commission on Human Rights: United Nations Voluntary Fund for Victims of Torture*, E/CN.4/1997/27 of 9 December 1996. See also UN Press Release HR/4300 of 23 July 1996, and Press Release GA/SHC/3388 of 13 November 1996.

29.   Danieli, Rodley and Weisaeth, eds, *International Responses to Traumatic Stress*, pp. 145–7, 179.

Part V

Final Reflections

12

On the Prevention of Torture

Manfred Nowak

In 1974, as a postgraduate student at Columbia University in New York who was shocked by the most abhorrent reports about torture in Chile, I wrote a comprehensive thesis about the phenomenon of torture. I analysed its practice as well as the various rational and irrational arguments attempting to justify it from ancient times through the Middle Ages until its abolition in the time of the Enlightenment and its twentieth-century revival under Hitler, Stalin and Pinochet. It was one year after Amnesty International published its first global report on torture. Together with other students I established an Amnesty International adoption group at Columbia University and actively participated in its campaign for the abolition of torture. When I interviewed the first victim of torture I personally had met, a Chilean refugee who had just arrived in New York, I (not my Chilean interview partner) had to interrupt the interview because I could not endure his stories any longer. In that time torture was for me something completely unimaginable, an act of barbarity which belonged to the dark history of the Middle Ages and which could only be invented again by the perverse minds of people like Hitler, Stalin and Pinochet. In other words: if the international community was able and willing to eradicate these types of evil tyrannies, it would at the same time abolish torture again. I was naive enough to believe that democracies were immune from torture.

In the meantime, I have met hundreds of victims and witnesses of torture and enforced disappearance from all regions and political systems of the world, have heard the most horrible stories during my various fact-finding missions, and seen the secret torture chambers where these human beings were tormented for weeks, months and even years. I do not believe any more that any society is immune from torture and that we will ever be able to abolish torture. We can perhaps abolish the death penalty, but we will never eradicate arbitrary and summary executions. Similarly, torture still is abolished (and will hopefully remain so) as a legally authorized method of interrogation and securing evidence, but in reality governments and private individuals resort to it as they commit other crimes.

This does not mean, of course, that we have to accept the practice of torture, which after all remains the most direct and brutal attack on the very essence of human dignity and on the core of the human personality. Yet we have become more realistic and modest in our aims as well as in the methods to combat torture and similar gross violations of human rights, such as enforced disappearances and arbitrary executions. We have tried to identify the root causes and to develop a step-by-step approach of measures aimed at eliminating the root causes and thereby preventing torture.

During the 1970s there was in principle agreement among the human rights community that the mere prohibition of torture under international law and the traditional methods of monitoring states' compliance with this obligation, such as the state reporting and the individual complaints procedures, were not sufficient to combat the revival of systematic practices of torture and enforced disappearance, in particular in Latin America. There was disagreement, however, about the most appropriate means to terminate and prevent such practices. One school of thought regarded impunity as the major root cause of torture and, therefore, favoured to combat it by means of domestic and international criminal law. This strategy resulted in the adoption of the 1984 UN Convention Against Torture (CAT), the 1985 Inter-American Convention to Prevent and Punish Torture, the 1992 UN Declaration on the Protection of All Persons from Enforced Disappearance, and the 1994 Inter-American Convention on the Forced Disappearance of Persons. All these instruments oblige states to make acts of torture and enforced disappearance offences under domestic criminal law, punishable by appropriate penalties, to thoroughly investigate every allegation of torture and disappearance, and to bring the perpetrators to justice. In addition, the crime of torture was made subject to the principle of universal jurisdiction in order to avoid 'safe havens' for torturers. Furthermore, torture is recognized as a crime against humanity in the draft Statute for an International Criminal Court and subject to the jurisdiction of the *ad hoc* International Criminal Tribunals for the Former Yugoslavia and Rwanda. The philosophy behind this is that the criminal prosecution of torturers and, to a lesser extent, perpetrators of acts of enforced disappearance will break the cycle of impunity and, thereby, have a significant preventive effect. The recent jurisprudence of the Inter-American Commission and Court of Human Rights and the UN Committee on Torture contributed to this philosophy by ruling that the right to an effective remedy in relation to the prohibition of torture and enforced disappearance entails the obligation of states to investigate such acts and to bring the perpetrators to justice.

In practice, this approach did not lead to the desired result. Although the problem of impunity for gross violations of human rights is one of the major topics in the human rights discourse of the 1980s and 1990s, states are extremely reluctant to implement their respective international obligations. Only very few states have enacted specific legislation to criminalize torture or enforced disappearance, with appropriate penalties which take into account the extreme seriousness of such practices. There are almost no cases in which the perpetrators of such crimes have been brought to justice. On the contrary, more and more countries resort to sweeping amnesty laws in order to protect the perpetrators from being prosecuted, often in clear violation of their respective treaty obligations. I am not aware of any case in which the principle of universal jurisdiction was actually applied in respect of these human rights violations, and the establishment of international criminal tribunals is too recent a phenomenon to have yielded any preventive effect.

The second school of thought focused on the purely non-judicial and non-accusatory systems of preventive visits to places of detention – that is, those places in which most acts of torture and enforced disappearance occur in practice. It is based on the philosophy of the International Committee of the Red Cross that the very fact that an independent international body may conduct unannounced visits to all places of detention may have a deterrent effect and thereby contribute to the prevention of torture and similar human rights violations behind closed doors. This strategy led to the adoption of the 1987 European Convention for the Prevention of Torture but similar attempts in other regions or at the universal level (draft Optional Protocol to the UN Convention Against Torture) have not yet been successful. Although the European Committee for the Prevention of Torture (CPT) is widely regarded as an effective body of international monitoring, investigation and mediation, I doubt whether the mere practice of carrying out preventive visits as such has the desired effect of deterring potential torturers. In order to conduct visits to a given country in an orderly fashion, such missions in practice have to be announced beforehand to the respective government, and the authorities have ample time to interrupt their practice of ill-treatment and/or to remove evidence of such practice.

The success of the CPT, and to a certain degree also of the UN Special Rapporteur on Torture and the UN Committee Against Torture, in exercising its power of inquiry under Article 20 of CAT, results, however, primarily from its practice of monitoring the general conditions of detention and of making recommendations to the respective governments as to how to improve such conditions with a view to preventing torture and similar human rights violations. Only in very few cases, such as Turkey, did the visits of the CPT, the Special Rapporteur or the UN Committee Against Torture actually establish evidence of torture. Nevertheless, these visits regularly revealed serious shortcomings regarding the general conditions of detention and the minimum rights of detainees as spelled out in various provisions of international human rights treaties or soft law standards, such as the UN Standard Minimum Rules for the Treatment of Prisoners, the Body of Principles for the Protection of Detainees or the European Prison Rules. The practice of the above-mentioned bodies clearly reaffirms the link between the right to personal liberty on the one hand and the right to be protected against torture and enforced disappearance on the other hand. The non-observance of the rights to personal liberty and the minimum rights of detainees, as well as inhuman or degrading conditions of detention, are an important indication for taking the human dignity of detainees not too seriously and prove to be conducive to more severe human rights violations which ultimately may result in torture, arbitrary executions and enforced disappearance.

The practice and recommendations of all respective international monitoring bodies, from the European and Inter-American Courts of Human Rights to the CPT, the UN Human Rights Committee and Committee Against Torture, the UN Special Rapporteurs on Torture and Arbitrary Executions or the UN Working Groups on Arbitrary Detention and Enforced Disappearances, lead therefore to the conclusion that the meticulous respect and ensurance as well as the strengthening of the various rights related to the concept of personal liberty are the most efficient means to prevent torture and similar forms of gross violations of human rights. If the rights laid down in the UN Convention Against Torture, the UN Declaration on Enforced Disappearance or the various soft law instruments were fully respected, such gross violations would soon be eradicated.

What are these rights? First of all, nobody shall be arbitrarily arrested or held in preventive detention. Second, every arrested person shall have prompt access to family members, a lawyer and a doctor of one's own choice and shall be immediately informed of these rights. Third, every detainee shall be held in an officially recognized place of detention and shall be brought promptly – that is, within 48 hours – to a judge. Fourth, an official up-to-date register of all detainees shall be maintained in every place of detention and a centralized register shall be established. Fifth, all interrogation shall be recorded on audio- or videotape and no evidence obtained as a result of ill-treatment shall be admissible before the courts. Furthermore, any allegation of ill-treatment, torture or disappearance shall be promptly, thoroughly and impartially investigated by a competent authority; all places of detention shall be inspected regularly by an inde-pendent body, and all prison and law-enforcement personnel shall receive a proper human rights training.

The observance of these rights would seem not to put an excessive burden on states. Most of them seem self-evident, at least in every demo-cratic society based on the rule of law, and their implementation does not require high financial investments. The question remains, therefore, why torture and inhuman treatment nevertheless occur as a regular feature in so many countries of the world, including in highly democratic ones. The answer lies first and foremost in the lack of a human rights culture in general, and a lack of respect for the human dignity of persons such as detainees who are considered as outcasts of the society irrespective of whether they are convicted hard-core criminals, pre-trial detainees to whom the presumption of innocence should be applied, members of minorities and other marginalized groups, or just 'illegal' foreigners and refugees who happen to come from a so-called safe third country. The development of a less discriminatory attitude to these categories of human beings and of a more humane prison culture would be an important first step on the long and winding road to the eradication and prevention of torture.

13

Challenges for the Future

Inge Genefke

Torture is carried out systematically in more than forty United Nations (UN) member states and is practised sporadically in many more. Many of the countries which have in fact ratified the UN Convention Against Torture still practise or tolerate the use of torture.

Former authoritarian regimes have generated a great number of torture victims and in some cases continue to do so in spite of the changing political climate. As the state undergoes a process of democratization, the experiences of these victims are often revealed. The effect is an increase in the number of victims coming forward and thus in the number of victims – both primary and secondary – in need of rehabilitation. Thus, the global number of torture victims should realistically be counted in millions.

Torture is used as a tool of power. The use of systematic and government sanctioned torture can be related to four different contexts. First, it is often used in dictatorships and by authoritarian regimes as a way of creating general anxiety in society and suppressing the opposition – for example, those who work for democratic development. Moreover, in armed conflicts, torture of enemies (both soldiers and civilians) is used as a strategic means to expand power and territory and to suppress opposition and national minority groups. It should also be pointed out that in new democracies, torture is a practice remnant from authoritarian regimes and a means of individual power abuse used by military or law enforcement personnel. Finally, torture is frequently used as a lawful sanction.

There are a number of major problems facing all those who fight against torture:

1. The limited recognition of and support to torture victims and a general lack of knowledge about the fact that professional rehabilitation is both necessary and possible.

2. The inadequate international funding available for rehabilitation and prevention activities worldwide, including multilateral, bilateral, and private funding.

3. The limited implementation of international conventions against torture and the lack of knowledge about the obligations undertaken by states parties to these conventions. These obligations include the responsibility to ensure education of law enforcement personnel and health professionals (UN Convention, Article 10), responsible for detained or imprisoned individuals, about their duties towards these individuals. The obligations also include the provision of assistance – including rehabilitation (Article 14) – to victims of torture and their families, and the effective prosecution of perpetrators responsible for torture (Articles 4–8).

4. The limited efforts undertaken by the world community towards the prevention of torture. This may be due to lack of interest, insufficient knowledge about the existence of torture, and the magnitude of the problem.

5. The lack of knowledge about possible means to counteract torture among individuals and groups exposed to torture.

The main obstacle is the limited attention and awareness regarding the extent of the problem. Where political torture is performed, torture is also often a routine procedure in the police stations. In many countries, police were never trained in democratic interrogation techniques. So, being taken to a police station in these countries is most often synonymous with being tortured. Besides, torture victims often feel ashamed. And that is why there are, beyond doubt, many more victims than the statistics show.

Future Work

Future actions could be based on more than twenty years of health professionals' working experience with torture victims. These years have given health professionals (including myself; I have been working in the field since 1971) an in-depth knowledge of torture methods, the effects of torture, short and long term, how to diagnose victims of torture, the aim of torture, and how to rehabilitate the victims.

The knowledge that torture produces a wide range of tragic physical and psychological after-effects on the health of the torture victims, that the primary aim of the torturers is to break down the victim's identity and personality, that torture is used as a tool of power against people working first and foremost for democracy and for better social conditions – this information has to be further developed and disseminated where it is most needed.

Attention must be devoted to make the information relevant to the audiences and to experiment with ways of communicating about torture that overcome emotional resistance towards involvement in an unpleasant topic. Special efforts should be made to inform and appeal to the authorities responsible for torture, as well as to create pressure on these when necessary. Finally, the persons affected through these efforts must be carefully selected in order to avoid endangering them.

I would maintain that an advocacy programme be produced in order to carry out three main activities, namely to accumulate, process and disseminate information about the practice of torture, the consequences of torture and the possibilities of rehabilitating persons who have been tortured, as well as prevention measures. Accumulation covers primarily the maintenance of documentation centres and the continuous collection of information. Processing includes analysis and systematization of information, eventually resulting in the production of publications, articles, and other means of communication. Dissemination is the presentation of information to specific target groups: for example, promotion and distribution of publications, press campaigns and speeches.

The activities mentioned above are naturally perceived to support the prevention of torture at global and national levels. It is of importance also to develop specific prevention activities directed at eradicating torture at society and community levels. Here one could talk of primary versus secondary prevention. Primary prevention aims at eradicating torture before it occurs. In order to do so, we must identify the causes of torture, the possible agents of torture, the systems that permit, organize and spread torture, and the high-risk groups that are in danger of being tortured in each specific country of intervention.

Advocacy for ratification and implementation of international legislative measures (e.g. the UN Convention Against Torture) are examples of primary prevention efforts. Informing about and increasing awareness of the malignancy of torture among decision-makers, opinion leaders and the general public are other examples.

The goal of secondary prevention is to limit the occurrence and consequences of torture, once it is manifested in a specific country, by early identification and documentation of the groups tortured and rapid crisis intervention using various methods of rehabilitation. Secondary prevention develops and mobilizes selected community resources in countries where torture has occurred, through education and training of health professionals and other professional groups, specifically law-enforcement personnel. During the last few years, encouraging results have been obtained by approaching high-level police and prison officers, and politicians responsible for law-enforcement personnel. Training has included not only human rights in general but also, very importantly, direct anti-torture knowledge with the aim of changing law-enforcement personnel's attitude towards torture. Secondary prevention also includes work against impunity for agents who have already performed torture.

This direct preventive work should of course have high priority, although the recognition of and assistance to the millions of torture victims, so important for achieving a more humane world, should also have our greatest attention.

The above-mentioned programme is based upon the fact that we today have enough knowledge about the phenomenon of torture: what torture is; why torture; when, how, where and who the torturers are. We have enough very good declarations and conventions, which – if they were implemented – would lead to a radical decrease in the use of torture. Again, what is needed is recognition of the problem and recognition of the magnitude of the problem.

Torture has always existed. During the last decades, however, new knowledge has developed concerning the phenomenon of torture. This may, hopefully, have the consequence that the world finally recognizes that the structure of our societies and their development are in close relation to the performance of this horrible tool of power. That may lead to the necessary change in the attitude towards torture, which is a first very important step towards diminishing its use.

About the Contributors

Juan Almendares Bonilla, MD, is Executive Director of the Centro de Prevención, Tratamiento y Rehabilitación de las Víctimas de la Tortura y sus Familiares 'Ole Vedel Rasmussen', Tegucigalpa.

Ingrid Ask, graduate student at Uppsala University, is a research assistant in the long-term research programme on human rights at the Swedish Institute of International Affairs, Stockholm.

Terence Dowdall, Ph.D., is Director of the University of Cape Town Child Guidance Clinic, Cape Town.

Bertil Dunér, Ph.D., is Head of the human rights research program at the Swedish Institute of International Affairs, Stockholm.

Ümit Erkol, MD, is Assistant Coordinator of the Treatment and Rehabilitation Centres of the Human Rights Foundation of Turkey (HRFT), Ankara.

Inge Genefke, MD, DMSc. h.c., is Secretary-General of the International Rehabilitation Council for Torture Victims (IRCT), Copenhagen.

Priscilla B. Hayner, MA (Columbia University), was previously Program Officer for international human rights and world security at the Joyce Mertz-Gilmore Foundation; she is presently an independent writer,

Lone Jacobsen, Registered Nurse, is Chief Nurse at the Rehabilitation and Research Centre for Torture Victims (RCT), Copenhagen.

Love Kellberg, Stockholm, is a jurist and former Undersecretary for Legal Affairs of the Swedish Foreign Ministry, formerly Member of the European Commission of Human Rights and the European Committee for the Prevention of Torture.

Lisa M. Kois, BA, JD, is a human rights lawyer specializing in the human rights of women, presently legal consultant to the UN Special Rapporteur on Violence against Women, Colombo.

Rita Maran, Ph.D., is currently lecturer in International Human Rights at the University of California at Berkeley (International and Area Studies Teaching Program).

Edith Montgomery, Ph.D., is Chief Psychologist at the Rehabilitation and Research Centre for Torture Victims (RCT), Copenhagen.

Manfred Nowak, Univ. Prof. Dr., Austrian Federal Academy of Public Administration, is Director of the Ludwig Boltzmann Institute of Human Rights (BIM), Vienna, and former Director of the Netherlands Institute of Human Rights (SIM) at the University of Utrecht.

Selim Ölçer, MD, is General Secretary of the Human Rights Foundation of Turkey (HRFT), Ankara.

Ann-Marie Bolin Pennegård, Master of Laws (Harvard, 1978), is Minister and Deputy Head of the Swedish Delegation to the OSCE in Vienna, chair of the drafting group of the working group on the draft Optional Protocol to the UN Convention Against Torture

Nigel S. Rodley is Professor of Law at the University of Essex, and United Nations Special Rapporteur on Torture.

Eric Sottas is Director of Organisation Mondiale Contre la Torture/World Organization Against Torture (OMCT), former Secretary General of International Movement of Catholic Intellectuals, Pax Romana, Geneva.

Bent Sørensen, is former Professor of Surgery, University of Copenhagen, former member and First Vice-President of the Council of Europe Committee for the Prevention of Torture (CPT), and presently Vice-Chairman of the United Nations Committee Against Torture (CAT).

Katarina Tomaševski, Dr. iur., is Senior Research Associate at the Danish Centre for Human Rights, Copenhagen.

Index